# of Men's Lives

FEARLESS 50s

Gender Rivalry

MANopause

Gender Crossover

Take This Job and Shove It

Opening the Spiritual Dimension

SEX

SURFING SEX

From Competing to Connecting

Post-Nesting Zest

INFLUENTIAL 60s

Growing the Brain

Don't retire! Redirect!

Black Tempest

Male Menopause

Age of Integrity

Age of Influence

SNUGGLING SEX

Lusty Winter

THE 70s

Nigel Holmes

Also by Gail Sheehy

LOVESOUNDS

SPEED IS OF THE ESSENCE

PANTHERMANIA

HUSTLING

PASSAGES

PATHFINDERS

SPIRIT OF SURVIVAL

CHARACTER: AMERICA'S SEARCH FOR LEADERSHIP

GORBACHEV: THE MAN WHO CHANGED
THE WORLD

THE SILENT PASSAGE

NEW PASSAGES

UNDERSTANDING MEN'S PASSAGES

UNDERSTANDING MEN'S PASSAGES

DISCOVERING THE NEW MAP OF MEN'S LIVES

GAIL SHEEHY

RANDOM HOUSE NEW YORK

Grateful acknowledgment is made to the following for permission to reprint
previously published material:
Farrar, Straus & Giroux, Inc.: Four lines from "To a Dutch Potter in Ireland" from *The Spirit
Level* by Seamus Heaney. Copyright © 1996 by Seamus Heaney. Reprinted
by permission of Farrar, Straus & Giroux, Inc.
Mark Strand: "About a Man" from *The Late Hour.* Reprinted
by permission of Mark Strand.
Villard Books, a division of Random House, Inc.: Brief quotes and summarization
from *The Ballad of Gussie and Clyde* by Aaron Latham. Copyright © 1997
by Aaron Latham. Reprinted by permission of Villard Books,
a division of Random House, Inc.

Library of Congress Cataloging-in-Publication Data
Sheehy, Gail.
Understanding men's passages: discovering the new map of men's lives / Gail Sheehy.
p.   cm.
Includes bibliographical references and index.
ISBN 0-679-45273-7 (hardcover)
1. Middle-aged men—United States.   2. Masculinity (Psychology)—
United States.   3. Maturation (Psychology)   I. Title.
HQ1090.3.S495   1998
305.244—dc21   98-9942

Random House website address: www.randomhouse.com

Printed in the United States of America on acid-free paper

24689753
First Edition
Book design by Caroline Cunningham

For Clay

I tramp a perpetual journey . . .
My right hand pointing to landscapes of
    continents and the public road.

Not I, nor any one else can travel that road for
    you,
You must travel it for yourself.

It is not far, it is within reach,
Perhaps you have been on it since you were born
    and did not know,
Perhaps it is everywhere on water and on land.

—WALT WHITMAN, *Song of Myself*

Author's Note

The vision that informs this book grew out of an experience with my husband. When his exhilarating career as a magazine editor began to wind down, he spent two years moping around and trying to find the opening to a new passage. He tried consulting, thought about writing a book, monitored his investments. But he was only going through the motions. Nothing came close to the challenge of seizing an idea, matching it to the perfect writer, and sending it out into the world to stir things up.

He needed to focus not on what was wrong with him but on what was right with him. He needed a new dream.

He made it a priority to search for an answer to the question *What else could I enjoy doing?*—to struggle with it, argue about it, dream about it *every day.* This kind of transition in middle life is not accomplished in a matter of months; it is more likely to take a year or two. At times, we both felt as though we were wandering in a dark wood, lost but not alone. We had each other, we were a committed team, and that was key.

Men today are not washouts at 40 just because they have been downsized out of a job, or at 50 because they have fulfilled the traditional roles and wonder "Is that all there is?" Life offers many rich and varied seasons through the forties and fifties and into the sixties and seventies and can still be active and productive in the eighties, even the nineties— for those who find new channels to express their passion and who feel they are making a difference.

So it pays to make an investment in a "new self" by struggling with questions such as *Why am I here? Where is the meaning? What parts of myself have been left out that I am now free to live out?*

When the answer came to my husband at last, it was clear as crystal. What he most loved about being an editor was identifying and shaping young talent. That discovery led him to trying his hand at teaching at the university level in New York. Voilà! He came out of the cave—that place of refuge where men retreat to nurse their wounds and figure out what they feel—and began connecting with old friends and helping strangers. One stranger, a friend of a friend, wanted advice on a book project. Clay gave the man a good deal of time and gentle direction. That led to a series of serendipitous communications and ultimately an invitation from the dean of the Graduate School of Journalism at the University of California at Berkeley. The dean wanted Clay to come out and explore the possibility of teaching there. Eventually, with the enthusiastic backing of hundreds of his former colleagues and disciples, who raised the money to endow a program in his name, Clay became director of a brand-new magazine center at Berkeley.

It meant turning both of our lives upside down and moving across the country to start all over again. Plunging into a new culture at a lesser income, we started from scratch to create a new nest and make new friends. This is very different from the spirit-deadening dilemma of coming to the end of one's primary career with no anticipation or preparation and feeling junked. This was an exhilarating change: we planned and precipitated it. This was our preemptive strike against sameness and sourness, against hiding inside the shell of identities that had once defined us.

Breaking out feels wonderful—at first, anyway. While trying out the area, we went back to living like postgraduate students: the rented two-bedroom apartment, the brick-and-board bookcases, the single telephone-booth bathroom and spats about "It's my turn!" But we also had more time for intimacy, for taking long exploratory walks and experimenting with strange restaurants and discovering a jogging path with a view high in the Berkeley hills, where we began our mornings with the mentholated tickle of eucalyptus in our noses. Our days were full of firsts again. We felt young.

Changes, even the most pleasant of them, always produce stress. But people who learn how to turn stresses in their professional life to productive or creative use seem to thrive and feel more alive. It wasn't easy for my husband to let go of the "make-'em-jump" authority he had wielded as a New York editor. He had to adopt a whole different approach to accomplishing his ends. Eventually, though, he found a style more appropriate to this stage of life: the Socratic method of asking questions and prodding students to dig more deeply for their own answers. It wasn't easy for me, as the following spouse, to leave my entire support system back on the East Coast—my children, all my friends and creative colleagues. "Be patient with yourself, Gail," I kept telling myself. "You're growing brain." That is literally true. If you continually introduce new learning situations and put yourself at some risk, even an older, developed brain can sprout new foliage and make new neural connections.

What's more, it is far too easy as we reach middle life to get stuck in the same circle of friends, where you know what they're going to say before you go to the party. Clay felt his mind growing sharper from being exposed to a very different ethos than that of the East Coast. Shaking up our lives demanded that we reach out and make new friends. And we became more attentive than ever to seeing, calling, writing, e-mailing, and planning adventures with the most cherished of our old friends—and collecting frequent flier miles with the persistence of pack rats.

Gradually, something happened to these two New Yorkers, accustomed to burrowing into their apartment to escape the winter ice or summer humidity. Awakening morning after morning, now in our new home in the Berkeley hills, to squint at the endless horizon stretching across the bay and see the sun hurdling over the foggy phantom of San Francisco, and finally spreading over the silvery Pacific beyond, works some magic on the spirit. Here there are no boundaries to one's dreams.

My husband is not unique. Most men as they approach 40 or later ages will run into passages for which they were never prepared. Faced with a change in his fortunes, my husband had (in Shakespeare's words) "courted his most auspicious star." "Did this change, with all its disruption, work out as well as you hoped?" friends ask him.

"Better than I could have hoped," he tells them. "It's a new life."

THE DISCOVERY PROCESS

This book is intended as a guide to self-discovery for men—and their wives or partners—who need to reinvent themselves for their increasingly unpredictable and elongated lives. The book is roughly divided by the decades of a man's life from age 40 on. Since there is such broad variation in the ages when the marker events of life occur today, do not take the age breakdowns too seriously. Many men in their twenties and thirties will recognize some of their concerns in the stories of men who have already reached their forties but still have unfinished work to do on earlier developmental tasks. Similarly, men in their seventies may be just as acutely concerned about male menopause, for instance, as men in their fifties. Read the table of contents in order to zero in on your age or stage.

Frankly, this wasn't an easy book to write. At some primitive level I felt anxious about wading into the most private corners of men's lives and reporting what I found there, for better or worse. Women may pull and tug at their men: *Tell me how you feel! Tell me how you feel!* And then they do. *Oh, no! That's how you feel? I didn't want to hear that! I wanted to hear the good stuff.* When men do talk about their inner experience, they use curse words, they don't spare feelings, they reveal hells and furies that wives and daughters cannot imagine them holding inside. Most women don't want to go into that pit.

But I have had the benefit of talking at a heartfelt, gut-wrenching level with hundreds of men who are the real authorities behind this book. My training is as a cultural interpreter. Margaret Mead, my mentor, taught me to use the anthropological method to place an individual's psychological journey in the context of the rules and rituals of his subculture. My mission is to be a recorder and conduit, a proponent of the possible, and a catalyst for action among men who want to capture a second life.

In 1989, I started collecting life histories of women and men who were living through stages beyond where my earlier book *Passages* left off. They tend to be achievers and risk takers, the first to sense or discover new passages made possible by an evolving world. They are the pacesetters in any society.

Radical changes have taken place so swiftly that many men were willing to unburden themselves to a woman writer—once assured it would be in a male-bashing-free environment. I found group interviews to be particularly valuable with men. With the generous assistance of social organizations and local or state universities with reentry programs, I was able to gather groups of men in every region of the United States for an evening's discussion of what it means to be a man in middle life today. In preparation, they filled out a confidential life history survey, the same omnibus questionnaire developed during my research for *New Passages* and answered by 7,880 men and women drawn from every region of the United States. This time the participants ranged from skilled blue-collar workers to middle-class middle managers and entrepreneurs, as well as professionals and high achievers in the arts or business world. Their family backgrounds ran the gamut from poverty and family violence to wealth or life fortune.

Men turned out enthusiastically in Atlanta, Boston, Dallas, Memphis, Miami, Minneapolis, New York, Los Angeles, San Diego, San Francisco, Tampa, and Washington, D.C. The palette was very colorful: twelve colonels sitting around a breakfast table at the Pentagon in Arlington, Virginia; creative men in San Francisco searching for meaning and honor in their lives; gutsy recoverees from male menopause in Texas; blue-collar Boston men seeking a college degree in midlife; Miami doctors who have been "HMOed" and are struggling to uphold their professional ideals; and in Atlanta, black men teaching white men from the stuff of their lives. The men who turned out were not the broken wings. The very act of turning out for a group discussion showed that they were still probing, open, looking for new solutions. Indeed, when some of the participants were asked to read and respond to early drafts of the chapters concerning them, they recognized a commonality of experience but wanted the book to go deeper: *How much of the way we are goes back to our primitive ancestors? How are the most evolved men changing? Why do we have to die earlier than our wives? What's behind the depression you see in so many middle-aged men?*

After selecting a total of one hundred men from the various groups, I followed up with personal interviews, often repeatedly, in order to render their life stories more fully and faithfully. Because of the highly personal nature of their disclosures, the men were offered the choice of being anonymous or revealing their real identities. In most cases, to their credit, they elected to be named. Those who preferred to remain anonymous were given pseudonyms, as noted, and although sometimes their professions and locales were altered, all the pertinent details of their lives and quoted conversations are verbatim.

Gay men were often present in the groups, and much of their experience resonated with that of the majority of heterosexuals, particularly if they were partnered. But I did not feel adequate to the task of decoding the mind-boggling changes that have occurred in the gay male life cycle in recent years. The process of understanding and accepting one's sexual orientation, and the decision to live with it, requires the courage to live outside many of the conventional markers of adulthood. This is a subject worthy of its own book.

Highlighted in this book are the "stars" among regular guys as well as public figures. These bold, feisty, imaginative men have wonderful stories to tell about how they discovered what was missing or found their passion and forged a new direction to invigorate the second half of the life course. They share a fantastic secret: *"Hey, I'm not as old as I used to be!"*

How does male sexual potency change across the life span?

The latter became a whole secondary line of research. It is only in the past few years that this question has begun to be the subject of scientific inquiry. Investigating male sexual health in middle life took me around to the best sex clinics in the country. I have kept in close touch with those few doctors who are trailblazers in diagnosing and treating male midlife sexual dysfunction. The section of the book dealing with male menopause emphasizes many avenues for self-cure and reports on the most exciting and effective new medical treatments. But the most revealing information of all came from discussing the subject frankly with men themselves, in groups or individually. The stories of men who have beaten the devil of impotence and seized a full new life may be more illuminating than all the data.

Behind the anecdotal evidence, the book rests on a bedrock of data that come from several years of work with the U.S. Census Bureau. The bureau's data are the broadest cache of sociological comparisons we have in the United States. The bureau's social scientists helped me to create my own microdata sample, a longitudinal data set that could draw upon fifty years of Census Bureau data, from 1940 to 1990. That allowed me to compare people in different generations and trace what has happened to a particular cohort—an age-sex group—over its lifetime. We extracted the same variables from each of the last six U.S. decennial censuses and cross-tabulated these against age, sex, and marital status. As the broad picture emerged, documented in hundreds of tables with tens of millions of numbers, it became clear as a bell: There has been an acceleration of change in the adult life cycle and all the stages within it.

As always, specialists in many different disciplines have generously worked with me to cross-fertilize their findings with my empirical data. The book has the benefit of contributions from the scientific community—cardiologists, urologists, endocrinologists, and bench scientists—as well as from anthropologists, historians, psychologists, and psychiatrists. Experts in employment and economic analysis have helped to illuminate the new male career cycle. Many social scientists at the U.S. Census Bureau and the National Institutes of Health and of Aging have provided a wealth of current data, some of them so new they are unpublished. A complete list of books, articles, academic papers, and unpublished statistics is included in the bibliography.

Acknowledgments

As a book grows and changes from the amoeba stage to a bloated manuscript that needs shrinking and rethinking until, one hopes, it finds the right form to say what it was meant to say, there is no greater solace to an author than a brilliant, constant editor. I am indebted to Robert Loomis, the distinguished executive editor at Random House, for his unflagging intellectual companionship. He is never afraid to break new ground.

I am also grateful to George Hodgman, the extraordinarily versatile editor with whom I work at *Vanity Fair,* who volunteered to read drafts of the book with his unerring eye. And for his stimulating challenges to my perspective as well as for his encouragement, I thank my live-in editor, my husband, Clay Felker.

My colleague in conducting many of the group interviews was San Francisco psychologist Melanie Horn, Ph.D., who was an insightful sounding board. Dr. Ellen McGrath, a friend and clinical psychologist with a bicoastal practice in New York City and Laguna Beach, California, and Harry Wexler, a New York psychologist who works with men, were both most generous in suggesting sources and helping to refine interpretations. Harriet Mayeri, a California market researcher, brought her special skills to moderating focus groups. As a connoisseur of poetry for the epigraphs, as always, I defer to my friend Muriel Bedrick, vice president of her family's publishing company, Peter Bedrick Books, Inc., in New York.

Words cannot properly acknowledge the omnibus contributions of Ella Council, my indefatigable household manager, who keeps the team together. I am also grateful to my friend and former editor Byron Dobell; my agent, Lynn Nesbit; my computer consultant, Josh Skaller; and to the quick-witted editorial assistance of Rebecca Donner, Janelle Gates, and Dede Lahman. I also want to express my pleasure in working with the gifted designer Nigel Holmes on the map and cover, and with the expert staff at Random House, including editor in chief Ann Godoff, Carol Schneider, Sally Marvin, Bridget Marmion, Suzanne Wickham-Beaird, and Barbé Hammer.

Contents

AUTHOR'S NOTE XI

ACKNOWLEDGMENTS XIX

PART I: WHAT DO MEN WANT?

Chapter One
IT'S A GUY THING 3

Are You Prepared for Another Life? 8
But I'm Not Ready! 11
The Need to Know and the Fear of Knowing 13
The Eight-Hundred-Pound Gorilla 14

Chapter Two
THE NEW MAP OF ADULT LIFE 17

The Wife's Nightmare 20
What to Do with All This Leftover Life? 22

PART II: FLOURISHING FORTIES

Chapter Three
WHY DO I STILL FEEL LIKE A KID? 27

The Vanity Crisis 29
A Flagrant Freedom 32
The Father-Son Midlife Power Struggle 36
When You Comin' Home, Son? 37

The Dead Father 38
The Midlife Delinquent 41

Chapter Four

MANHOOD ON TRIAL 45

Yuppie Playing Catch-up 46
Banker "Excessed" at Home 47
The Sole Breadwinner's Insecurities 47
The Idealist's Angst 47
A Hard Time to Be a Man in His Forties 50
Confronting the "False Self" 52
Are You What You Smoke? 53
"The Big Impossible" 55
The Reluctant Father 58
First Fatality Jitters 60
Moving Up the Mortality Markers 63
Honor Among Men 64
Manly Sports: More Than Just a Game 66
Current Manhood Models 69

Chapter Five

MARRIED AND MORTAL 78

The Aha! Moment 78
The Heart of the Matter 81
The Stonewaller's Defense 85
The Trouble with Wives 88

PART III: FEARLESS FIFTIES

Chapter Six

PASSAGE TO YOUR SECOND ADULTHOOD 95

The Samson Complex 97
Mature Masculinity 100
Former Pro Football Star 102

Geezer in Graduate School 103

Globe-trotting Journalist Turns Gardener 103

The Fearless Professor 106

Beyond Power 108

Barry Diller's Search for Self 112

Prospero's Passage 116

Welcome to the Age of Influence 118

Chapter Seven

REDIRECT YOUR LIFE BEFORE THE HAMMER FALLS 121

The Dark Night of Joe O'Dell 122

Destructive Defenses 125

The Comeback of Joe O'Dell 127

They'll Never Fire *Me* 128

The Rebirth 131

The Window of Opportunity 133

Midlife Money Realities 135

What Could Spook John Wayne? 136

Give Up "I'm the Big Shot" 137

Building a Team 139

Opening the Spiritual Dimension 141

Find Your Passion and Pursue It 144

Chapter Eight

LOVE AND WAR WITH WIVES, FATHERS, CHILDREN 146

From Competing to Connecting 147

Gender Crossover: Comfort or Crisis? 149

Coaching the Coach 151

Withholding Sex 155

The Safety Net Wife 157

Making the Crossover Work 160

Brain-Sex Changes 161

Mellowing Out 162

Empty Heart 163

Mr. Mom 164

Father Hunger 166
Letting Go of a Growing Son 167
How Many Men Friends Can You Count? 169
The Nest Is Empty—Are You Ready for Love in the Morning? 172

PART IV: WHO'S AFRAID OF MALE
MENOPAUSE?

Chapter Nine
THE MALE SEXUAL LIFE CYCLE 177

Magical Expectations 178
The Male Sexual Life Cycle 181
The Unspeakable Passage 185
Men Behaving Intelligently 189
Mind over Manliness 191

Chapter Ten
SECRETS OF PERPETUAL VIRILITY 193

Would You Rather Have Steak and a Smoke Than Be a Sexual Athlete? 194
Magic Bullets 196
When Sunday-Afternoon Football Is Better Than Sex 198
Free Testosterone! 200
DHEA: A Man's Master Hormone 202
Chemical Machismo 202
Couples Work 205
The Testimonial Woman 209
Teaming Up to Find the Right Treatment 210

PART V: INFLUENTIAL SIXTIES

Chapter Eleven
PASSAGE TO THE AGE OF INTEGRITY 215

Secrets of Well-being in the Sixties 216
Imagining the Paul McCartney Retirement Home 219

Don't Retire! Redirect! 220
Looking for Your Postcareer Career 222
His and Her Retirement Fantasies 224

Chapter Twelve
PROGRESS VERSUS DESPAIR 227

The Black Tempest 229
Don't Back Up, Severe Tire Damage! 231
Help Is Not Hard to Get 233
I Am *Not* Having a Heart Attack! 236
Absorbing the Blows of Fate 239

PART VI: WHAT KEEPS A MAN YOUNG?

Chapter Thirteen
UNCONVENTIONAL WISDOM 243

Do Men Have to Die Earlier Than Women? 245
*Un*retired Champions 248
Growing and Regenerating Brain 251
Spiritual Hunger 253
Love in the Twilight of Life 254
A Lusty Winter 255

APPENDICES

APPENDIX A 259
Chapter Six: Passage to Your Second Adulthood
Coping with Job Loss 259
Strategies for Surviving Job Loss in Middle Life 260
Resources: Career Counselors 261

APPENDIX B 263
Chapter Eight: Love and War with Wives, Fathers, Children
Resources: Couples Therapy 263

APPENDIX C   264

Chapter Ten: Secrets of Perpetual Virility

Shopping for a Doctor/Male Health Clinic   264

Resources: Physicians and Therapists for Sexual Health Issues   265

APPENDIX D   267

Chapter Eleven: Passage to the Age of Integrity

Preretirement Couples Exercises   267

APPENDIX E   268

Chapter Twelve: Progress Versus Despair

Warning Signs of Depression   268

BIBLIOGRAPHY   269

INDEX   275

PART I

WHAT DO MEN WANT?

While we sleep here, we are awake elsewhere and . . . in this way every man is two men.

—Jorge Luis Borges

Chapter One

_____

IT'S A GUY THING

It has traditionally been assumed that age is kinder to men than to women. My research over the past eight years has revealed a surprising reversal: many men 40 and over are having a harder time today making a satisfying passage into the second half of their lives than are most women. Why?

Women feel pangs over losing their youth.

Men feel dread.

"It's the dread of losing potency!" says my friend Fitzgerald. "It's imagining yourself as an actor onstage who has lost his voice."

There are some inevitable changes as we tramp the journey of life. Men usually hit them as they would a brick wall—and then may fall apart. If they knew what to expect in advance, it could help them to master those changes and profit from them.

The point of this book is to help men and their partners to outwit the inevitable changes ahead. Today, particularly for men under 50, the timing of marker events—finishing school, first grown-up job, marriage, parenthood, empty nest, retirement, golden years—has turned out to be unpredictable. What a man is supposed to do, and when, is not clear. It is both exciting and disorienting, like sailing for a new world but wondering if you will drop off the edge of the old one first. The maps and charts are all out-of-date. Any man who feels a little lost is hardly alone.

The first step is to understand the passages that men go through after age 40, and then to discover, within the new map of men's lives, how you can travel these new passages for yourself with greater awareness and a passport to renewal. Even on a subject as threatening as "male menopause," the news is good and getting better. It is gradually becoming recognized as a mindbody syndrome that is perfectly normal, widespread, treatable, and often reversible. Pharmaceutical companies are racing to offer men perpetual virility—by popping a pill. As immediate and compelling as is the concern most men have with how their sexual performance might be affected by getting older, there is much more involved in restoring vitality and virility than putting more lead back in the pencil. Mind-set matters at least as much as bodily changes. The whole gamut of causes and the impressive armamentarium for fighting male menopause are spelled out later in the book.

Why single out men? It's not as radical a departure as it might seem; I have been writing about the predictable and unpredictable changes of adult life for both sexes since the publication of *Passages* in 1976. But after twenty years of probing the psyche and interpreting the impact of cultural shifts on both sexes, I faced a humbling admission:

Men don't understand women, but at least they know it. Women don't understand men, but they *don't* know it. Does the following dialogue sound at all familiar?

"What's wrong?"

"Nothing."

"Why won't you talk to me?"

"What about?"

"About why you seem so down."

"I'm just tired."

"But you just sit around watching TV. Sometimes, you can get the most tired from doing nothing."

"I'm not doing nothing! There are things I have to think about."

"It seems like you've come to a point in your life where things are changing for you. How does that make you feel?"

"It's just something you have to go through."

"I'd like to help. Won't you talk to me about it?"

"What is there to say?"

"What is it you want out of life? Just make up your mind and be straight with me."

"*I don't know* what I want."

Most of us have had such conversations. I know I have survived a few of those trying-to-help-but-only-making-it-worse dialogues. The presumption among women is that they know what's wrong with their men, and that they could fix it if only men would listen. But do many women really know what it's like for a man today?

Milton Glaser, a legendary graphic artist and a wise and cherished friend, made this observation of the cultural lag between the genders: "Women are developing a new belief system; a new way of viewing life is coalescing. Most men don't know what's happening to them. They don't have any idea what to believe in. For a lot of us, the values we grew up with have been subverted and changed. Men are astonished at this change; they haven't formulated a response to it. It's a time when men are very, very uncertain."

Men may not equate change with growth. Generally speaking, they associate change with loss, giving up, being overtaken, failing. It is not seen as a positive part of inner growth and the road to a new kind of power. Particularly in the first half of their lives, men are rewarded for putting blinders on and pursuing their narrow career path: life seems straightforward.

"In my corporate life, I'm always telling company leaders how important it is to step back, look at trends, see what the future might bring, and plan ahead for it," says a New York public relations man, "but in my personal and career life, forget it." He expresses a male view as old as time: "I just keep moving forward in a kind of dumb-beast way, seeing the next opportunity and throwing my spear at it, taking my lumps and hoping everything will work out for me. Whether as men we are hardwired to think that way or it's the steady process of socialization, we just don't like to change."

You may have been speeding along the route you set in your twenties when, suddenly, the road turns bumpy. Or you hit a washed-out patch and cannot move forward. Or the juice simply drains out of your batteries. How do you recharge yourself? Change gears? Who do you turn to for help?

It has become a cliché to say that men don't like to ask questions. Obviously, this is not always true. (My husband has stopped at the nearest gas station to ask for directions at least once.) But men have not been taught to ask questions about their sexual life cycle or their health or psychological well-being. They don't think they have the time or need for such consultations—unless disaster strikes. Studies show that men make far fewer visits to doctors than women, and when they do go, they generally don't ask any questions. Beneath the silence and stoicism, however, most men over 40 sense that the playing field of life is radically different from the world of their fathers.

An economic revolution equivalent to the Industrial Revolution is pitting mature men against younger, computer-savvy digerati. Experience may no longer count for as much in marketplaces focused on the now. Not only are new skills demanded, for which several generations—older baby boomers, the "Silent Generation," the World War II generation— are not prepared, but a different attitude is required. The rules of the game between employer and employee have changed. You used to be able to count on the corporate father—the farseeing, benevolent giver of rewards and reprimands. Now the corporation is a virtual father—amorphous, nonhierarchical—and you can never be clear where you stand.

The ground of relations between men and women has also undergone an earthquake of change. Men of the baby-boom and earlier generations were socialized, as boys, to assume a clearly prescribed role in the benign patriarchy portrayed in popular culture by shows such as *Ozzie & Harriet* and *Leave It to Beaver.* As young adults they were thrown off balance, ridiculed by the women's movement, and later dismissed by some academic activists as belonging to a continuum of "dead white men." In middle life they find themselves competing with a newly confident species of younger professional women. Add the pressure to remain youthful and demonstrate perpetual virility, and many of today's men over 40 are in trouble. If a man keeps playing by the old scoreboard and the old timetable, he is likely to strike out.

In this climate of uncertainty, hundreds of men have talked to me candidly about all kinds of forbidden subjects: their concerns about aging, the ebbing of physical strength and athletic prowess, their fears of losing their jobs and their fathers, the meaning crisis they face at the midpoint of their lives, their envy of empowered working wives, their wish to be closer to their children before they lose them, their preretirement anxieties, and the whole question of potency in all areas of their lives.

Perhaps you never thought these questions would concern you. You've never thought about not being young. A well-known entertainer was shocked the first time he went through the supermarket line and the checkout girl looked right through him. Still handsome, though his jaw-line is now somewhat softened, he is less cocky and less confrontational; he seems to have calmed down and warmed up—qualities that would presumably enhance his powers of attraction. Yet when we talked, he could focus only on the negative aspects of these changes: "You feel separated from youth at the same time you're feeling diminished in physical strength and stamina; you start being passed over by younger men; the sex isn't as great as it was; an incredible desire to be young again comes over you."

When I ask men if they ever talk over these questions with their male friends, they almost always shake their heads: "No."

Why not?

"It's a guy thing."

Most of the time they don't even discuss these matters with their wives, who are often preoccupied with their own midlife changes. After a lecture in Pennsylvania, I was stopped by an energetic-looking woman with a book bag slung over her shoulder. "I started back to school in my late thirties," she said. "I'll celebrate my forty-second birthday by getting my diploma as a clinical social worker. My husband kept complaining, 'You're changing. Why? *I'm* the same man you married twenty years ago.' *Bingo!* That's the reason we're getting divorced."

The husband probably thinks that remaining the same, and hiding his feelings and frustration, is being manly. He may feel stuck, even trapped, by his financial responsibilities. He expects himself to be the same provider, the same aggressive competitor he always was, expecting his body to take punishment and burn fat and attract women the way it always did. But beneath the bravado he probably doesn't feel the same thrill of the chase he did in his twenties. His whole identity is tied up with the status he has achieved so far. If he lets go even a little, what else is there?

He cannot imagine how to change. Why should he?

When women in midlife go back to school, start new careers, or leave stifling marriages, for the most part they are exhilarated. Even if their salary and status is not as great as a man's, they derive greater satisfaction—because they started with so much less. The men they leave behind are often resentful, even jealous, having likely helped to finance a former wife's emergence into the status of "being my own person" at the expense of their own revamping.

Linear reasoning is likely to lead a man to think, "Once I achieve certain things, *then* I'll be happy." But it is not only titles and material accomplishments that matter. And when those external achievements fail to provide meaning and joyfulness on schedule, men become frustrated. Confused. Angry. And ashamed to admit it.

This male malaise has no name. It is a dark continent. Most men don't recognize—or refuse to accept—that they continue to go through different stages throughout their adult lives. And few men I have studied are even aware that important new passages still lie ahead—after 40. These crossroads demand a full stop and a pause to look inward. They present a man with a chance to stretch and progress, or to lock in and regress. It is necessary to let go of a little control during these times of passage so that an old shell can be sloughed off and space made for a yeasty, multi-dimensional "new self" to grow.

Transitional periods are always unsettling, *for anybody.* But a lack of awareness makes it more likely that a man may slide into depression and do all sorts of self-destructive things. More often than not, men are not even conscious of being depressed. They begin slipping down the cliff, inch by inch, while clutching frantically for anything to hold on to or simply numbing themselves to what feels like an inevitable descent down the back side of life.

This book presents a brighter outlook, based on research with today's new men. It is men in middle life who have the best chance to become masters of their fate—better lovers, better fathers, truer to themselves and their own values, freer to express their feelings and exercise their creativity, more influential, more collaborative, more spiritual. They need only knowledge and a mind open enough to receive it.

But time is running out! Not nearly as fast as you think. In fact, the middle years are the stage of potential highest well-being in the lives of healthy educated people today. You don't believe it? Consider some facts:

ARE YOU PREPARED FOR ANOTHER LIFE?

We are living through the greatest miracle in the history of our species—the doubling of life expectancy since the Industrial Revolution. Back when the United States was founded, life expectancy at birth stood at only about 35 years. By 1900, it reached 47 years. One of the most stunning developments of the twentieth century has been to stretch the life cycle by an average of thirty years—more than the total gained over five thousand years going back to the Bronze Age! Another shock of good news on life expectancy appeared in September 1997 in *The New York Times:*

> In 1996 *alone,* American men added *six months* to their life expectancy and reached a new high.

That was according to an analysis of U.S. vital statistics by the Centers for Disease Control. The average male life span is now 73 years. It is also

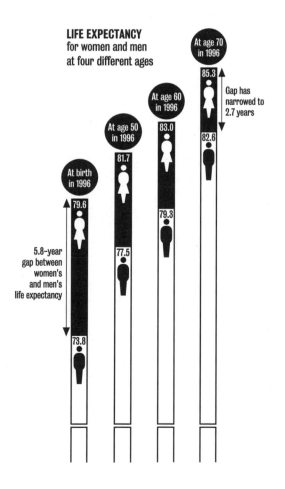

LIFE EXPECTANCY
for women and men
at four different ages

At age 70 in 1996
85.3
Gap has narrowed to 2.7 years
82.6

At age 60 in 1996
83.0
79.3

At age 50 in 1996
81.7
77.5

At birth in 1996
79.6

5.8-year gap between women's and men's life expectancy

73.8

catching up with the female life span (now an average of 79), as the number of AIDS deaths and the incidence of heart disease and cancer decline. Between now and the year 2030, the proportion of people over age 65 will almost double. And this will be true, even sooner, all over Europe.

Fine, you may say, but if an extended life span means spending years with my bulb dimming and my body falling apart, forget it. We all look to our fathers and mothers as mirrors of our own aging. Those are miscues in many ways. When our parents turned 50, we thought they were old. *They* thought they were old. Since 1950, unimagined advances have been made in medicine; and, more pertinent, public health education through the mass media has prompted profound changes in personal behavior. People in middle life today have a very different life profile from that of their parents, who were expected to turn off their mental engines in their fifties. They didn't dream of running marathons or gulping down hormones to keep them randy until their eighties.

People are maturing earlier, physically, but taking longer to grow up emotionally, and much, much longer to grow old. For the middle classes, adolescence is now prolonged until the end of the twenties. Our First Adulthood only *begins* at about age 30. Somewhere around the midforties we enter a major passage into what used to be a rather staid, if not stagnant, middle age.

Yet we seem to be more reluctant to grow up than ever before. Of the hundreds of men over 40 whom I have interviewed, most believe they are five to ten years younger than that imposter whose picture somehow slipped inside their passports. Today the midpoint of adulthood is no longer necessarily 40—it's more like 50.

> Fifty is what 40 used to be.

If you are a man now in his thirties, forties, or early fifties, you can adjust your lens on aging. Beneficiaries of the boom in men's health, biotechnology, and brain research, you belong to a species unprecedented on the planet, a species whose life span will *routinely* extend into your eighties and nineties. This means you must prepare for the possibility of another life—beyond the traditional roles and responsibilities—because the years from 40 to 80 or 90 offer you a whole new playing field: what I call your *"Second Adulthood."*

In Second Adulthood you begin to learn that fulfillment in life is not a result of simply racking up points on a single scoreboard. Rather, there are a number of different scoreboards—as son, mate, father, friend, colleague, mentor, community wise man, benefactor. The crucial innings of Second Adulthood are neither played by the same rules nor scored in the same way as a young man's game. But most men are so focused on winning in the first half, they usually miss the signals that can prepare them with a winning strategy for middle and later life.

Gary Markovitz, for example, was a good soldier. Having served in Vietnam and returned to college to train as a technocrat, he had defined himself for seventeen years totally within the context of his company. "When people asked me what I am, I was an IBMer," he admits. "Not Gary who worked at IBM, but an IBMer."

By his midforties he began to wonder if his batteries were wearing down, but it didn't occur to him to wonder what else he might enjoy doing. He heard about his company's buyout offer while on a business trip to San Francisco. At first he had no interest in it. But on the plane ride home he found himself thinking about a friend's recent funeral. The man had come up through the ranks at IBM with Gary and had suddenly passed away from cancer.

Gary found himself ticking off, finger by finger, just how many people could be counted on to show up for his own funeral. He didn't get very far. What value did he have outside IBM? He thought about his oldest son, who was already 25. Before long, there would be a grandson sitting on his knee. Innocent and adoring, the boy would ask him, "Grandpa, what did you do that meant something?"

I made money.

"It didn't pass the grandfather test," Gary decided. "I could be doing better things."

BUT I'M NOT READY!

A man in his late forties in a Minneapolis audience expressed a common concern of men: "Give it to me straight. Do I have to lose power as I grow older?"

On the contrary. The power of mind, rooted in experience, only increases as we meet the predictable crises and accidents of life and discover our resilience. A whole new stage has opened up in the middle of
life: the "Age of Mastery," a bonus stage from ages 45 to 65. The passage from First to Second Adulthood and into the Age of Mastery actually transforms the idea of power.

Baby boomers need a guide to *their* middle life. Theirs will be a brand-
new journey, full of surprises. Four out of every ten American adults belong to the baby-boom generation, which, based on my research with the
U.S. Census Bureau, must be divided into two subgenerations. The leading edge can be called the "Vietnam Generation" (born 1946–1955).
This is President Bill Clinton and British Prime Minister Tony Blair's
generation, which they describe as being strong in ideals but indifferent
to the old ideologies. Boomers now in their early forties to early fifties
came of age *expecting* that everything would always get better, and for
most of them, it did. The spirit of the sixties formed their utopian consciousness, and vestiges of that spirit are still with them, tempered by the
cynicism of the times.

The younger half of the boomers—the "Me Generation"—came of
age in the 1970s (born 1956–1965) and missed much of the idealism
of the Vietnam Generation, but focused more on personal development. They dreamed of achieving the perfectly balanced life and thus
continue to postpone taking on many of the responsibilities of full
adulthood. But they are far more tolerant of egalitarian marriages, gay
partnerships, single parenthood, and other social experiments. Both
halves of this dominant generation have always been highly individualistic and thus irreconcilably divided. But on one issue they seem to be in
total agreement:

> Boomers do not accept middle age.

Boomer men do not see themselves as getting older. And they certainly
don't anticipate any changes in their peak sexual performance—*it may
happen to other guys, but not to me.* Yet secret doubts lurk, and a single episode
of slackened sexual ardor can raise the question: *Is this the beginning of the
dreaded falling off?*

THE NEED TO KNOW
AND THE FEAR OF KNOWING

In lectures based on my last book, *New Passages,* one question is always certain to come up: *"Is there a male menopause?"*

There is a need to know and an equally weighty fear of knowing. When I first became aware of the phenomenon, the evidence from men was mainly anecdotal. Six men sitting around a midtown Manhattan bar after work—virile sales managers and successful retailers—all of whom appear to be backing up the hill from their midforties toward the great divide at 50. They have a couple of drinks, and, within my earshot, one brassy boyo challenges the rest: "Tell the truth. How many times have you faked being asleep when your wife gets into bed with a glow in her eyes?"

Every man laughs. Then a crevice falls open in the conversation. The man in the power tie who posed the question reaches out for a lifeline: "I mean, doesn't that happen to you guys?"

"Sure, Mr. Winkie doesn't like to drink," another man says, chuckling. The rest chime in, putting off the problem on overwork, stress, having a few too many.

But these occasional factors do not do much to illuminate the mystery of why so many men in middle life gradually lose their vitality and virility. They see slightly older friends change from being bullish, buoyant, and decisive into being down, depressed, listless, and lustless. They wonder: *Will it happen to me?* Of course, being men, they refuse to talk about it. At most, the subject is couched in jokes and jibes.

> An older man is walking down the street when he hears a frog talking. The frog says, "If you pick me up and kiss me, I'll turn into a beautiful woman."
>
> The man picks up the frog and puts it into his pocket.
>
> "Aren't you going to kiss me?" the frog complains. "I'll turn into a ravishing woman and you can have me all you want."
>
> "I'd rather have a talking frog in my pocket."

What is happening? Are we talking simply about getting older? Yes, but also about a larger challenge to a man's view of himself—an identifiable phenomenon with physical, hormonal, psychological, and sociological components—that is now trendily referred to as "male menopause." "We do not yet have a term for this five- to twelve-year period of midlife in men, but we know it is shared by both genders," acknowledges Dr. Eliot Sorel, president of the World Association for Social Psychiatry and clinical professor of psychiatry and behavioral sciences at George Washington University School of Medicine.

It soon became apparent to me that if menopause is the silent passage, male menopause is the unmentionable passage. It is just as fundamental as the ending of the fertile period of a woman's life, because it strikes at the core of what it is to be a man—the thing a man has always counted on to bring him pleasure, the thing that has worked for him hundreds of times, mindlessly, like a machine, by himself or with any number of partners, the source of his fantasies, the sword of his dominance, the very root of his evolution as *Homo sapiens*—his youthful sexual drive and performance.

In the April 1993 issue of *Vanity Fair*, with Sharon Stone on the cover stripped to the waist and cupping her naked breasts, my male editors allowed me to publish one of the first full discussions of the subject: "The Unspeakable Passage: Is There a Male Menopause?" Ever since, men and women have been talking privately to me about this problem without a proper name. Interviews with more than a hundred men between the ages of 40 and 70 about this subject revealed that most have been shunted from the urologist to the psychiatrist to the surgeon and ended up totally confused. I have also observed the work of some two dozen medical experts in this narrow field who study and treat men over 40 suffering from some degree of sexual dysfunction in mid- to later life. While the broader medical establishment still by and large ducks the subject, the mass media also remain wary of touching the subject, and I found out why.

THE EIGHT-HUNDRED-POUND GORILLA

One day in the fall of 1996 I got a call from a dynamic young producer on the serious CBS magazine show *48 Hours*. Chuck Stevenson had read my work on male menopause and interviewed some medical experts, and he wanted to put together a piece about men in middle life in sexual crisis. Chuck was only 41. A little young to be thinking about male menopause?

"Actually, I'm finding the subject fascinating," he said. As he saw it, "The precursor to men's midlife crisis is reduced sexual ability, which then triggers all these various psychological feelings."

I was delighted with Chuck's enlightened approach. He and correspondent Erin Moriarty came out to do the interview in the garden of my home in Berkeley, along with a three-man production crew.

For the interview, Chuck wanted to touch on "technical menopause— that small percentage of guys who really don't have the testosterone."

What I really wanted to talk about was not the small percentage of men who are already so incapacitated they might seek surgical relief. My concern is the whole middle range of men who don't know what is normal and who, when their sexual habits or performance changes, become so embarrassed or ashamed that they pull away from any intimacy. On camera, I described the most common scenario:

> The longer this problem remains unspoken between a couple, the more monstrous it grows, until there is an eight-hundred-pound gorilla in the bedroom. Nobody mentions it for six months, two years, five years; meanwhile, the pair stops hugging, stops holding hands, stops touching altogether, moves to separate beds, to separate rooms, and ultimately separate lives. They become estranged in all forms of intimacy because of this sexual shutdown.

When the shoot was over, I asked the producer how the piece would be titled and promoted. "That's going to be the hardest thing for us," Chuck Stevenson admitted. "How do we make this segment move without scaring off men? We can't say 'midlife crisis' or 'change of life.' " Ultimately, the segment was titled "Undercover," which was inoffensive but meaningless. Nothing was left in about the eight-hundred-pound gorilla. Chuck acknowledged that the piece did not work. The reason, he told me with regret, was the enormous sensitivity of senior network executives to letting us talk about impotence.

But it was the reaction of the TV production crew that proved the most intriguing. Ordinarily, a camera crew tunes out while filming and just focuses on doing its job. While we discussed the male menopause, these three men blanched and reddened, but they hung on to every word. After the shooting they stuck around to talk.

"I wanted to hear about it," one of the cameramen said candidly, "but I don't want to talk about it."

"It was hitting too close to home for me," admitted another crew member. He was in his forties and living through divorce hell. She was the one who left. "What really needs to be said is the fact that when a man has a midlife sexual crisis, people often say, 'It's all in your mind, snap out of it.' "

"But it's really part of the natural course of events," one of the cameramen tried to reassure him.

"That's right," said his colleague. "I can see now where you could get that rhinoceros in your bedroom, or whatever you called it—"

"An eight-hundred-pound gorilla."

"Yeah, and blocks could form."

"That made sense to me, too," said the cameraman, "because when communication breaks down in a marriage, it's all gone." All at once his colleague had an Aha! Moment—one of those little epiphanies that suddenly throws a floodlight on what one's life is really about.

"That's what happened in our marriage! Nobody really talked about the gorilla. We just grew more and more apart. I don't feel like it was my fault. I was doing my duty, doing what I was supposed to do. I was just waiting it out. She got tired of waiting, and it happened all of a sudden—the marriage fell apart."

Doing one's duty and not talking about the inner collapse of one's whole idea of oneself is an all-too-common "manly" stance at midlife. This book is meant as a friendly guide out of such dead ends. No man should squander his precious life "just waiting it out." And once he discovers the exciting new map of men's lives, laid out here in facts as well as many living examples, he should be lured to explore new continents of imagination and experience never before dreamt of by past generations.

Chapter Two

THE NEW MAP OF ADULT LIFE

For tens of thousands of years men lived as warriors, hunters, and providers, dominant over women and indispensable as breadwinners. Their brawn was admired and feared, and they were usually employed in work that required the strength of a male physique. The idea that a man's moral superiority is related to his physical attributes harks all the way back to the ancients.

In the past few decades—an evolutionary eye blink—men have been asked to cool their aggressiveness, "share" their emotional secrets, and be more polite about their sexual predatoriness. Missiles are now launched by fingers tapping computers, food is "hunted" using laboratory manipulations that increase livestock and crop yields, gathering is accomplished by a global network of fax modems and the World Wide Web. Even the visible winners among men in American life are doubting themselves. "I would definitely say we are dispirited," CBS television correspondent Bill Geist told *The New York Times.* "We've lost track of whether we're supposed to be acting more manly or more sensitive. . . . It might be that men are winding down and becoming unnecessary."

"Is it true that the 'sensitive man' is out and the 'macho man' is making a comeback?" I was asked by a young man recently graduated from college and faced with a highly competitive job market. His girlfriend had gone straight from graduation into a high-earning position. Yes, predictably, there has been a backlash. Men revolt by wagging their phallic cigars in smoking clubs, gorging on bloody steaks and dry martinis. Some warm to TV shows such as *Men Behaving Badly* or magazines like *Loaded* that celebrate the eternal adolescent. Much more extreme and ugly forms of backlash are seen in domestic violence and most blatantly in the resistance to women in the military.

At the same time, a new model—postpatriarchal man—is in the process of formation. Mostly he is forming among well-educated, well-married men under 40. You may spot Mr. Mom happily suckling his baby son with a bottle at the café table or Dad cheering his daughter at the hockey game while she whacks in a goal. But it is hardly likely that men will ever come to define themselves primarily as fathers. Deep down, the way men see their role has remained surprisingly consistent. This is confirmed both by cross-cultural studies and by interviews with hundreds of men who came together in the group discussions I held across the United States. Being a good provider is still the primary way men define themselves. What has changed so drastically is that fewer men, and more and more women, can fulfill that role.

As husbands, men are finding themselves in partnership with their wives, since two incomes are usually necessary for a middle-class lifestyle. The economic crunch of the 1980s and early 1990s meant that most men slid backward in real income. Two startling statistics put the enormity of this change into perspective:

In 55 percent of American homes, women now bring in at least half the income. And almost *one third* of the working wives in America (29 percent, or 10.2 million women) now earn more than their husbands.

This arrangement is modeled by the first families of the United States and the United Kingdom. Both Hillary Rodham Clinton and Cherie Booth Blair have had dazzling public success as lawyers. In 1996 the president of the United States earned $200,000. His wife made almost three and a half times as much—$742,852—from her own activities, writing and promoting a book. The wife of Prime Minister Tony Blair was made a Queen's Counsel at the age of 40, a title held by only the top 10 percent of English barristers. Known as Ms. Booth in her wig and gown, she too has long been the family breadwinner, with an annual income estimated at more than $350,000. Yet we would hardly suggest that the prime minister of Great Britain and the president of the United States are superfluous men. The partnerships they enjoy with their wives have only magnified their own possibilities and helped them win.

Further statistics suggest that women will continue to gain in educational and economic clout. More women than men are graduating from colleges and graduate schools (except at the doctoral level). More women are working full-time for a longer portion of their lives. Even as a confident new generation of women has been climbing the greasy pole of corporate America and launching the majority of the country's new small businesses, older women fueled with postmenopausal zest have been climbing the steps of state legislatures, expanding their voice in Congress, and breaking through gender barriers to hold posts such as the nation's top law enforcement official and the voice of America in foreign affairs.

Men still vastly outnumber women in public office and power positions in corporate life. But now they have to make room for women and work with them. No wonder that rumbles along the gender fault line are louder than at any time since the shrill beginnings of the women's movement. Who knows what the new roles and rules are? Can the fields of battle and sports empower women to become champions without making men feel emasculated? What is an egalitarian marriage? What does it mean to men to see hordes of young women choosing to have children without fathers? Side by side with the welcome display of the new post-patriarchal dad, we have the shocking statistic to which Senator Daniel Patrick Moynihan constantly refers: in the fifty largest cities in America, an average of *half* the children are being born to single mothers. There has previously been no such experience in the history of the species.

When our social organization changes this dramatically, it provokes general chaos. Not because it's impossible to create more balanced lives, but because it's all so *new.* For all the cries and whispers of "Who needs him?" or "What's a woman doing here?" men and women need each other more than ever as partners in facing an increasingly demanding and accelerated pace of life.

THE WIFE'S NIGHTMARE

Women constantly ask me, "What can we do to get our men to see the light? How do we *talk* to them about their fear of change and aging without making it worse?"

The life-and-death importance of their concerns struck me when I visited the young widow of a high-profile lawyer. He had shattered his second family and shaken up his colleagues by dropping dead from a heart attack in the middle of his customary five-mile jog. He was scarcely over 50 and, it appeared, in optimum health. But a year and a half before, he had been dropped from his firm's executive committee.

I asked the widow if her husband had expressed his feelings about being fired, in private. "He was brought up not to show feelings," she said. "Stoic. His father always said, 'You never bring your problems home.' I certainly gave him a million openings, because I was so upset for him. Being the wife, maybe we express it for them. But he brushed it off. He said, 'Honey, it's just business.'"

Although her husband had had regular physicals, his wife wondered if he might have had symptoms and ignored them. He had never mentioned any chest tightness, angina, or shortness of breath. He followed his motto to the end: *Gut it through.* But like *half* of the men who drop from a heart attack suddenly and unexpectedly, her husband never got up.

Over the past few decades, a link has been scientifically established between exposure to loss and a host of physical and psychological illnesses. "Exit events" that begin to pile up in the second half of life—loss of social status, the departure of grown children, sudden deaths of friends— these and other common occurrences are now considered portents of physical problems. The literature remarks on how frequently an individual under high stress—especially a man—is unaware of its existence and its impact on his life.

This is a problem for all men who define their manliness by expecting themselves to be eternally strong and able to overcome any obstacle alone. They cannot take advantage of today's unprecedented longevity unless they anticipate and deal with it. Men cannot go on living the same way their fathers or even their mentors did. They must be prepared to make changes in their lives consciously, preemptively. Many are not ready.

Society has not prepared them for this potential bonus stage of life, and few have developed the skills and inner resources to manage it well.

In the movie *Moonstruck*, a frustrated Olympia Dukakis kept asking, "Why do men chase women?" Finally, Danny Aiello gave her an answer she didn't expect: "Because they're afraid of death."

There are real reasons men fear death more than women. The risk of dying is greater for males at every age than for females. Beginning at three months' gestation, the chances of a miscarriage with a male fetus is about twice that for a female. Men age faster than women, get gray hair sooner, lose their sexual drive earlier, rise to anger or frustration a lot quicker, and may experience the shock of change—such as unemployment—a lot harder.

"The reason men fear death more than women is because they are not directly related to the birth process," observes artist Milton Glaser. "The woman who delivers a child understands that she is in the world again, forever. The continuity of human experience runs through the mother. Men don't feel the sense of continuity a woman does. Men are bystanders."

For women, change is a given. They lead interrupted lives, in and out of work and domestic realms. Their bodies ebb and flow through regular monthly cycles. They become accustomed to the immensity of changes that occur throughout pregnancy and childbirth: seeing their bodies swell out of all proportion and then gradually regain a familiar shape. If such astonishing changes can take place physically and result in the miracle of new life, then change is seen as good.

Even when men have all the advantages of money and position, it is hard to take the risk of change or to see the point of altering the familiar game plan. And nobody can do it all alone. Women in middle life reach out and form intricate webs of nurturance; as their youthful competition for men is replaced by the conviviality of shared experience, their friendships multiply and deepen. The opposite seems to be true for men in middle life. Wary of allowing other men to glimpse any cracks in the armor or sores on the soul, men tend to raise their guard even higher than before. They rarely make new friends. They may become emotionally dependent on their wives, even dangerously so. Men rarely read books about their health or stop to reexamine where they have been in the journey of their lives before plunging ahead to the next stage. Psychiatrists tell me that so often men who come to see them about feeling "stuck" or "in a rut" cannot allow themselves to make a change, not even when their wives are pushing and coaching. Some men literally have to break down—have a physical blowout or a mental plunge into depression—before they can give themselves permission to make a major change. And yet there is so much more to live, and to live for.

WHAT TO DO WITH ALL THIS LEFTOVER LIFE?

All the early explorers of the life cycle—Charlotte Buhler, Erik Erikson, Carl Jung, Daniel Levinson, Bernice Neugarten, George Vaillant—observed that the character of adulthood changes markedly between early and middle adulthood. Back when those scholars were studying the adult life cycle, however, educated men were assured of entering the command stage by their midforties. Many could coast through their fifties and plan on a predictable retirement in their sixties. Now millions of men at all social levels who expected to be secure by middle life are facing interrupted lives, even as they are enjoying longer and healthier ones. With thirty or more years to fill up *after midlife*, there is time enough to reinvent yourself. You can make the decades after 40 the most exciting and deeply meaningful of all.

The book is divided by the stages of the new Second Adulthood:

The "Flourishing Forties" are the peak decade in many ways. But now is not an easy time to be a man in his forties. Traditional manhood models are outdated; new definitions and demonstrations of manliness are needed. A new concept—one that celebrates the strengths particular to today's postpatriarchal man in early midlife—is sought in the stories of men who are society's pathfinders. How are they redefining their roles as warriors, providers, mates, fathers? Where do they find honor in everyday life?

The "Fearless Fifties" today offers the possibility of regeneration. Men can tap many new wellsprings of meaning, love, and intimacy to refresh themselves in middle life. But they need to give themselves permission to redirect their lives *before* the hammer falls. As their fathers die off, their children grow away, and their wives come into their own, it is essential that men in their fifties consciously prepare to replace what they feel they have lost in zest, energy, and joy.

"Who's Afraid of Male Menopause?" traces the male sexual life cycle and the greatly exaggerated expectations many men have today that can inhibit their performance as lovers. The male middle-life slowdown is discussed holistically, as a mindbody phenomenon. Secrets of perpetual virility are catalogued through both individual stories and solid information from medical experts. The fears and frustrations of wives of men with potency problems are fully acknowledged. Experts agree that the best "sex therapy" is done at home. Couples work is suggested.

The "Influential Sixties" leads to truly uncharted territory. Today, another stage is being inserted into the life cycle by healthy people beyond their midsixties—the "Age of Integrity"—in which millions of men are finding, to their astonishment, "Hey, I'm not old yet!"

> Sixty is what 50 used to be.

Retirement is becoming an obsolete concept for boomers. Having defined themselves largely by their work, they are often bothered by the question "What do you do when it stops?" Traditional retirement connotes hanging up one's gloves, sitting around playing cards with bossy widows in patio pants, and waiting for the sun to go down. What's more, most boomers will not be able to afford to stop working, at least part-time. Having started their families late, they will be trading in sunset cruises for college parents' weekends. Working retirement offers a man a way to keep his mind agile and a hedge against the fear of irrelevance.

In this stage power can be transformed into a more enduring imprint: influence. It isn't just living longer that matters; it is what one chooses to do to make something more meaningful and rewarding out of those years than has been the custom, something that in the past has been accomplished by exceptional men such as George Washington, Benjamin Franklin, Pablo Picasso, Winston Churchill, and Charles de Gaulle. The Age of Integrity, then, is a stage that almost has to be consciously created.

Finally, the book looks at "What Keeps a Man Young?" Being connected to the future through enlivening links to all generations allows men to be active and useful up to a year or two before they die. And it is increasingly likely that these men will have a mate to share their later years. An American woman who arrives at age 50 today and remains free of cancer or heart disease can expect to live to the age of 92! These estimates by demographers usually produce as many groans as gasps. Whoever prepared us for the possibility we might live long enough to see our *grandsons* go bald?

Men who are open to gaining fresh insight, however, can make a leap into twenty-first-century manhood, combining the best of their *biological* instincts with a new *psychological* potency. True, change is usually painful. But if a man welcomes the challenge of new passages after 40 and sees them as opportunities to stretch himself and gain more skill at life, he will surely grow.

PART II

FLOURISHING FORTIES

Chapter Three

WHY DO I STILL FEEL

LIKE A KID?

Jim Edwards, a popular radio talk-show host in West Palm Beach, Florida, voiced one of the most common comments of men in their forties: "Why do I have a problem thinking of myself as a grown-up? And I'm going to be forty-three in a couple of months!"

Most baby boomers recoil from the very mention of middle age. They took longer than any generation to grow up, and they'll damn well take longer than any other generation to grow old. Desperate to hang on to their youth, many simply refuse to move forward.

"I sometimes feel like I'm still that nineteen-year-old kid who's now struggling to deal with the responsibilities of being a man," admitted the San Francisco restaurant manager on the slippery slope of turning 40. He can still get away with dressing like a boychick in his Andre Agassi surfing trunks and pecs-popping Gap T-shirts, and he hoards all his old Prince CDs as if to maintain by osmosis a respectable level of horniness, but he is also married with children and a lawn and insurance payments. "I can't believe that here I am, an adult, and no beam of light ever came down and imbued me with parental or adult powers."

The work of adult life is not easy. Each stage not only presents new tasks but requires letting go of some of what worked before. With each passage some magic must be given up. Some cherished illusion of invulnerability must be tempered by reality. And the "kid" identity that has come to feel comfortable must eventually be cast off like an outgrown overcoat. If you want to grow, you must be willing to change.

Tim Allen, the TV comedy star of *Home Improvement,* reacted to starting his midlife crisis years by titling his book to reflect his generation's collective denial: *I'm Really Not Here Now.* He described in a TV interview going out to dinner with a group of his fortyish men friends. They all sat glumly around the table, saying almost nothing, until they let out a tribal sigh: *Huuggghhh.* "What's the problem?" Nobody knew. Maybe they were all just tired.

"Some of the guys decided that at forty years or fortyish your gas tank's half empty," Allen said. "Or you're half full, depending on how you look at it. So people are thinking, 'This is really what I'm going to be doing,' and if it really wasn't what they wanted, they got kind of depressed about it."

It is only natural to feel some disillusionment when measuring the heroic dream of one's twenties against the more prosaic reality of life at 40. Somehow, the reality is never quite as grand or good as the fantasy. No matter what rung of achievement he has reached, the man of 40 often feels stale, restless, overburdened, and underappreciated. He begins to worry about his health. He is disgusted with himself when he can't have a few drinks and still be a tiger in bed. He can hardly avoid the maudlin question made famous by singer Peggy Lee: *Is that all there is?*

"Forty? Forty wasn't bad at all," quipped screenwriter Erik Tarloff. "Forty-one was the killer. That's when I knew the forties meant business."

In many ways men reach their peak in their forties, but it's not that simple. Matters both material and spiritual that may never have crossed your mind before will be revealed as you make the long journey from First to Second Adulthood. Farther along the journey you will find yourself at the top of the mountain with a breathtaking 360-degree view in all directions, from the terrain you have already covered to the unmapped frontier ahead of you. But the early glimpses of this forward view can be unnerving.

Terry South, a 43-year-old middle manager on the West Coast, articulated the queasy sensation: "I'm forty-one, and the most I have to show for it is a nice house with a big mortgage and a good title on my business card and a fancy office—that's pathetic. I have kids that I'm happy and proud of, but if I piss my life away, it's my own fault. I have gifts that have been locked up in a suitcase for years and years that I've ignored. Chasing after something that I don't even care about, something that was dished out to me. It's the meaning thing."

But let's be honest. The first changes a man notices at 40 severely challenge his mental image of himself as still being that 19-year-old kid.

THE VANITY CRISIS

You back out of the shower at the health club feeling all tight and stoically sore. You peek over your shoulder in the mirror at a buffed-up body you cannot help but compare to the male bodies that have become the dominant advertising icons. . . . Haahhhh, you may be getting older but soon you'll be as ripped as those gods in briefs in the Calvin Klein ads . . . and then you catch a sudden glimpse of double reflection. What's that pink skullcap doing on the back of your head? Ohmigod! You're *balding!*

"The jolt of mortality that hits is *amazing!*" Steve Perrine, a magazine editor, marks that day as the start of a repeating series of embarrassments. He kept finding himself confronted with the abysmal view of the back of his head. "It was like a moon following me around." And he isn't even out of his thirties! But that is the monstrously unfair thing about men's hair: it starts aging way before they do.

"There's nothing wrong with *being* bald," says Perrine, "but there's something terribly upsetting about *balding.*" This state of dynamic defoliation can last for fifteen years. The important thing is not to panic. Michael Jordan found a creative way around premature hair loss. Men looked at his shaved head and said, "Hey, that works." Voilà, it has become a trend, virile at any age.

Perrine is a deputy editor at *Men's Health,* the phenomenally popular male fitness magazine, which has soared from a zero market share to 1.3 million readers in its ten-year history, supported by a male grooming industry that rings up over $3 billion in sales of various tints and oils, hairpieces and hair removers, goos, and even girdles. Around many American corporations, he says, status is measured by a man's waistband. A thirty-two-inch waist is optimum, of course, but for men in their forties and fifties, the high-status number is thirty-four. "It's as clear a delineation of class as the color of your collar," insists Perrine. The editor is intimately aware of the primary concerns of his readers in their forties: "Your gut, your hair, your butt."

The vainest men in my focus groups are not those in their serene sixties or seventies, but men on the slippery slope of early midlife—forty-ish, still young by today's standards. They are the ones who moisturize their skin or dye their hair or consider a lunchtime skin peel.

What is all the fuss about? This is the first glimmer of mortality, and as such, it is the most sobering and overstressed.

> The fear of losing hair is the fear of losing control.

"It's the first time in life when you realize you *can't* control it," as one man succinctly stated in a midlife passage group discussion. The physical changes are a signal to start listening to voices inside, which are likely to be more insistent: *What do I really want to invest my life in? What do I really care about? How can I construct a life that fits the me of today as opposed to that know-it-all kid of 21 who decided I would be happy being a dentist (or an electrician, an actor, a cop, a suburban househusband) for the rest of my life?*

Stay with those inner voices. Don't get sidetracked by obsessing about the outer shell. Falling prey to the truthless marketing of the hair transplant industry, for instance, and ending up with the doll's-hair look (oddly spaced hairs combed back over a skull of scars) is a dead giveaway of something much more damaging to your image than a little sun reflector on the top of your head: it screams insecurity.

As this book was going to press, the Food and Drug Administration approved the first-ever antibaldness pill, Propecia, and the toupee and transplant crowd was about to throw their rugs and weaves in the air. Then came the qualifiers: none of the men who took the pill in experiments grew back a full head of hair, although two thirds of them showed some improvement. Then the other shoe dropped: the principal side effect of Propecia is a slight risk of impotence. The very prospect is enough to make even Kramer lose some hair.

"I love the statistic that says the average person will spend seven to eight years combing, drying, and fixing their head of hair," says John T. Capps III, founder of Bald-Headed Men of America. "That's seven years that I can do other things."

One man in his midforties described to me a whole mythology he has invented around the shedding of the pelt that is leaving a broad and sexy forehead above his bushy brows. "I just tell my wife I don't need the fur anymore. It's dropping away until it will leave a completely naked phallic symbol. I don't need to stay in the cave anymore. I'm entering the stage where I can be out naked in the forest."

Watch Al Gore over the next few years. The boyishly handsome Vice President, whose disciplined physical conditioning always distinguished him from burger-lovin' Bill Clinton, has grown a prominent gut while in office. And despite his efforts to avoid being filmed from the back, his hair is clearly thinning on top. What will he do about it? Go to close-cropped? Adopt a face-the-music stance? Stay tuned. The Vice President will be the poster boy for aging male baby boomers.

The other marker of the approaching end of youth is the decline in athletic prowess. Your preteen son leaves you in his tire tracks while mountain biking. You strain a tendon from running on the beach and go back the next day—you'll beat it—but you end up pulling a hamstring and being immobilized for weeks. The struggle over relinquishing physical dominance is, for men, as fierce as the struggle over surrendering youthful beauty is for women.

No one has discovered a cure for the common signs of aging. You can curse the phone book and watch TV news instead of squinting at the newspaper, but sooner or later almost everyone in the early forties finds the fine print blurring. How to combat the creeping suspicion that you are falling apart?

> Buck nature
> Suck gut
> Test your physical limits

Terry Anderson, the former chief Middle East correspondent for the Associated Press who was taken hostage in Beirut in 1985 and held for seven years, was forced to fall back on his inner endurance and mental discipline. He came out of captivity with the clarity to write a book about it—*Den of Lions*—and became a popular lecturer. But he, too, admits to a small vanity crisis in his midforties.

"I was thirty-seven when I took my long 'vacation,' " he told me. "I came out seven years later having seen no mirrors. I still felt young, but now I was forty-four. And every camera that ever passed me focused directly on my bald spot." Shocked at seeing the TV footage, he thought, *My God, I am old.*

His wife dissuaded him from doing any cosmetic work. She accepted him as he was. The support of a loving partner has value beyond measure. "Women seem to be able to switch roles a little more easily than men," he mused. After living on the edge for so long, it was even harder than normal for Terry Anderson to feel engaged by the more mundane efforts of everyday life. Men's trajectory in first adulthood is all about challenge and risk, moving upward as swiftly as possible. What could he do to feel confidence in his strength again?

"I took up downhill skiing at the age of forty-five, and I love it," he reports. "There's something about roaring down a hill knowing you are on the verge of breaking something." But he probably won't break anything, because now he has the judgment to calibrate and control risk.

Many men go through a Marathon Man phase. They start pumping iron or training for their first marathon at 40 or so. The reintroduction of risk or novelty in conjunction with learning anything new has a powerful effect on the brain, raising hormone levels and resulting in a burst of well-being. Best of all, the more blood and oxygen you manage to pump around your circulatory system, the better lover you will be. And if you can do fifty wide-grip pull-ups, it doesn't matter that you're 45! Desirable women will pick up your scent. One may ask if she can spot you while you bench-press. (I made that up, but you can always hope.)

A FLAGRANT FREEDOM

The central issue for many men at this stage is the struggle against settling in to real adult responsibilities—and the resistance to giving up their independence, which is tied to youth.

"Forty was wonderful," says Luis,* a second-generation Mexican American who works successfully in the building trades in Los Angeles. "I never felt smarter. I never felt sexier. I got together with the woman who would become my second wife, and life seemed like, *wow*, finally, after all the struggle of the twenties and thirties and the family interference and fighting with my first wife and the shame of divorce, forty was like a great broadening out of the river." And then the realities: "The notion of becoming truly responsible—hey, step back, be an adult—means you may have to make a sacrifice because others are now depending upon you." He admits, "I was resisting because it meant I had to change." A common gender passage.

Jerry,* a son of working-class Jewish parents on Staten Island, spoke to common sources of youthful identity for men. "My cock is me. The drinking is me. By going out and drinking when I was eighteen, that was the way to show I was me. It wasn't my father, it wasn't my mother, it wasn't my teachers, it wasn't the temple. I could make any fantasy come true when I was a young guy. I was very proud that I could seduce a woman within one night. Of course, it got me into a load of trouble when I was older and my first wife found out."

Why do men want to feel like they are still kids in their early forties? Because fully becoming a grown-up means giving up some of their more flagrant freedoms. Men who have enjoyed drinking or doing drugs or chasing women or gambling, and who have become addicted to these habits as a way of demonstrating their manliness and showing off for other men, now find to their dismay that there are painful consequences in middle life. The body eventually rebels. Friends get caught. Wives find out. Children act out. Pressure builds on a man to give up his boy privilege.

> No! I'm still my own boss! And I can do whatever I want to do!

It is natural for a man to feel challenged and resist. The first awareness of the evaporation of youth, the faltering of physical powers you have always taken for granted, the fading purpose of stereotyped roles by which you have thus far identified yourself, the spiritual dilemma of having no

---

* A pseudonym.

absolute answers—any or all of these shocks can throw you into the agitation commonly labeled "midlife crisis."

Critics of theories of adult development seem increasingly intent on discrediting the idea of a normal, predictable midlife crisis. The term "crisis" comes from Erik Erikson and was never meant to connote a catastrophe or any sort of breakdown. It was used to suggest that there are critical turning points along the life cycle when one's vulnerability is exaggerated but one's opportunity for growth is also heightened.

"What about me? I didn't have a crisis," some men will say.

That's why I replaced that confusing label with a less loaded word for the critical transitions between stages and called them "passages." According to one scientific study, half the middle-life men denied obvious evidence of a midlife crisis. Some men I have interviewed, looking back on their forties, only recognize in retrospect, *I went through a dark patch back there, but I don't remember much about it.* In all of us, however, somewhere between the midforties and midfifties today, the passage out of our First Adulthood and the rebirth into our Second Adulthood makes sweeping changes in personality possible. And some degree of personality change is probably inevitable.

In First Adulthood we are generally preoccupied with crafting a "false self"—a front tailored to please or to pass—that is useful in earning approval, rewards, and recognition from the external world. But as a man grows older, a dissonance grows between this made-to-order self and his more authentic self. The search for meaning in whatever one does becomes a universal preoccupation of Second Adulthood.

These changes may allow a man to let his narrow occupational and economic definitions fall away, to relax the "tight blue suit" and rely a little less on his polished "false self." He then becomes ready to look for a sense of purpose that is truly his own. Once he can permit a truer expression of his emotions, he may also be able to achieve a new intimacy between himself and the ones he loves.

But men still want to protect at least one area of life that is their province: *This is my freedom zone.* The old Thursday-night poker game served the purpose; now it may be an adventure weekend, sport fishing, or a men's group retreat. Some men, however, will go to self-destructive lengths in the attempt to hold on to their boy privilege.

Bill Clinton, like many successful people who escaped from traumatic childhoods, became very ambitious and productive in the effort to overcome past injuries. And like many such people, Clinton never really had a boyhood. "Abandoned" by his natural father, who died before his birth, left by his mother for his first four years while she chose to pursue a nursing degree out of state, then living with an alcoholic abusive stepfather, Clinton had to assume the role of grown-up in a chaotic family situation. He was the dutiful and dependable one. But he also had a secret life, back then. His mother, a pleasure seeker, often took him along as an adolescent to her favorite nightclub in Hot Springs, where he had a peek into a world of illicit gambling, drinking, and prostitution. She also taught him how to be seductive. Coming home from her all-night nursing duty, she would routinely say to her young son, "Nobody's told me yet today how pretty I am."

An exceptionally bright victim of that kind of childhood learns to deny and compartmentalize the trauma, but it still lies there, a deep river of sadness and lovelessness, and unless addressed it continues to shape one's life choices. Clinton is happy only when he is seducing people— and he is equally potent in "seducing" both men and women, or just about anyone he meets. Since boyhood he has been seeking love and approval by running—literally running—for president. Yet he has always exercised flagrant freedom of action in another area, recklessly seeking pleasure outside of marriage. He hurts and mystifies those closest to him by constantly jeopardizing his hard-won, respectable status and goals in life with this behavior. How could he be so reckless as to carry on in the White House? Clinton is a classic example of the *puer aeternus,* a Jungian archetype.

> The *puer aeternus*—the eternal boy—remains stuck in an adolescent orientation toward life.

What's more, he became entangled with a White House intern when he was facing his second and final campaign for the presidency. As a youthful boomer, he was also approaching the dreaded age of 50. His emotional anchor, his adored daughter Chelsea, was preparing to leave the nest. Clinton's behavior might be seen as the mother of all midlife crises. What's next for the President? It's the one question he never discusses.

For some men, the forfeit of their more flagrant freedoms appears desirable only when they become fathers for the second time around. The

Staten Island man quoted earlier is now a midlife father of two boys under 10. "The first time around, I didn't change one dirty diaper, and I was proud of that," he says. "My father never did it, so why should I? But the second time around, I finally got it. My kids would really trust me if I showed I could take care of them in a basic way. If they sense I'm not going to run off to get shitfaced or get laid or any other quick fix, but they *know* I'm going to be there, I'm going to hang in, it makes a huge difference in the kind of trust and closeness we have."

He readily admits, "I wasn't built that way. I had to learn that in my forties."

THE FATHER-SON MIDLIFE POWER STRUGGLE

Historically, men have looked to their fathers to mirror for them how to be a man. Father knew best. But the superiority Father assumed and the narrow, tightly collared roles assigned to him belong to an era when men fought the wars, dominated the home, drove the workplace, and set the public discourse. Today, a man in his forties can take very few cues from his father. This is another reason men at this stage ask: *Why do I still feel like a kid?*

The transition into early midlife is usually a muddle of inner contradictions. Just as the kid-man gathers enough proofs that he can make it on his own, eager to "show his stuff" to the father who once seemed overpowering or who stood in the way, Dad begins to decline. Turn soft. Dad wants to rely on him. He can't lean on his father anymore, and he isn't ready to be leaned on. He may become irrationally angry at his father for deserting his post before he has been able to steal the "magic." He may also, underneath, feel guilty for superseding the old man. It is a confusing period between sons and fathers.

The father of the midlife son has his own inner battle. He is being required to relinquish his role as the strong, all-knowing one. As the younger man struggles to assume mastery of his own life, the older man is left feeling weak, passive, and even helpless in relation to another man, his own son, his guarantor of immortality. If the father has never felt confident about himself as a man, he will find ways to continue to block his son's fully growing up—with subtle put-downs or outright criticism—all the while admonishing him to "be a man." Even a more secure father may swing between reasserting his authority, reaching out for reassurance, and withdrawing. An essential shift in the power balance must occur between father and son, but it is often a painful transition on both sides.

> A grown-up son makes his father feel redundant.

There are many aspects of the father-son power struggle, any one of which may exaggerate the son's feeling of vulnerability on the brink of midlife or, alternatively, accelerate his growth. We will examine several common scenarios.

WHEN YOU COMIN' HOME, SON?

The number one talk-show host in a midwestern city, a 36-year-old father of two, lives on the air. He loves filling the airwaves with his thoughts for three hours a day, five days a week. "My show is who I am." Gary,* the talk-show host, begins talking about the trouble he is having separating his identity from that of his father.

"Even as an adult in my late thirties now, I still feel like I'm the little boy and he's my dad. I'm still embarrassed to admit to him my mistakes, and I still want his praise. I'm afraid of his retribution if I make a mistake."

With me while I was in Gary's studio was a contemporary of his, Rick Shaughnessy, a smart, strapping public relations man who had recently become a new father but with the bittersweet coincidence of losing his own father. He told Gary he used to feel the same way about his dad, but that he now regretted having disconnected from him.

The host's father is now 65 and retired, he tells us, with time for regrets on his hands. He is always asking Gary to go biking or hiking or out drinking with him.

---

* A pseudonym.

"I want to have time back with you," the older man says.

Gary is torn. He remembers waiting and waiting as a little boy for his father to be finished. He wants to tell his father, "Great, but now I'm a package, Dad. My new job's a stress and the kids have the flu, and I have a wife now, but it's sure nice talking to you, Dad," as Gary paraphrases the lyrics from the haunting Harry Chapin ballad about a father whose son repeatedly asks, "When you comin' home, Dad?" only to be told "I don't know when," until the father retires, the son moves away, and the dialogue is reversed. Gary continues rehearsing the conversation he'd like to have with his father: "See me as a grown-up with the full responsibilities of manhood. Don't see me as a little boy who should be able to be told, 'We're going biking this weekend.'"

Gary stiffens, his voice self-righteous: "I just don't have time for that closeness now—just like he didn't have time for me when I was growing up."

Rick Shaughnessy butted in with a deep and fervent warning: "Make it happen before you bury your father, man. When your dad's sixty-five, it can happen anytime."

THE DEAD FATHER

It is normal for a man to fear that his father might die before they get things straight between them. The emotional gulf between fathers and adult sons is perennial enough to have been the subject of some of the world's greatest drama and literature. That is gradually changing for younger fathers. Still, the cultural revolution that is beginning to shape the first postpatriarchal man makes it difficult for a son in midlife to accept guidance from his World War II or Silent Generation father or to fully endorse the old man by following in his footsteps. The son may be torn between the need to demonstrate his independence—*Hands off! I know exactly what I'm doing!*—and his yearning to have proof of love and acceptance by his father before it is too late.

· When it does happen that a father dies abruptly, before a son feels prepared to take his place at the head of the family, it can precipitate a long and rocky midlife passage. Not only do you lose someone you love, but you are suddenly out there all alone. There is no one more grown up ahead of you. It may be experienced by the son as a desertion and even lead to a period of desolation.

Frank,* like many men in their midthirties, felt a need to get closer to his father. Tony-the-Life-of-the-Party, his father was nicknamed. "You would never have known my dad was laid off by two different companies in his fifties," Frank said. "He wouldn't listen to anyone who suggested he might be depressed."

Hoping to talk to his dad, Frank had driven back with him to Pennsylvania coal country for a family reunion. His father sat stiffly in the new suit Frank had helped him choose, an extra large to accommodate an aspic of fat that had solidified since the layoffs. But when they visited Frank's grandparents' grave site, his father refused even to step out of the car, retreating into some inner sanctuary and shutting his son out. Frank remembers brushing his lips across the man's cheek: Did he feel it? Did he like it? The next time he heard about his father was a call from his mother at the hospital: *Your father was at the company Christmas party. Dancing with a group of secretaries when he hit the floor.*

Frank took a taxi through the foggy December night, numb, looking for the hospital in Passaic, New Jersey. His mother had not said if Tony-the-Life-of-the-Party was dead, and he had not asked. Frank pushed through the doors into the phosphorescent glare of an emergency room and found it absurdly populated with people in sequined gowns and shiny black dinner jackets, their faces flushed from celebrating. Having hurried over straight from the company Christmas party, they hung along the white corridor like ancestral pictures slightly askew. He could hear their slurred whispers.

"That's his son!"

"It's his boy, Frank!"

"Oh, God, does he know?"

Frank insisted, "I want to see him."

The suit he had picked out for his father only three weeks before was slit up the front. Tubes had been pulled out. The exposed putty-colored

---

* A pseudonym.

flesh was inert. This was not his father. This shape was no more human than the chalk outline of a victim on the highway. Frank felt a shock of rage.

"Why did you do this to me?"

The father's eyes were still.

"You knew you had a weight problem. Mom and I kept telling you. You wouldn't stop. *How could you do this?*"

Frank knew, incontrovertibly, that his father was no longer in the room. His soul was uprooted. The father he had idealized had abandoned him before Frank had accomplished the project of emerging from the family and becoming his own man. Who was there now to perform for, to prove himself to?

For the next few years Frank, a New York TV producer who gave every outward sign of being on the fast track, felt his own soul adrift. For comfort he turned to work and cocaine, but he found little comfort and greater loneliness in this familiar quick fix. His marriage came apart. He traveled extensively with TV crews, and in the field there was no check on his drug use or his carousing. His work addiction served to mask his loneliness and anxieties. But he felt himself becoming hostage to these inanimate companions. So he asked his boss if the company would offer him a buyout. Not a chance.

"Then I'll have to take a leave," he told his boss.

A leave of absence, a moratorium or delay of decisions, might have given Frank time to incorporate his father's death and to gather some separate strength. But his own identity was too shaky. He felt he would be sucked into the same life path as his father unless he fled. Frank walked out of the big network office that day. Two weeks later he drove out to California and never went back. I asked Frank what he had felt the day he left the big network office.

"Fear. Absolute fear." He leaned forward, his hands moving like a boxer's, ready to buffet any blow. "Because I didn't know what was going to happen. I was always afraid of uncertainty. I shunned uncertainty because I didn't believe in myself. I didn't know what my values were. I didn't know what was important in life." He struck out on his own anyway, which was an important developmental step. "It was something I had to do in order to prove to myself I could stand on my own two feet."

THE MIDLIFE DELINQUENT

If there is anything certain about a passage, it is uncertainty. In ordinary circumstances, without the blow of a life accident, the doubts about your outgrown identity, shifting values, and the meaning crisis—all issues linked to the midlife passage—are revealed over a period of years. You have time to adjust. But when they are thrust on you all at once, as they were for Frank, you cannot immediately accept them. The downside of life comes too hard and fast to incorporate.

The real reason Frank came unstuck was basic: he had physically left home, but he did not feel like a grown-up. Moreover, he didn't *want* to grow up. But, you might say, the man was already in his midthirties. Amazingly, of unmarried American men between the ages of 25 and 34 today, more than *one third* are still literally living at home. A brief rebound or two during the twenties is predictable and probably healthy. But the long stayers either haven't yet found a solid career direction or can't find (or keep) a wife, so they languish in a sort of halfway house between indulged son and tryout adult. They have not accomplished the first task of adult development: pulling up roots.

Frank's mother became dependent on him once his father died, and he was sucked back into the warm but womblike infantile position of Sonny Boy. He was confused about what code of manliness he should follow. And now the father he had expected to teach him was gone. Frank was in conflict about what was important in life. In his twenties he had chosen money and power. He bragged that at 26 he was already making $80,000 a year. But look what those same goals had done for his father, and look where they had landed Frank: with a wrecked marriage, a drug problem, and an even greater problem with intimacy. Approaching 40, he was alone except for the comfort of his two best friends: cocaine and work.

The major task of midlife is to give up all your imagined safety providers and stand naked in the world, as the rehearsal for assuming full authority over yourself. Frank wasn't ready. The more inadequate he felt, the more desperate he was to flaunt his independence. Although the specifics of his story may not equate with those of people in your experience, a period of delinquency in midlife is not an uncommon reaction.

Men like Frank who desperately need to preserve the unruled and unruly independence that is the prerogative of young manhood often use drugs, drinking, gambling, compulsive sex, or other addictive behavior to mask their fear of growing up. Some, like Frank, are loners. Others run in packs. They may go on business trips together, blow into a town, get drunk, find women to pass the night with, do business the next day, and fly home. A pact of silence protects them from being caught, until the first wife finds out. Once the first divorce occurs, the other marriages collapse like dominoes. This form of resistance to accepting the responsibilities of adulthood is not limited to the professional and white-collar classes. Steelworkers do the same thing: they may leave the factory, go to a bar, take a whore out to a Winnebago, get laid, and roll home by nine at night with a load on.

Midlife male addictive behavior may be far more widespread than any statistics would suggest. "It's a little like white-collar crime—it's taking place, but it's hidden," says Dr. Harry Wexler, a national expert on substance abuse. He can produce all kinds of numbers and graphs on male addiction based on urine samples of the prison population, but middle-class abusers seldom show up in the criminal justice system. However, as a member of the Alcohol/Substance Abuse Expert Working Group of the American Psychological Association, Dr. Wexler notes that the classification of "addiction" is broadening beyond illicit drugs and alcohol to include food and sexual addictions. "The net is being cast much wider."

Such behavior may have worked reasonably well up until now as a mask over unexplored wounds from earlier in life, or as a patch job over the daily frustrations of ambition and longing for sexual variety. But as these men move into their forties, they are about to hit a huge bump in the road. Their bodies rebel against the abuse. Or they are in danger of going over a cliff as their mates get fed up and threaten to pull out the safety net that holds up their emotional stability. They risk losing the things that are most important to them but that they take for granted, because the addiction obscures both the bad and the good.

Frank realized he would never be able to create a decent relationship with a woman as long as he was dependent on these adolescent escapes. He tried going to Alcoholics Anonymous and other twelve-step programs and was told that he needed more contact with men, older men he could talk to in place of his father, men who could serve as role models.

Joining the oldest men-only AA group in town, he became friendly with men who had 25 to 45 years of sobriety. He was amazed by the way they opened up to one another and offered genuine friendship, love, and support. "All they talked about is relationships," he recalls, still amazed by the insight. "I thought, wow! I have to start practicing and cultivating successful relationships with men and women."

Starting all over again as a graduate student at thirty-five, wearing kid's clothes, he was still rehearsing for full participation in the adult world at forty. Teaching while studying paid for a marginal existence and gave him time to study and practice meditation. Given the breathing space for awareness, he discovered what there was about his father to truly honor. Once he realized that it was not necessary to compete with and beat the dead father in material success, it freed him to pursue his real passions, teaching and writing. A lapsed Catholic, Frank found his way through meditation back to using the rosary as a daily form of worship and spiritual growth.

He didn't come fully alive to himself until he was 42. A year later, he attended a men's group interview with me in San Diego. A friendly and talkative man with a boyish hood of red-brown hair and a trim beard lightly dusted with grey, Frank still wore the uniform of the graduate student—chinos, loafers, and a Gap sport shirt—and was enthusiastic about teaching a large lecture class at a major California university. He had written his first book and was about to finish his Ph.D. in mass communication.

"Look at me now, six years later." He grinned. "It's a total hundred and eighty degrees. I'm working just above poverty level, but I'm happy. Why? Because I'm bringing my life experience to students rather than trying to compete in a shrinking market for TV producers in Hollywood or New York." His greatest achievement, however, was to find the woman of his dreams *and* to be ready to win her as his wife.

The *transformative woman* often plays a major role in allowing a man to renew himself in midlife. In Frank's case, he thought long and hard to conjure up the qualities in the woman he needed and in so doing released the feminine in himself. He married a caregiver. But she is also a mature Asian-American woman, highly skilled and highly paid, who makes it possible for him to pursue his choice of academic life over corporate life. His new identity and his new wife have enabled Frank to redefine the masculine code that killed his father. He has graduated out of midlife delinquency.

"Now I'm more comfortable with uncertainty," he said. "I feel more diversified and far more successful *inside* than ever." His voice gentled. "I just wish my father were still alive so I could enjoy my success with him."

Chapter Four

MANHOOD ON TRIAL

It is a February morning in Memphis, and seven men sit around a conference table, suspended between the uncertain boundaries of their lives as husbands and fathers and the offices they will soon go to, dreaming of themselves as heroes of their own quest. They have put aside their reticence about joining in a group interview because they have hit some unexpected obstacles on what they thought was their one true path in life. From questionnaires they filled out in advance, it is clear that all of these men want to fulfill the traditional male role of breadwinner, preferably as sole provider. They are all trying hard to do right by their families. Their loyalty and commitment are stunning. Yet most of them admit that their partners are dissatisfied. Only one man is divorced, and he sounds miserable.

Satchel Paige, the legendary African-American baseball pitcher, made famous the following question: *"How old would you be if you didn't know how old you wuz?"*

This is the opening question in all my group interviews with men. Invariably, among educated middle-class men, the answers they give range

from five to fifteen years younger than their actual age. Given this cogni-
tive dissonance, a whole decade can slip away, as it had for Rick Smith.

YUPPIE PLAYING CATCH-UP

"I'd be thirty," Rick Smith says.

Tall, lean, the cradle of the South in his softly featured face, Rick, if
he were to hold to the facts, would need to add nine years. He is actually
almost 40. "But I feel like I've lost that last decade. My wife and I spent
too much time focusing on our careers all through our thirties. We never
had children. Now we feel like we have to play catch-up."

It had become painfully evident to Rick's wife, five years into their
marriage, that she was physically unable to conceive. In her midthirties
she wanted to explore adoption. Rick ducked and stalled at every turn.

"Look at all we've got going for us," he would counter. "And where
would we find the time to be parents?" He went to bed thinking about
work, he woke up in the middle of the night thinking about work, then
he and his wife would go their separate ways and both would expend
most of their energies and passion in ten-to-twelve-hour days at work.
They belonged to the Me Generation, after all. Their contemporaries
wanted to skin the world alive, and given the bloated salaries and inflated
titles being passed around during the 1980s, the benchmark of success
rose higher and higher.

"You had to keep feeding the monster," says Rick.

His wife became more insistent that they consider adoption. But the
more open she became to change, the more rigid was Rick's opposition.
"No, we're not going to adopt, period!" So Rick and his wife lived in the
antic present, anesthetized by activity to what was missing at the center
of their lives.

"What do you worry about every day?" I ask.

"Can I keep this marriage together while I make this transition?"

The previous year he had been pushed out of his comfortably dull job
in the printing industry. His wife had taken up the slack while he looked
for another position. He had found an exciting new direction, but at a
much-reduced income level, and he felt guilty about not sticking to the
traditional script.

BANKER "EXCESSED" AT HOME

A blond man named Danny Garrick,* 46 and separated, cannot hide the anger aflame in his face. He tells us that when his job as a bank vice president was "excessed" in a merger, he felt worthless. "For the last few years before the merger, my job responsibilities were expanded and I was required to put in more and more hours on the job. But at home, I kept getting pushed farther and farther out. Then, finally, I got pushed out the door." What does he worry about?

"When the divorce is all over, how will my children feel about me?"

THE SOLE BREADWINNER'S INSECURITIES

Tad,* a robust 42-year-old with a swag of thick black hair across his forehead, looks like a solid soccer dad who used to have all the answers but suddenly doesn't anymore.

"Can I ever be secure financially, or, um, emotionally?"

To avoid relocating his family, he switched fields a year ago and gave up corporate benefits to start his own advertising company. "We had a third child—a whoops! Now my sport has changed from baseball to kids."

Tad wants desperately to carry off the traditional role of sole breadwinner. So, to fulfill their commitment to Christian values, he and his wife decided that she should give up a heady career as president of her company to be a stay-at-home mother. "But now she's exchanged adulation for indignation," Tad says, utterly perplexed. He is having a crisis of confidence.

THE IDEALIST'S ANGST

Sean,* the idealist of the group in a tweed jacket and horn-rimmed glasses, asks rhetorically,

* A pseudonym.

"How do I express myself, my ideals?"

"I thought it would happen in my work, but all I do is help to clean up society's messes." Sean works in the district attorney's office in Memphis, which is a racially divided urban battlefield of the Deep South. He is painfully aware every day of being a white male. Fatigue and a few fine lines of despair already have settled into his young face. He has been cleaning up after rapes, robberies, homicides, and abandoned crack babies for twelve years now, and he feels locked in: "This is not a job with a lot of victories."

He begins to tell a story about a murder case that won't let go of him. It concerns a single mom who left her 2-year-old son with a pot-smoking boyfriend for the weekend and came back to find her baby burned to a crisp. The boyfriend had punched the baby in the stomach to stop his crying, then torched the house to cover up the baby's death.

"She came into my office to talk about it," Sean says, "this young black girl, product of a crack mother, and she just cried and cried and cried." His serious face blotches with emotion. "The mask I wear as a tough D.A. dropped for a second, the mask she wears as a black female dropped for a second. I was in awe. I felt as if I had glimpsed her soul—that we had made some connection even if only for a second." He sighs. "I felt privileged."

His story moves the other men.

"I hope you won that case," one says.

"I didn't."

Bringing his frustration home is disrupting Sean's otherwise solid, long-standing marriage. And now time is beginning to press. His uncle's death last year toppled him, prematurely, into the gulf of midlife crisis. Sean felt the first mortality jitters. "It was the first time in my life that I realized death is for real—that it would get me too!"

When Sean pulled into his driveway after the funeral, he froze. The arithmetic of life hit him. "I'm thirty-eight, my uncle was only fifty-five. There's really not that much between thirty-eight and fifty-five." It was a shattering experience, but he believes it did him a lot of good. "I realized I couldn't be angry anymore. I have to make some changes in my life. I have to, in effect, grow up."

Did any of them feel diminished, as males, by the social and economic upheavals of the past few decades? I ask.

"As males, most of our self-confidence has to do with our positions," Tad says. Chests sink. Several of the men are victims of the Darwinian downsizing phenomenon of the early nineties; the rest wonder when it might be their turn. "I'm glad it happened to me," rallies the lean and handsome Rick, "because I never would have walked away." Having been "excessed" by the printing industry, Rick had recently bought into a small community newspaper. "For the first time in my life, I honestly want to get up and go to work," he enthuses. "That was a real shock." But the tonic of this new challenge is diluted by feeling diminished in his wife's eyes.

"The difficulty I'm having with defining masculinity is, at a time in my life where I should be able to ignore what people think of me, I went from a fairly large income to my wife being the breadwinner," Rick confesses.

Is his partner dissatisfied because his new career means a comedown economically?

"Maybe that's what stunted our sexual drive," he mumbles.

That brings forth a few startling admissions from the others about their flagging libidos. The men look mildly astonished at the things that are coming out of their mouths in front of other men. At one point the assistant D.A., sweating, opens his jacket, loosens his tie, and unbuttons the top of his shirt, as if to show us *This is how exposed I am.* The conversation palls. The men roll their shoulders. Rick speaks a doubt they probably all share: "I don't know if I've crossed the bridge and it's all downhill, or if I'm just entering another phase of life and I'll move on."

> This is what a midlife passage feels like. It is normal, temporary, and necessary.

The Memphis men are still young. They have not even reached their zenith. Yet each of them is in some danger of becoming lost.

Rick, if he continues to resist becoming a father, could lose his marriage.

Tad, if he continues to insist upon the role of sole breadwinner, could lose his shirt.

Sean, unless he courts Shakespeare's "most auspicious star," could lose his capacity for doing good in the world.

These are among the predictable tempests that beset today's men as they prepare to cross the rough channel between a youth they knew and a strange new territory that is unknown. Confusion and even terror are natural. But tempests blow over. Rick, Tad, Sean, and the others can also grow immeasurably by changing course—before they capsize. Yet in their uncertainty about how to be manly today, these traditional southern men were hanging on for dear life to the same old course, even though that course was not sustaining their families financially or keeping their wives happy.

So what's the problem? Something isn't working, and these well-meaning men are not sure what it is.

A HARD TIME TO BE A MAN IN HIS FORTIES

Headlines and recent books have trumpeted the notion that manhood is on trial—"Masculinity Under Siege," "The End of Patriarchy"—or they propose that it is dead altogether, as in John Stoltenberg's book *The End of Manhood.* No less a male icon than Clint Eastwood calls himself "the last cowboy." The character he played in the hit film *The Bridges of Madison County* describes himself in the Robert James Waller book as among "a certain breed of man that's obsolete." He thought of himself as belonging to an historical continuum of men who were given courage so they could throw spears long distances and fight in hand-to-hand combat. Today he sees computers and robots replacing men of courage. "Men are outliving their usefulness. All you need are sperm banks to keep the species going. Most men are rotten lovers, women say, so there's not much loss in replacing sex with science."

Two male writers who strutted like giants up and down the American cultural landscape for a quarter of a century, Norman Mailer and Gay Talese, both championing the double standard of men's wanton sexual privilege and women's wifely subservience, sound much more tentative these days. "A man's world now is very vague indeed," says Talese. In the battle to keep *Esquire* magazine alive as readers and advertisers were slipping away, Mailer, at 74, lodged an almost pathetic plea: "I would like to see a men's magazine survive. Let's keep these few Mohicans alive."

Meanwhile, women's magazines flaunt ever-more-aggressive cover lines, encouraging a woman to be the sexual hunter and instructing her in how to satisfy her increasingly rising expectations.

"You Always Have Orgasms . . . Then Suddenly You Don't"
—*Cosmopolitan*, December 1996

"Be Your Own Best Sex Teacher"
—*Cosmopolitan*, May 1996

"Who Says You Can't Enjoy Sex Without Commitment?"
—*Cosmopolitan*, January 1996

"Seize the Night! Your Sexual Peak Is Now!"
—*Glamour*, December 1996

" 'I Wish I Enjoyed Sex More' (You Can)"
—*Glamour*, October 1996

The torrent of feminist writing on sex and gender in the past two decades has expanded our knowledge of women's capacities and desires. Meanwhile, the cults and codes of manhood remain virtually unchanged. The state of being a "real man" is more uncertain and precarious than ever.

"This is a very hard time to be a man in his forties. Men feel quite threatened and attacked. On the work front and at home they feel expendable." The speaker was my lunch partner, John Munder Ross, a pioneer in the study of men who teaches psychoanalysis and human development at the medical schools of Columbia, Cornell, and New York universities. "Many women begin to look for positive changes in their forties and early fifties, when their years of total parenthood are winding down. They become more invested in their careers and often initiate separation from their mates. Men are much needier and more dependent and have greater separation anxiety than we like to acknowledge."

CONFRONTING THE "FALSE SELF"

It is commonly believed that men are hardwired to act aggressively and suppress emotion. Certainly, in the more brutish eras of our evolutionary history these traits made the difference between surviving to enjoy the evening's meal of wild boar or *being enjoyed* as the wild boar's evening meal. Even today, in studies of temperament, one of the most striking gender differences is a man's ability to remain cool under physical attack. Aggression and dominance, rather than sensitivity and submission, have been cited in studies as responsible for superior self-esteem in *both* men and women.

Yet there is also a basic need for intimacy—human closeness—that becomes more persistent as a man grows older. And that need is in direct conflict with the younger man's egocentric need to display his physically aggressive side.

What confuses this natural process for men today is the erosion of traditional male roles and privileges that were taken for granted under patriarchy. While college enrollment is down for Generation X men, as mentioned, women now make up more than half of the degree recipients at all levels of higher education except the doctoral. The pattern is repeated all over Europe. And with their better educations and natural social skills, females are improving their job prospects relative to males in the new "knowledge-based" global marketplace.

The Bureau of Labor Statistics forecasts that the fastest-growing kinds of work between now and 2002 will be computer data processing, health services, child care, and business services—and all are dominated by women. Sectors that are declining most rapidly—such as weapon making, shipbuilding, trucking—depend on brawn or war and were historically man's work. The participation of adult males in the U.S. workforce is down from 87 percent in 1948 to just over 75 percent now.

Which sex has watched its wages remain flat or decline over the past two decades?

American men *in every age group*, except those over 65, saw their median money income (in constant dollars) hit a plateau, decline, or show only a modest gain from 1970 to 1990. During the same two decades, women in every age group drove ahead from their formerly low wage levels. For men aged 40 to 44, working full-time, the median income increased over the twenty years from $32,400 to only $34,600. While men in their late forties and early fifties have not been able to break a median wage of $41,500 in their peak earning years, women have steadily climbed in earning power during their middle years, from the depths of $22,000 to $26,500 for older boomers. It's no wonder the percentage of two-paycheck families is steadily climbing. And the more women become economically independent, the less likely they are to remain in a miserable marriage.

But before you leap to the conclusion that women are stealing men's jobs, let us be clear about the real reasons for these gains. Far more women are in the workforce, and working full-time, often to support families where the fathers have been laid off or are underemployed, absent, or nonexistent. And there is still no occupation where the average wage for women is more than 90 percent of what men earn for the same job.

ARE YOU WHAT YOU SMOKE?

The scene is the Big Smoke in San Francisco at Embarcadero Center. A thousand men, having paid $150 a head, are here to smoke big cigars, sip free booze, get a little buzz, and show off. Big men. Big steak-and-potatoes men with slaphappy smiles strut around the display booths with thick brown protuberances sticking out of their mouths, sucking and puffing, rolling their free imported "sticks" across their lips, holding them proudly as if holding a perfect erection. They stop to sample different shapes and sizes. At the Bering booth a poster shows off fifteen different shapes of perfect Honduran hand-rolled (supposedly on the thighs of naked women) upright cigars, the most popular of which, according to the salesman, are the short, thick ones, the Robustos; as they get longer they get thinner, all the way up to the master of them all, the eight-inch Grande. "If you smoke it slowly," the salesman promises, "it will last for three hours."

It's an almost exclusively male heterosexual crowd. Well, there are some babes, a sprinkling of them, their breasts and thighs displayed behind net tops and tiny spandex skirts like boneless chicken parts under shrink-wrapped plastic. But they are mostly hired models who pass out free champagne and brandy to police captains with pistols poking out of their hip pockets, white-collared priests, corporate execs, and salesmen with prominent facial hair.

At the center of the swirl is the short, thick figure of Marvin Shanken, the prescient editor who more than anyone else is responsible for the cigar-smoking mania in America at a time when men are hungry, no, famished for exclusive ways of expressing their maleness. Shanken's insight into how to ride this trend took the form of launching a magazine, *Cigar Aficionado*, which celebrates smoking cigars, driving fast cars, eating red meat, all of which is saying to women—and here Shanken uses an Italian gesture, flicking his fingers under his chin and out in your face—"I'm dangerous, reckless, devil-may-care, bulletproof. I'm a tough guy, take it or leave it."

When Shanken launched *Cigar Aficionado* in 1992, nobody understood it, he says. The antismoking wave was at its peak. The cigar market had dropped like a stone, with only 100 million hand-rolled cigars produced in the whole world. Over the next four years the sales of premium cigars more than doubled. And Shanken's magazine, thick and glossy and crammed with a hundred pages of ads just for cigars, saw an increase in circulation to 400,000. Why would a man slap down forty dollars to renew his subscription to a bimonthly magazine about *cigars*?

Shanken saw cigar smoking as a way for men to reassert an exclusively male preserve and adorn themselves with a status symbol that is considerably cheaper than the luxury cars or boats that were the totems of successful Yuppies in the go-go eighties. The prototype of the man who attends his promotion parties in major cities is a successful show-off who trades sports talk and dirty jokes and whose every third sentence starts with "The bottom line."

So what's wrong with hanging out and smoking cigars? Nothing, in the short run. (Although if he were alive today, Sigmund Freud, a habitual cigar smoker, might have something to say about becoming smoke-dependent: he died of mouth cancer. A big cigar contains more tobacco than a whole pack of cigarettes, and cigar smokers end up just as dependent on nicotine as cigarette smokers.) Cigar smoking in male packs was an understandable, if superficial, attempt by men to take back part of their lost, exclusive world. The fact that sexy women like Demi Moore copied them added a frisson of glamour to the behavior. The trend has peaked and is on the wane. Why? Such behavior does not seriously address the confusion over a code of manliness appropriate to today. It is an elite version of a larger movement among men who feel displaced, disappointed, and "dissed." Men need ways and places they can get together with other men, and many of those opportunities have been lost as a result of long-overdue laws against sexual discrimination.

"THE BIG IMPOSSIBLE"

Men's problem with defining and proving their masculinity is an eternal one. True manhood is an elusive status beyond mere biological maleness. In aboriginal North America, for example, among the nonviolent Fox tribe of the Iowa area, real manhood was described as "the Big Impossible." It was an elevated status that only an extraordinary few could achieve.

"Masculinity is not something given to you, something you're born with, but something you gain. . . . And you gain it by winning small battles with honor," wrote Norman Mailer in *Cannibals and Christians.* Current anthropological observational studies would support the novelist.

A man is *made a man.* There is no parallel belief among most of the peoples studied by anthropologists that girls need to be *made* women.

Cultural anthropologist David Gilmore conducted a fascinating retrospective cross-cultural study of manhood and masculinity. He found that across cultures, from primitive to contemporary urban cultures, attaining the status of "real man" is an uncertain and precarious endeavor. On every continent, among the simplest hunters and fishermen as well as sophisticated urbanites, there is a critical threshold that boys must pass, through harsh testing, before they can gain the right to the gender identity of manliness.

In Christian Crete, for example, men must show their "manly selfhood" by stealing sheep. In the Balkans a "real man" is one who drinks heavily, spends money freely, fights bravely, and fathers many children. In Mediterranean countries, rigid codes of action as husband, father, lover, provider, and warrior often reflect an inner insecurity, writes Gilmore. "Effete men, the men-who-are-no-men, are held up scornfully to inspire conformity to the glorious ideal."

The break from the world of women is initiated by a boy's father. A second and more forcible separation from mothers and nursemaids has historically taken place later in most societies, around "age seven plus or minus one," according to Dr. Munder Ross. In ancient Greece, for instance, the child Alexander (later to become Alexander the Great) was handed over to a male tutor named Aristotle, to be instructed in the manly arts and ways of the world. This ritual still holds in much of the Middle East and Asia even today.

Closer to home, the English tradition of separating well-born boys from their mothers and nannies at the age of seven and banishing them to the all-male rites and rituals of boarding school—cold showers, cauterized emotions, often physical violence if not homosexual assault by authority figures—was traditionally meant to toughen men up to take their place in the future ruling class of the British Empire. The empire may be gone, but boys headed for Oxbridge are still subjected to the same tests.

> American men seem to be particularly insecure—why?

"American men have no history because we haven't known what questions to ask," according to the central thesis of a new book, *Manhood in America*, by historical sociologist Michael Kimmel. He argues that the quest for manhood has been one of the formative and persistent experiences in men's lives.

"Over our two centuries of history, American manhood became less and less about an inner sense of self, and more and more about a possession that needed to be acquired," observes Professor Kimmel. He proposes that the story of American men's efforts to prove themselves "is a story of a chronically anxious, temperamentally restless manhood." If most men define their masculinity not so much in relation to women but in relation to each other, what happens when they have no shared heroes or collective benchmarks?

As Gilmore points out, there is no single line that, once passed, confers manhood, as there is for girls, who are officially women at menarche. Even in their late twenties, young men admit to me they are confused about what constitutes the code of manliness today. A beefy blond Gen Xer of 28 raised in the American West with a natural alpha male presence told me without noticeable envy, "With my parents, there was a relationship of clear dominance and submission. My dad was a surgeon.

He acted with godlike certainty. I mean, he *assumed* prerogative. My mother was a nurse. They both worked, but she assumed it was her role to show deference to him and please him."

Did he find he couldn't take many cues from his father about how to be a man today? I asked. The revelation startled him, but Greg agreed. He summed up the historical shift in a sentence:

> "There are no rules for how to be a man today."

The line is even more vague for men entering Second Adulthood. Women have the marker of menopause. Men have no such clear marker to signal them that they are changing and need to adapt to that change to make it work for them. In *A New Psychology of Men*, William Pollack and Ronald F. Levant attempt to redefine and expand the meanings of masculinity. They are among the most thoughtful of scholars attempting to rescue men from the confinements of rigid role expectations that have emphasized competition, toughness, and emotional stoicism and goaded men into a "pseudo-self-sufficiency."

It is no use to segregate males into rigid either-or camps: the effeminate man who is sweet but weak versus the "he-man" who has to slap his wife around to show he's boss or live uncommitted and probably emotionally famished. Mostly, men deny what is ambiguous and contradictory in their nature. They are always on guard against the two great dangers they feel, as described by Dr. Munder Ross in his book *The Male Paradox:*

> The danger of succumbing to their feminine side—becoming a "wuss."

> The danger of affirming their masculinity through repeated acts of aggression or self-destruction—becoming "killers."

The answer to the manhood puzzle, suggests anthropologist Gilmore, must lie in culture. "We must try to understand why culture uses or exaggerates biological potentials in specific ways." When I sit with a group of nice guys like the Memphis men and hear about their futile struggles to live up to the old traditional model of masculinity, my heart goes out to them. They are trying to accomplish "the Big Impossible." For some time now, women have been defying all the stereotypes they grew up with—the narrow roles, the gender-punitive rules, the outgrown myths about age—and women are measurably happier in midlife than they have been in any previous generation.

It is time that men recognize that their gender-punitive roles and rules are virtually impossible to live up to in the contemporary world. Trying to do so only limits their otherwise exhilarating possibilities for custom-designing a happier middle life.

THE RELUCTANT FATHER

RICK REVISITED

"I was a jerk to say no, we're not going to adopt."

Three weeks after my meeting with the Memphis men (see page 45), Rick Smith, the reluctant father, was cradling his adopted newborn son and recalculating the chronology of his life. "I'd always been perfectly comfortable with the thought of dying at sixty," Rick had told the group. (He was the 39-year-old Yuppie who felt he and his wife had lost a decade by focusing exclusively on their careers.) "What I might be doing in my seventies really never entered my mind, because we didn't have children, and we'd be old and I'd be useless by that time." But by the end of our interview, he had vowed that he and his wife would go into "catch-up mode."

Forty was around the corner for Rick, and the hollowness of self-absorption had begun to wear down his resistance to taking on the obligations of parenthood. When a child became available, he stopped stalling at last.

I spoke to him nine months after he had become a father: he sounded deliriously happy. "Whatever self-absorbed nature I still had at thirty-nine disappeared the day we took the child home," he said. "I'm definitely a different person now." He and his wife had recommitted to their marriage, because now they shared a sacred trust. And once the baby had begun sleeping all night—miraculous!—the interest in intimacy had reawakened in both partners. Rick's resistance to having his own needs upstaged by a child had actually deprived him of the attentions and ardor of his wife. He could see that in retrospect. "It drove a wedge into almost all aspects of our relationship, all because of my stupidity."

His dark fantasies of the future—being the only 50-year-old dad at the church picnic—were beginning to fade. "I used to imagine all the other thirty-year-old fathers playing softball with their sons while I'm being helped around in a walker." Rick's picture of middle life was, of course, drastically outdated. Forty is still young for fatherhood today. In many urban and suburban communities, gray-haired dads are nothing unusual anymore. And 50-year-old fathers are doing triathlons or having arthroscopic surgery so they can keep playing baseball.

Now that Rick has a Second Adulthood worth investing in, he is thinking of his work life in a new and serious way. He doesn't mind so much sharing the breadwinner role with his successful wife. He sees himself as essential again. "This baby makes us look at life with a much larger perspective," he told me. "Now I'm thinking, when I'm sixty, my son will only be twenty. So I've got to hang around a lot longer."

Fathers really do matter. The New Father is one of the strongest culturewide shifts in the manly ideal. Some 90 percent of married fathers now witness the births of their children, which connects them to the birth process and the sanctity of life from the very start. Another recent poll found that 80 percent of fathers said they wanted to take a greater role in parenting than their fathers had. Still, there are very few good data on fathers and their importance to their children. Incalculable damage has been done to the family by social welfare policies that assumed the absence of fathers, policies that became a self-fulfilling prophecy.

Today there is a very vigorous grassroots father's rights movement. It is led by men who feel disenfranchised by divorce and a legal system that has been slow to recognize their loss of the role of father in most divorce settlements. Judging by the postings of men's movement organizations on the Internet, this is the issue around which the most common grievances coalesce. Out of 123 listed men's movement organizations in the United States and Canada, more than 40 are devoted specifically to father's rights—from the American Fathers Coalition to Dads Against Discrimination to Fathers Are Parents Too! to a Men's/Father's Hotline, as well as a Father's Exchange in San Francisco that invites men to join a group called Nurturing Today.

One of the greatest benefits of entering midlife is that a man can take off the blinders of the young warrior, driven by hormones to compete and "kill off" rivals, and see that he is not expendable. He is necessary as a continuing partner in marriage and a lifeline for his progeny. He is a member of a community and a society that desperately need his unique contribution. The enlightened man in his forties can now see his life as part of the larger continuum of history.

FIRST FATALITY JITTERS

TAD REVISITED

Another member of the Memphis men's group had stalled in the middle of his midlife crisis. Tad was the 42-year-old who wanted desperately to reclaim the traditional role of sole breadwinner. He had been a corporate officer with handsome stock options when he left the computer industry to start his own advertising business, rather than relocate his young family. He had taken a significant decrease in compensation to make the change. Believing that it was important to their religious life as Christians, he and his wife agreed that he would provide and she would leave her high-powered professional position to stay home and take care of their three children. But she couldn't afford any household help, and she began feeling indignant. Tensions had taken a toll on their sex life.

Tad was a little shaky when we checked in nine months after the Memphis group discussion. His partner in the new business, who was close in age, had been diagnosed with a brain tumor, and six weeks later he was dead. In talking about this sudden tragic event, Tad's voice drained of feeling and became mechanical, ticking off his practical decisions rather than stirring up his feelings about the death. "I decided it was best for us not to proceed with this company," he said. "So I basically backed out. Backed away from my business. Informed my partners. We sold off the assets. So I guess I am technically unemployed. I'm doing a little consulting work, so I am not devoid of income. It's not particularly uncomfortable for me—I have lots of options. It's more uncomfortable for my wife."

This sounded like a brave front. Tad had been unemployed for four months. He had assumed responsibility for full support of five people: him and his wife, two children in private school, and a 2-year-old. He was right at the beginning of his midlife passage and already having a crisis of confidence when he hit a trauma. The confluence of entering one's forties and having a close contemporary die can magnify the natural mortality fears at this age to a terrifying proportion.

In his phrase "backed away from my business" one could almost hear a more primitive fear: *I backed away from whatever it was that killed my partner.* "What I have become comfortable with, emotionally and intellectually, is that there really isn't any security anywhere. It's just the nature of our financial lives today."

> I am alone. There is no one who will always take care of me.

These are painful recognitions common to entering midlife. Tad's relationship with his wife was also fraying badly. "There is increased stress," Tad admitted, and then, without irony, he added the comment, "I honestly don't know why."

His wife had given up the gratification of being president of her own company to play her part in an idealized scenario that has become a luxury. The couple's best intentions had left the family a few paychecks away from disaster.

Given the economic realities of today, it is very difficult for a middle-class family to depend on a single earner with a stay-at-home wife. Yet Americans are more reluctant to give up the traditional family role structure than are people in many other countries, according to an international Gallup Poll of adults in twenty-two nations. Nearly half of the Americans surveyed said the ideal family structure was one in which only the father earned the living and the mother stayed home with the children, compared with only about one fourth of those polled in Germany, India, Lithuania, Spain, Taiwan, and Thailand.

Both Tad and his wife, he admitted, had become quicker to anger; both felt grievances common in this circumstance. "I'm sure she feels that since I am unemployed, I ought to be doing more things to help around the home," Tad said. "And I think there are more things she should do to help me or support me."

SEAN REVISITED

Another member of the Memphis group had confronted a mortality crisis but had used it differently—as a prod to take the risk of expanding
his world. Sean, the assistant district attorney, had expressed all the frustration of the disappointed idealist. He was the white lawyer with "establishment" written all over him who worked downtown with mostly
poor black men in a racially tense city. He wanted to do good in the
world. Instead, he felt as though he was cleaning up society's messes and
no one really gave a hoot. His heroic quest as a lawyer was not being fulfilled. Society wasn't what he wanted it to be. He was almost forty, and
he envied his wife for having more rewarding work (she runs her own
adoption counseling agency). A man on the edge of midlife can spend an
awfully long time nursing such narcissistic wounds and taking out his
angst on other people.

His wife, Claire,* took the brunt of his brooding. "I used to twist myself into a pretzel about it," she recounted. "I have a lot of freedom to
do more emotionally satisfying work because of the higher income he
brings in. I felt bad about it." Finally Claire confronted her husband. He
couldn't work twelve hours and then use their precious time together obsessing about the lack of meaning in his work. "I recognized that the
frustration I feel at work is not my fault," Sean told us. "I didn't create
the situation. Frankly, as a white male in Memphis, I don't see I have a
great future. But the job doesn't define me."

Realizing that "the job doesn't define me" is a first step toward deil-
lusionment of the early dream; it allows a man to move toward a more
inner-based merit system.

The death of Sean's uncle had precipitated a passage. As he told us,
suddenly "death was for real. I couldn't be angry anymore. I had to grow
up." He fantasized about changing careers, about becoming a deacon or
a priest. But realistically, as a father of two young children, he would have
to put such dreams "on ice" for ten years until his family responsibilities
lessened. So he opened up his thinking to explore other ways to answer
the calling of his better nature. He began studying Asian culture. Visits
to the public Japanese garden in Memphis suggested new philosophical
principles; he planted his own Japanese garden in the backyard and be-

---

*A pseudonym.

came interested in Zen Buddhism. It was a spiritually refreshing outlet. He had also been serving in the Army National Guard as a military lawyer. When the United States approved sending troops to Bosnia, Sean volunteered to pull a month of active duty to assist in preparing the troops for deployment. "I enjoyed it immensely," he said. "To me, the military comes closest to living out those ideals I believe in."

In the summer of 1996 he was asked to be part of a fascinating project: The American Bar Association wanted him to assist the War Crimes Tribunal at The Hague on the war in Bosnia. He would go to The Hague to review unindicted cases and help to make decisions about which war criminals to pursue. His world was expanding.

"If someone thinks enough of me as a lawyer to ask me to support the War Crimes Tribunal, then I must be pretty good. I think in many ways the best is yet to come for me."

MOVING UP THE MORTALITY MARKERS

In the days before modern technological medicine and transportation, most people saw death up close among family members while they were relatively young. As recently as twenty years ago, when I wrote *Passages*, I described the "deadline decade"—when we first become aware that we are perishable—as being somewhere between ages 35 and 45. Today, it is commonplace for people to be insulated from death and to delay the confrontation with their own mortality by ten years, putting it off until closer to the midforties.

Although this can be a gradual passage with no particular outer event to mark it, eventually we all confront the reality of our own death. And somehow we must learn to live with it. If our life course is interrupted during this time by a life accident—one of those untimely events that we cannot predict or prevent—it can accelerate and exaggerate the mortality crisis. We are not prepared for the idea that time can run out on us or for the startling truth that if we don't hurry to pursue our definition of a meaningful existence, life can become a repetition of trivial maintenance duties. Nor are we anticipating a major upheaval of the roles and rules that may have comfortably defined us in the first half of life but that must be reordered around a core of strongly felt personal values in the second.

Tad and Sean both had a mortality crisis, but they dealt with it very differently. Tad's may have been more severe, since his partner's death also shook the security of his new company. He was not ready to make a transition and retreated into a smaller circle: family, church, a few friends and people he might meet through his consulting work. He was limited in what he could envision for himself. In contrast, Sean's vision of himself enlarged. He was studying other philosophies, extending his interest in both the military and more meditative pursuits such as gardening and Zen. Sean was able to see outside the box—beyond Memphis, beyond the United States—to explore what he might do in the world. He was also beginning to score himself differently: "I don't want to regret the big issues of life. In the past, I compared myself to other people. Now I only want to have been the best father, husband, lawyer, the best human being I can be."

Underneath the shock of experiencing a death up close for the first time is the fact, as yet unacknowledged, that there is a downside to life, a back of the mountain, and that you have only so much time before the dark to find your own truth. As such thoughts gather thunder, the continuity of the life cycle is interrupted. They usher in a deadline decade that today spans the midforties to the midfifties. During this time the dissonance between the false self and the authentic self reaches its maximum tension, and most people will have a full-out *authenticity crisis*.

HONOR AMONG MEN

"What men need is men's approval," notes playwright David Mamet. Traditionally, men have demonstrated their masculinity through displays of honor. The fields in which they were best able to do this were sports, politics, business, and war—all fields that until very recently excluded women.

I asked men in group interviews if they still found opportunities to demonstrate honor. To a group of San Francisco men I put the question "Does the concept of honor still have any relevance for you today?" They all began scribbling furiously on yellow pads.

"Honor means knowing your true path and sticking to it," asserted Bill O'Connell, a highly respected radio personality featured on KDFC, a classical music station in San Francisco. He seemed to feel that changing one's path might not be honorable.

"It's doing the right thing," offered Paul Couenhoven, a 42-year-old attorney.

David Mainehardt, a 48-year-old photographer who went back to college in his forties to get a Ph.D. in order to broaden his horizons, related "honor" to "being self-directed but geared toward a goal larger than yourself."

I noted that in the traditional sense, honor was demonstrated through being challenged, being put on the line. At the extreme, one gained honor by risking one's life for something larger than oneself; or, in a smaller way, by putting others' welfare before one's own and saving a village or an institution.

"To me, the whole idea of honor means living by a set of values no matter what the cost," said Couenhoven. Among historical figures he suggested Sir Thomas More, the leader of the Catholic Church in sixteenth-century England, whose execution for his values was dramatized in the play and movie *A Man for All Seasons;* or the thirteenth-century Scottish patriot William Wallace (played by Mel Gibson in the movie *Braveheart*), who united his people and led a ramshackle yet courageous army determined to vanquish the superior English forces and reclaim the Scottish throne from the ruthless English king who had seized it: "Wallace was willing to risk his life for what he believed in, while everyone else could be bought off."

Since women have made inroads into all of the traditionally male-exclusive fields—business, politics, sports, and even war to some degree—how did this group of men see women vis-à-vis the concept of honor?

A former public defender, Couenhoven speculated, "In this day and age, women are probably more honorable than men. Election surveys show that men are much more likely to vote on money issues and women are more likely to think about how social and economic policies are going to impact people."

Terry South, the middle manager we heard from at the beginning of Chapter 3, expressed regret that the corporate world shows no recognition of the ancients' truth of leading by serving. "We have a lot of women in our business [TV]," he said, "and I feel like I learn more about that whole idea of leading by serving from women much more often than

I do from men. By serving, I mean looking out for the interests of the collective group, rather than self-interest."

But the cultural truth remains, as Mamet and Mailer reflect, that men care most about what other men think of them.

> Men are driven to prove themselves—perpetually—especially to other men.

A man's greatest fear is of being dominated, or humiliated, by a stronger man or in front of other men. How, then, do men in middle life continue to demonstrate their manliness even as their physical strength wanes?

MANLY SPORTS: MORE THAN JUST A GAME

"It's just a game," women often say in exasperation while their mates sit transfixed for hours before TV images of men running around a field chasing a football or soccer ball, swinging at a baseball, or laying up with the grace of a flying marlin to sink a basketball. The average American man watches twenty-eight hours of TV a week, and much of that is sports. Many of those men are in midlife or older, "Joe Six-Packs" who are no longer participants in highly competitive sports. So what's the great appeal?

"You live through these godlike men who are performing feats you can almost believe *you* are doing," says one armchair sports fan. Basketball, baseball, football, soccer, and other manly sports are more than games; they constitute a culture, arguably the dominant male culture today. Perhaps always. Back when the New York Yankees were the undisputed gods of baseball, humorist James Thurber wrote, "Ninety-five percent of American men put themselves to sleep at night by striking out the batting order of the New York Yankees." In the summer of 1997, the famous participatory journalist George Plimpton turned up at a party in

East Hampton looking sleep-deprived. "Last night I put myself to sleep by playing Pete Sampras in the finals at Wimbledon," he told me, "until five in the morning."

In a fascinating book titled *The Stronger Women Get, the More Men Love Football*, a former professional basketball player, Mariah Burton Nelson, points out that "Manly sports comprise a world where men are in charge and women are irrelevant at best. . . . Sports offer a pre–civil rights world where white men, as owners, coaches, and umpires, still rule."

Sports also permit shared passion between men. Just watch: it is most often the over-40 guys in the stands at football games or soccer matches who shriek and groan and weep, uncovering raw emotions they would contain in front of men in almost any other setting. Sports allow grown men to *feel*.

Most pertinent to our discussion of forging a new masculinity ideal are the lessons in emotional control, and true athletic stars are champions at emotional control. If they weren't able to psych themselves up, meditate to dilute their anxieties, channel their anger, blot out the jeers of the crowd, they would never have the cool and concentration necessary to kick that crucial field goal or come back from losing the first set to hammer winning serves in the second. As Nelson writes, "When they fight, the fighting is deliberate masculine theater, not a momentary loss of control. The decision to [lose one's temper] involves rational considerations: not losing face, trying to win games, fulfilling expectations of fans and teammates, and appearing on the evening news."

If ever there were a metaphor for facing what appears to be insurmountable in middle life and changing your strategy to adapt and triumph, it is the historic heavyweight championship fight between Muhammad Ali and George Foreman in Zaire.

It was the Prince against the Champion. Ali was bragging up and down that he would take his title back. But Foreman was the meanest charging bull to come along in heavyweight circles for many years. The retinue of Muslims around Ali was merely praying that George wouldn't *kill* their man. Ali told everybody he was going to dance, and everybody expected Ali to dance: the dance around death.

Ali came on strong in the first round, throwing rights at Foreman's skull, punching offensively with all the authority he could muster. Foreman roared forward, his gloves thrust out like the horns of a bull, and forced Ali into a corner. *Start dancing,* his corner men shrieked. But he lay back. Writers George Plimpton and Norman Mailer leapt to their feet, and one shouted to the other, "Oh, Christ, it's a fix!" But Mailer thought he saw fear in the Prince's eyes as the first round finished. He was up against an immovable force greater than himself.

No one was prepared to see the great boxing balletomane back himself into a corner in the middle of the second round. Ali changed tactics entirely and lay back on the ropes—"traditionally a sort of halfway house to the canvas for the exhausted fighter who hopes perhaps the referee will take pity on him and stop things," as described by Plimpton in his book *ShadowBox*—and from that position, looking like a bosun hanging off the mast in a storm, Ali worked the rest of the fight. To the sixty thousand fight fans writhing in their seats and to the world TV audience, it appeared that Ali was in constant danger, maybe even wimping out. But as Mailer later recounted in his book *The Fight,* Ali was "demonstrating that what for other fighters is a weakness can be for him a strength. . . . Ali uses the ropes to absorb the bludgeoning."

Imagine the emotional and physical control it took for Ali to endure the humiliation of appearing passive, allowing Foreman to pummel him while he absorbed and absorbed some more, conserving and consolidating his own strength while he waited for his opponent to tire himself out.

Foreman never changed. As his rage gradually spent itself, his punches grew weaker and weaker, until Ali saw his moment. When finally the Prince came off the ropes, he gave Foreman three rights in a row, then a left, and then a projectile. Foreman was utterly startled. His arms flew out to the side, and in a long, collapsing two seconds he glided down to the mat.

"My God," said Mailer to Plimpton in a tone of wonder, "he's champion again."

Think about this scene when you hit the ropes in midlife. How do you adapt when you're overpowered? How well prepared are you to change your game plan? How willing are you to try new tactics? Or to bide your time in a defensive stance before you see an opening to move forward again?

Foreman, having lost his honor when he lost his title, sank into a two-year depression. But he made some deeply important passages of his own and came back into the ring at what is considered for boxers middle age, starting a trend. At 48, Foreman was still fighting.

CURRENT MANHOOD MODELS

Men are finding different ways to bolster themselves in this time of confusion—let's call them postures. A spectrum of these postures is suggested below, not as neat pigeonholes but as different expressions of manhood in contemporary life. A man may move from one to another, depending on his mood or circumstance.

One of the strongest trends of the nineties is men reverting to an old, prefeminist, pre–Alan Alda form:

RESURGENT ANGRY MACHO MAN (RAMM)

The RAMM movement encourages a man to return to his primitive "nature" as the "strongman" or "wild man," with fire in his belly and a strong arm to put women back into their place. The prototype is the American cowboy. The tough loner who shoots from the hip, doesn't need love, doesn't stick around with women, doesn't react to loss was the cultural ideal through the 1950s, immortalized in the most successful advertising campaign ever: the Marlboro Man. Riding horseback through wild nature with a cigarette dangling from his mouth, he was a symbol of virility and raw, vigorous health. But on closer look, the Marlboro Man was uneducated, smelly, lonely, and destined to die young from lung cancer. In the 1990s he was found out as a dangerous imposter, hunted down by antismoking forces, and banished from billboards.

The best of the RAMM model is displayed in arenas where men must steel themselves to pain and emotion in order to fight or protect their families or their kind: combat soldier, cop on the beat, prizefighter trying to get out of the ghetto. But even here—or especially here, in formerly exclusive male preserves—some men are so desperate to display their dominance and control that they open themselves to ruin.

The effort to integrate the U.S. military, while in many ways successful, has etched into our consciousness the names of more memorable battlefields than a small war: Operation Tailhook, Aberdeen, the Citadel Virginia Military Institute. Only now the enemy is women. When the Supreme Court ruled that VMI had to admit women, a defiant senior cadet told *The New York Times,* "We were burned during the Civil War and shelled by the Union. We'll endure this too."

Shocking revelations of rape, assaults, and sexual abuse have resulted in trials of high-ranking noncommissioned officers and the ruination of the pioneering military career of the first female B-52 pilot for adultery and lying to cover up her sexual indiscretion. As *New Yorker* writer Roger Angell summed up the gender insult, "Flying the B-52 . . . is macho Valhalla, and the arrival of a fully trained and qualified woman on the flight deck must have been cause for consternation somewhere in the collective unconscious of the old-line flyboys who make policy decisions in the Air Force." Even in the Marines, women now shoot live ammunition from heavy weapons. The Army, to its credit, having finally investigated and found sexual harassment to be pervasive across gender, rank, and racial lines, is attacking the problem by revamping its whole approach to leadership and training.

A symbol of manhood who has held up for several generations is John Wayne. Some polls still find him number one among Americans' favorite movie actors, ahead of Clint Eastwood and Mel Gibson, even though he has been dead for many years. As described by Garry Wills in his book *John Wayne's America,* he is the embodiment of the country's receded frontier, "untrammeled, unspoiled, free to roam"—a flagrant freedom in the flesh. Wayne remains an inspiration to men of the RAMM type, such as conservative presidential candidate Pat Buchanan and Congressman Newt Gingrich, the latter having grown up emulating Wayne's swagger and taking his male codes from movies such as *Sands of Iwo Jima.*

"I was a fifty-year-old at nine," Gingrich told me in an interview. "I had imprinted John Wayne in his midforties as my model of behavior." The character Wayne played in *Sands* was a friendless, combat-hardened unit leader of a marine rifle squad who makes a victim of a new recruit. His behavior was not unlike that of Gingrich's father and stepfather toward the young Newt.

"They're both angry," Newt said of his two fathers. "They both served in the military. They're both physically strong. They both believe in a very male kind of toughness. They're both totalitarian." Given a childhood shaped by a natural father who abandoned him and a stepfather who belittled him, Newt came to politics with a psychic need so great that only the praise that attends a savior can fill the vacuum inside him. "I found a way to immerse my insecurities in a cause large enough to justify whatever I wanted it to," he told me. He had described that cause in a newspaper interview in 1985: "I want to shift the entire planet.

And I'm doing it. This is just the beginning of a twenty- or thirty-year movement. I'll get credit for it."

But in 1997, Newt Gingrich, with his aggressive RAMM behavior as speaker of the House of Representatives, earned the lowest approval rating of any politician in the United States. It is not insignificant that both Gingrich and Buchanan managed to stay out of the Vietnam War, just as their hero, the hawk Wayne, who in real life, according to Wills, "called on other generations to sacrifice their lives and called them 'soft' if they refused," was the same man who adroitly kept himself out of being drafted to serve in World War II.

The opposite philosophy . . .

SENSITIVE NEW AGE GUY (SNAG)

Initially, this was a guy who unexpectedly (or by default, as in the movie *Kramer vs. Kramer*) discovered his nurturing side. In the extreme version, he switched roles and assumed the prerogatives of Mr. Mom. He expected his kids and wife to idealize his contribution, his hours would be discretionary, and he wouldn't be responsible for mortgage payments. Or, having fought for custody after divorce, he was determined to prove he could outdo Mom. The results among men who try to perform this role alone, or without working outside the home, are mixed. They can usually develop the necessary empathy and patience to care for children, but to forgo career ambitions and male posturing may eventually make them feel desexed. And they often find themselves left behind by their women, who desert or divorce them to seek wider horizons themselves.

However, many successful men in midlife have disclosed to me their yearning to enjoy a period as Mr. Mom. It is a genuine cultural change, still small but growing. It could be a very healthy way for a man in transition to exercise his nurturant side and feel useful while he is figuring out a new direction. In the group discussion with San Francisco men on how they define "honor" today, Paul Couenhoven, the 42-year-old attorney, told how he had left the public defender's office in order to work fewer hours so that he could spend more time with his four-year-old daughter. He came closest to describing the gradual developmental process by which a man stops needing to act out his flagrant freedoms in exchange for the rewards of respect and love paid to a responsible man: "A sense of honor comes from building a sense of self-worth and not compromising it. I think being a father is all part of that sacrifice. Left to our own devices, if we followed every impulse that we had, we wouldn't be very good fathers. Once you've accepted that responsibility, you've got to stick to it. There are people now depending on you, and you don't have the freedom that you used to have."

The currently popular Hollywood model of the SNAG is an enviably successful but egocentric Yuppie who almost loses what is most important to him but is saved in the end by growing out of his macho posturing. One of Hollywood's top-grossing stars, the zany putty face Jim Carrey, scored a big hit with *Liar, Liar* by depicting a driven lawyer whose five-year-old son magically transforms him from a narcissistic no-show dad into a sensitive hands-on father.

The 1997 film hero Jerry Maguire, a fortyish bachelor sports agent, also learns from early success and humiliating failure how to make a comeback as a SNAG—less arrogant and more empathetic and nurturing. Pushing the boundaries of the SNAG still further, Kevin Kline launched a trend in the comedy *In and Out* toward depicting the gay man as having more fun. "Real men don't dance," drones the instruction tape Kline listens to; but Kline's character, an outwardly starchy English teacher, can't help himself boogying to beat the band. He turns out to be more honorable than any of the hetero males in the movie.

DOMINANT MALE MODEL (DOM)

These are the world-beaters, the wunderkinder, the high achievers who have to be on top to be happy. In Shakespearean times, the DOMs were the dukes of Milan, like Prospero in *The Tempest.* In more contemporary terms, they were the hotshot bond traders of the greedy eighties so memorably labeled by Tom Wolfe "Masters of the Universe." In the nineties they are personified by the rogue elephants of the information and entertainment colossi: Bill Gates, Rupert Murdoch, Sumner Redstone, John Malone, Michael Eisner, Donald Trump.

MESSENGER OF GOD (MOG)

A fourth philosophy, propounded by a new wave of Christian evangelism, calls upon born-again Christian men to band together in mass movements based on spiritually inspired twelve-step programs. Men are recruited to these movements by powerful autocratic figures. Louis Far-rakhan, a militantly anti-Semitic Muslim, presided over the Million Man March of mostly black American men. Bill McCartney, a messianic for-mer football coach who says he was called by God to create the Promise Keepers, announced in 1997 his plan to "sweep the nation, and then, in the year 2000, Promise Keepers is gonna go global!"

Both movements tap into a longing for ideals, discipline, spiritual guidance, and a regeneration of male authority. They appeal particularly to boomers and Gen Xers with rock music, an athletic "uniform," mar-tial speeches, pointed exclusion of women, and permission for hetero-sexual men to show love for one another. Surrendering themselves to tough love and chastisement for their irresponsible behaviors, adherents recite vows to be better fathers, husbands, community leaders, and enlist-ees in a "godly army" dedicated to restoring "biblical values." Men are commanded to "take back leadership of the family." Based on a carefully edited passage of scripture, wives are told to "submit" to husbands.

"If we don't change, we will be irrelevant in the world to come," as a keynote speaker summed up the sense of threat that pervaded a recent Promise Keepers revival rally.

The appeal of being a MOG is strong, especially to men who cannot compete anymore on the basis of brawn alone and who have felt dis-placed in the workplace and at home. Historians call McCartney's Promise Keepers one of the fastest-growing religious revivals in Ameri-can history. He demonstrated it by summoning his troops to a Stand in the Gap rally in Washington, D.C., in October 1997, which was widely covered on national TV.

The scene is the Washington Mall—men packed tight as nail heads and stretching a full mile from the nation's Capitol to beyond the Washing-ton Monument. It is a diverse company. The most astonishing impres-sion—given that the numbers gathered here rank with the largest events ever held on the Mall—is the silence. In all of this hairy, high-testosterone crowd of decidedly heterosexual men with bulky shoulders, thick necks, and mostly short hair or buzz cuts, there is no commotion, no snacking, no conversation. They stare straight ahead. Most wear Promise Keepers baseball caps with the bills turned straight forward and white T-shirts with sayings such as "Let go, let God." Except for occasional bursts of "Je-SUS, Je-SUS," repeated like a defense cheer at a football game, and the Christian hymns interspersed between the religious speakers, they are hypnotically quiet in the brilliant sun.

An orator whose image is projected on eighteen giant TV monitors exhorts the men, in trembling tones, to "confess the sexual sins of our lives": *"Get down as low as you can get before God so that you can't get down lower. Prostrate yourself on your face."*

Obediently, hundreds of thousands of men spread themselves out, nosedown, on sidewalks and streets, motionless, the soles of their Reeboks face up.

"Take out a picture of your wife, your kids, somebody that you have abused."

A man nearby, fortyish, in jeans and a velour polo shirt, cups a photo of his wife in his palm and his eyes squint shut. His cheeks color and his ears turn crimson as the speaker confesses for him and others. The men remain prostrate for ten minutes, humps of bodies as far as the eye can see. Tears run in rivulets down unashamed faces.

The few wives here stay on the sidelines, working press and crowd control. According to a survey, the majority of these men are already active in their churches. Their median age is 37, and they are unusually well educated for a mass movement—more than half say they have at least a bachelor's degree. Eighty-eight percent are married, and the great majority of their wives work. But despite the executive positions they might hold in the outside world, most Promise Keepers' wives accept that the husband is the head of the household because, they believe, that is the word of God.

Male bonding is intensely cultivated. An auburn-haired father of 36, Mark Sienkiewicz, who has brought his young son with him from Minnesota, says he feels a different relationship with other men at a Promise Keepers event than at a sporting event. "They seem more like they love you here. Football, you talk football, and that's about it. You don't talk about real things. Men tend to hold it all in." Another young dad is here to try to correct the instructions he was given by his own father. "He believed man's role was to provide, and that's fine. But what was missing," he says, was "love, sensitivity, understanding, patience. Stuff like that."

Coach McCartney, who has long been a supporter of Operation Rescue, the militant antiabortion organization responsible for violence in clinics, comes onstage at last, shouting "Hallelujah!" He barks an order to the men "to obey your leaders and submit to their authority." His eyes are shielded by amber-tinted shades, his expressionless face is sharply divided by a nose that looks as if it's taken a punch or two—as traditionally masculine an image as a colonel. McCartney organizes his movement with a classic military-style top-down chain of authority. The leaders are designated pastors referred to as "battalion commanders." Each pastor selects a "key man" in the parish to act as a staff sergeant and report to a regional "ambassador." Men are recruited as assiduously as college football players and grouped into "task forces."

Since the Promise Keepers have been accused of being almost entirely white, an effort was made to recruit others for this event and to emphasize racial unity. On stage is a spectrum of religious leaders—several African-American pastors, a Latino professor who speaks in Spanish, an Asian-American preacher, an American Indian in full headdress, a Messianic Jew who accepts Jesus, plus a deaf person—every kind but female pastors, rabbis, and homosexuals. McCartney says unequivocally, "We see homosexuality as sin."

The exclusionary aspects of Promise Keepers worry many groups. Some see this appeal to men as "the hottest religious right marketing tool since televangelism." Sixty religious leaders have formed an anti–Promise Keepers coalition to protest the exclusion of female clergy from PK events. Some progressives fear that the group's ultimate goal is to resegregate society along gender lines. Leaders of the National Organization for Women asked McCartney to insert an eighth plank into the PK manifesto, stating simply "We respect women as equals," but the coach says it is not necessary. Asked by Tim Russert on *Meet the Press* if he thinks the man is the head of the household, McCartney said, "I do believe that if there needs to be a decision made where it can't be reconciled, then tenderly and gently the man needs to take authority." In other words, a kinder, gentler patriarchy.

It must be said, however, that Promise Keepers is the first movement that has even attempted a mass liberation of men from the old, repressive definitions of manhood. It is the largest men's movement in the United States—although its numbers are declining from a high in 1996, when attendance at twenty-two stadium events reached 1.1 million, outdoing the attendance at basketball games of one of the world's most popular sports teams, the Chicago Bulls.

Many, probably most, of the men who attend these rallies with heavy hearts or broken lives genuinely desire constructive change. The awesome experience of being in the company of hundreds of thousands of other men and urged to express their emotions, let go of their anger, accept responsibility for their actions, and change their assumptions about what it means to be a man, can be a healing experience that is transformative. The cultural changes that ensue from these individual experiences will ultimately have a political impact.

PARTNER AND LEADER (PAL)

A true grassroots movement is evident in the United States: men are finding ways of bonding in small groups that form spontaneously— among men cruelly downsized at a workplace, men shut out of their children's lives as noncustodial fathers, or through a school or church connection. In these smaller groups, men are encouraged to act as partners as well as leaders, rather than being led by any higher authority. They are bonding not for the historical purpose of attacking or defending turf but as *chosen brothers* who can offer one another support and solace. Some want to unlearn the socialization that keeps their inscrutable feelings locked up inside. They are part of the new *flexible network society* that has been given great impetus by the Internet and the World Wide Web. Today, it is easy to create one's own attitudinal tribe. By surfing the newsgroups or interest categories on the Net, men can be found who share the same values and attitudes and respond to the same myths and symbols.

These groups are usually not religious, but some are part of a much broader spiritual awakening. Men are rediscovering their faith on their own individualistic terms, within and mostly without organized churches. Thousands of Christian and Jewish study classes have sprung up in workplaces around the country, as have Buddhist and Muslim groups. This broader movement generally welcomes wives as full partners. It calls men to spiritual transformation, but as described by inspirational writer Bob Buford in his book *Halftime*, it stresses their movement from success to significance. Religious counseling may be blended with psychotherapy. The new manhood ideal here is "servant-leader."

In truth, men's lives today call upon a full range of capacities from brute force to gentle empathy, and it is no longer necessary or useful to lock oneself into the old either-or stereotypes. That leads only to alienation from oneself. There is much that is still valuable about the traditional model of masculinity, but the model is no longer so mortally confining. In more warlike times, men conscripted into armies of conquest or defense had to resign themselves to being expendable. With military confrontations increasingly being replaced by trade wars, men in postmodern, post–Cold War countries (with exceptions such as Israel with its compulsory military service) have a greater chance to develop new "manly arts"—reinventing the way we live and die by using computers and biotechnology, for instance—and using their individual gifts for purposes other than protecting and defending.

To speak of "the end of manhood" is both absurd and destructive. New ideals of manliness are indispensable to the healthy functioning of any culture, to give men a purpose in life regardless of their age, and urgently necessary to bind men psychologically into the family and community.

Chapter Five

MARRIED AND MORTAL

THE AHA! MOMENT

The gray stone Gothic church on upper Fifth Avenue would normally be dozing unnoticed during the week, but strangely, on this sunny business day in September 1997, black limousines ring the block like sentries surrounding a head of state. Many carry personalized license plates with "TV" in the title. More than a thousand mourners have packed the Church of the Heavenly Rest. But there is something wrong about this memorial service. It's the hair. Most of the men still have their hair. TV is a young business, and the deceased was too young and dynamic to go to his heavenly rest.

> Winston Cox, former chief executive of Showtime Network, died on Saturday after collapsing at a Manhattan health club. He was 55.

It was an obituary that sent shock waves rippling through boardrooms and men's clubs of the highest and mightiest of Manhattan immortals. For some men still in their forties it marked an Aha! Moment—a little epiphany.

Tom Romano* is younger than Tony Cox, still in his forties, still young. Well, almost. He has a birthday around the corner. But as a talented TV executive himself, he looked upon Cox as a role model. He said that when he heard that Tony died, he himself felt chest pains. Tom's only conscious concern about moving beyond his midforties was the dissonance he felt between the young fathers he saw in the park and himself—one of today's delayed dads: he has a newborn at home. He and his wife feel like 20-year-olds approaching parenthood with 40-year-old bodies. He even was tempted to send Levi's a complaint: Why didn't their pants fit him anymore? He was at Woodstock—it wasn't fair!

The deceased himself believed he was immortal. Winston Cox believed he was going to outlive everybody. And why not? To look at him, anyone would have said, "Now, there's a robust, healthy man." The kind of man who would create a rugby team at Princeton, which he did, because he liked to compete only in the toughest of contests.

> He always wanted to be the guy who was up at the plate in the bottom of the ninth with two outs in a World Series.

He had the dimensions of a natural athlete—185 pounds solidly packed into a nearly six-foot frame—and a personality even bigger. Everybody called him "Boss." He loved a party. On Halloween he would dress up as his idol, Bruce Springsteen, and dance in surfer shorts. Even in a business suit, Tony Cox lit up any room he entered. He was a *presence.* Survived by a second wife and two young children as well as two adult children from an earlier marriage, here was a man with all the natural advantages and everything to live for. Why didn't he get his life's worth? There was only one ripple of unrest in the obituary:

> Cox resigned from Viacom early in 1995 after a corporate reorganization.

---

*A pseudonym.

Polite ambiguity on the part of the obituary writer eclipsed the fact that this was an involuntary resignation. Prominent among the brace of Showtime executives in the church's center pews is the reddish cockscomb of Sumner Redstone, the *über*boss, chairman of Viacom, the parent company that owns Showtime Network, and his (then) second in command, Frank Biondi, the man who had recruited Tony Cox to head up Showtime. Biondi was Cox's mentor, his patron, and the man with whom he had bonded most closely throughout his career. Biondi had hired him. And Biondi was the man designated to fire him. The corporate shake-up occurred after Redstone gobbled up Blockbuster, the nation's leading video rental company, a move made with the intention of becoming a $90 billion "global entertainment colossus" but that only created a debt-ridden Brobdingnag that ultimately resulted in Biondi's dismissal as well.

As mourners stream out of the memorial service, there is a glazed look of disbelief on many faces. The widow, young and slender and beautiful, is buffered by friends and the fertility doctor and nurse who helped the Coxes to create a new family. "Their children are so young, they couldn't even attend," someone whispers. The conversation of other top executives close to Tony's age has a tone of restrained panic.

"So shocking."

"He was on the damn treadmill."

"Didn't he run?"

"Are you kidding? Tony was a fitness fanatic," says the heaviest among them. "Tony was working out for years."

"He and Heidi were at the gym together."

"Now I don't want to go on the treadmill anymore."

"I'm reluctant to take the stress test. Pushing your heart rate to the max—"

"That's all I think about. It's like, wait a second—do these doctors really know what's good for you?"

The entire conversation is confined to externals. The men are all grasping for some simple, physiological explanation that will put distance between them and the larger issues stirred up by Tony Cox's untimely death.

An impeccably dressed man with a sculpted goatee stops to chat with Tom. "It should not have happened."

Not to Tony, Tom agrees. It just should never have happened.

They look away, each man juggling his grief with disbelief. The other man was CEO of a major sports complex until it was bought up and devoured and he, like Cox, was purged. It seems as if they are everywhere, these bright, successful men whose work is being taken away in the middle of their lives. Stripped of action, cut off and set adrift, "castrated" if you will, even these alpha males belong among the new at-risk population for depression and anxiety disorders. And younger men wonder: *Could it happen to me?*

THE HEART OF THE MATTER

Male friends talk about Tony the way a man talks who has lost his father. Indeed, that was the nature of their bond. A bonded male relationship is usually unarticulated. There is no language to express the depth of feelings one heterosexual man has for another. After a while it is assumed. Then, if anything happens to sever that bond, the one left behind cannot help but wonder if his love was ever returned, or if it was all in his imagination.

A man takes a huge leap by opening himself up to be hurt. Once you have a bond, male to male, it strips away your defenses and you bare yourself. It's a very hard relationship for men to accept. When you do accept it, you have so much more at risk—ego and pride and machismo. If it's ripped away from you, for whatever reason, it's hard to recuperate.

Tom Romano admits that he went through a dark passage when he lost his father and first glimpsed the shadow of his own mortality. It is apparent that he is itching to broaden his life in some way. He does not want to have to *prove himself* anymore. But wasn't that what Tony Cox said over and over again?

Cox had reached the stage of life, at 54, where he believed he had proven everything he needed to prove. Then to be blindsided by a corporate merger, stripped of his status, taken down in self-esteem—did something die inside?

If so, nobody would have known it. People who worked for him used to call him "Old Buck Up." People took all their troubles to Tony. He absorbed everyone else's angst, implacably. No matter how dire the problem, his advice was always the same: "Oh, your leg was crushed under a subway train? It's just blood—buck up!" His colleagues marveled at how Tony was able to keep everything inside.

Cox kept up a brave front as if nothing had happened. He had spent the past year continuing to go in to the old Viacom offices. Every day. They gave him a desk and phones. He rode up and down on the same elevators. His old employees still called him "boss." Headhunters pumped him up. He was considered a "hot file." He had all the same outer structure, wore the same old uniform, but he was no longer a player. While Viacom gave him a project, he wasn't offered another network or a movie studio or a Fortune 500 company to run. Finally, he began dabbling with a chain of on-line coffee shops in Cambridge. Cox wanted to play with this little company for a few years and take it public and make a bunch of money. But he had no passion for it.

Cox intended to make important changes. Having remarried just shy of 50, his second family was a source of special delight. He loved being able to dally a little longer in the mornings with his new wife, they laughed every day, and the babies she had given him tugged at his heart when he finally did leave. Indeed, he had begun telling his wife, "I'd like to just take care of the kids for a while—you go back to work." He talked about wanting to give something back. Maybe teaching young people. He had all the right instincts for making a transformative change at this critical turning point in his life, but he didn't get to do everything he intended.

He didn't reveal any signs or symptoms of heart trouble. He followed his motto to the end: Buck up. But like *half* of the men who have a sudden coronary, Tony Cox never got up. The initial report gave as cause of death a freak arrhythmia. After a full autopsy, doctors told his family he had severe coronary disease. His maternal grandfather had died of a heart attack, also at 55, a fact that Cox never mentioned to his doctors or to his wife.

If a man has underlying risk factors for heart disease, emotional stress can greatly exaggerate his vulnerability to a heart attack. How large a role stress played in this particular case is hard to say, but the loss of self-image, the injury to his ego, and the possibility of disguised depression would have exacerbated whatever risk factors for heart attack were hidden beneath his stoic facade. Dr. Dean Ornish, the pioneer of nonmedical reversal of heart disease, has noted in his research that the elaborate effort to support a false front is one of the most stressful things a man can do in inviting a heart attack. Dr. Harold L. Karpman, a professor at UCLA Medical School and attending cardiologist at Cedars-Sinai Hospital in Los Angeles, cites a study of 170 news reports of sudden death and the life circumstances that had preceded the people's deaths. The top five circumstances were:

1. Collapse or death of a close friend or relative
2. Threat of loss of a close person
3. Acute grief
4. Mourning or the anniversary of loss of a close person
5. Loss of status or self-esteem

In the opinion of top heart specialists, such nonphysical factors can prompt a change in blood pressure or the heart's pumping rhythm. Dr. Harvey B. Simon, practitioner of preventive cardiology at Massachusetts General Hospital in Boston and founding member of the Harvard Cardiovascular Health Center, reports that a stress-induced surge in adrenaline raises blood pressure, alters the heart's pumping rhythm, speeds the pulse, and can cause the heart to skip a beat and produce arrhythmias. While most arrhythmias are not harmful, in people with heart disease they can cause abnormally low blood pressure, loss of consciousness, or sudden death.

The trigger is not a specific level of stress; it is an *individual's mental reaction* to the emotional stress that can protect that person from—or promote—a blowout in his particular soft spot. Denial of loss is a huge risk factor, as are withdrawal and social isolation. Dr. Simon states unequivocally that "social isolation can increase the risk of heart disease and premature death." He cites one startling study involving 2,832 men and women over twelve years that found that "even after taking other risk factors into account, mild to moderate depression was associated with a 50 percent increase in fatal heart disease, and severe depression was associated with a 100 percent increase."

The important question is: What can a man—or his wife or partner and doctor—do to help ensure that a great loss at midlife does not put a man in peril of a heart attack?

Dr. Isadore Rosenfeld, one of the world's top cardiologists and holder of the Ida and Theo Rossi Distinguished Professor of Clinical Medicine chair at New York Hospital–Cornell Medical Center, offers this observation: "It may be especially significant in situations where a man has this kind of dramatic life event to look at *other* risk factors to which this emotional state can render him more vulnerable." The most important risk factors to explore are:

- His lipid levels
- His blood pressure
- His weight

There has been an explosion of new information about the immune system. "As this knowledge increases," says Dr. Rosenfeld, "it is my prediction that we'll find *everything* has an impact on the immune system—emotions, stress, even diet. And that will affect a person's vulnerability to a wide variety of diseases, from infections to cancer to coronary disease." Dr. Herbert Benson, the famous cardiologist who founded the Mind/Body Medical Institute at Harvard Medical School, has demonstrated indisputably that by inducing a "relaxation response"— through meditation and proper breathing—a man can modulate his reaction to stress and greatly reduce his vulnerability to a heart attack. Recent studies have shown that a daily dose of baby aspirin is very effective in reducing the risk of heart attack or stroke. But the longer-term resolution to great loss in midlife requires a thorough life review leading to conscious change.

I asked Tom, who I had met at the memorial service, if he knew any men ten or twenty years his senior who had reinvented themselves for the second half of their lives, men who might serve as models for him? He thought a long time, and shook his head: No. The charming and successful executive gave every sign of being at the edge of his own midlife passage, but he was bobbing and weaving around the crisis of authenticity. My next question was tough:

> If you do nothing to change your life, will the juice still be there in twenty years?

That was hard to say, he responded candidly. He knew he couldn't go on doing what he was doing now for the next twenty years. He's done it already. And it's not going to get any better. But he enjoys a high profile in a very small industry. When his biggest shows go on the air, he's in the control truck and the signal is seen around the world. That probably comes close to the dream of most men: being in the "control truck" and extending one's reach around the world. But Tom is realist enough to know that the Punic Wars in the communications business are far from over, that no position is safe. So at this present moment, he can't say he will be in this position in twenty years, or that it would make him happy. But he is still too comfortable to think about how to open up a parallel track.

Is a catastrophic event necessary as the catalyst for a man to engage fully in this search for his authenticity?

A financial planning executive who works with men of fifty and over on planning for retirement says, "I've never seen one of them get it—and reinvent themselves—before they run up against a career wall. Or suddenly they lose big in corporate warfare, or they're diagnosed with prostate cancer, or they have the first heart attack. *Then* they get it."

THE STONEWALLER'S DEFENSE

Any woman can tell you that men avoid emotional conflict by going off by themselves. Psychologists confirm that the two most common ways that men cope with domestic disputes are withdrawal and stonewalling. They flee from the emotional roller coaster. It is literally an act of self-protection. What is a man so afraid of? Here is a classic example.

"My interest in sex has plummeted."

"Since when?" I ask the expressionless man.

"Around the time we were working on having our first child—we started late."

"Do you talk about it with your wife?"

"We mostly avoid it. Then pressures build up. She gets on my case about little things. I can't take it—I just have to go off by myself and cool down."

This man happens to be a 45-year-old white public school principal in Los Angeles, in a modern mixed marriage with a Latina woman, but he could be speaking for Everyman. He complains that his wife is always criticizing or challenging him.

His spirited wife, Elena,* an administrative secretary whose lapsed dream is to be a voice teacher, is fixated on getting pregnant one more time before she pursues her dream. Or, as she puts it, "I'm desperate to get the cake in the oven before my fortieth birthday." Noel* and Elena's only child is now two and a half, and the couple's whole apartment has been transformed into a day care center for him.

"We have to set dates to make love," grouses Noel. "OK, now it's time to try for baby number two."

The stage is set for an ongoing marital conflict.

Wives are generally in charge of intimacy, so they bring up the sticky issues. Elena's complaints are those of Everywoman: "He has such a short fuse." And "As soon as I bring up the major issues between us, he either goes off like a firecracker or disappears into his den." She becomes more frustrated when Noel "won't hear me." He retreats rather than revealing that he is out of control. Once deep inside his fort, he fortifies the walls and disconnects emotionally from the whole family, leaving his wife to wail, "Why does he shut me out?"

> Men are stonewallers. Marital conflict is hazardous to their health.

Males, relative to females, have an exaggerated physical reaction to stress. A considerable body of research on gender shows quite consistently that men's bodies pump to higher elevations of stress chemicals and blood pressure than women's do in reaction to sudden danger or even a startling noise. Men also remain angry or vigilant longer, until they have a chance to retaliate. If and when they are able to counterattack, their blood pressure and stress levels subside. These findings by the guru of heart reactivity research, Stephen B. Manuck, Ph.D., at the University of Pittsburgh School of Medicine, may seem contradictory to an observation made earlier in this book about male temperament: the ability to remain cool under physical attack. "Cool," however, refers to the ability to disconnect *emotionally* while the body remains on high alert *physically* to repel physical danger.

---

*A pseudonym.

Especially in the ring of love sport, men tend to have shorter fuses and longer-lasting explosions than women. That fascinating physiological fact comes out of the "love lab" of marital researcher John Gottman, a psychologist at the University of Washington who has been studying couples' interactions for thirty years. During marital confrontations between his subjects, the man's pulse rate is more likely to rise, along with his blood pressure, and his heart rate will stay elevated longer than his wife's.

> When overwhelmed by marital tension, men suffer from "flooding" with stress chemicals.

And when he experiences that "flooding," he must either fight or flee. If a man has been schooled all through boyhood to suppress his aggression so that he doesn't become violent, he will probably choose to flee from emotional confrontations. What's more, the physiological arousal itself makes it very difficult for him even to *hear* what his wife is saying.

What would explain these profound physiological differences between the sexes? Responding to centuries-old programming, men still overreact in response to danger—whether that danger is being chased by a wild tiger or being cornered by an angry spouse—and men's animal instincts don't distinguish between the two forms of threat. Drawing upon four decades as a pioneer in hormonal research, Dr. Estelle Ramey, professor emeritus and physiologist at Georgetown University, has deduced that the male body was designed to have these "flooding" responses as well as surges of testosterone, which enable men to be quick on the attack or the defense—but only until roughly the age of 35. "Now that men are living so much longer, their hearts cannot keep up, given the continuing stresses of everyday life," says Dr. Ramey.

Dr. Gottman proposes two more explanations: First, the male's autonomic nervous system, which controls much of the body's stress response, appears to be more sensitive and to take far longer to recover from emotional upset than does the average female's. Second, when men withdraw from an argument, they are more likely to repeat negative thoughts that keep them riled up: "I don't have to take this crap" or "It's all her fault" or "I'll get her back for this."

In his paper "Why Marriages Succeed or Fail," the perceptive Dr. Gottman writes, "This may explain why women are so much readier than men to dive directly into potentially explosive issues." It is much harder for a man than for his wife to let down his guard and say, "C'mon, honey, let's talk about it."

It also explains why men are much more likely than women to be stonewallers—85 percent more likely, according to Dr. Gottman—and often with destructive results. If asked by the psychologist about his state of mind, the stonewaller says, "I'm trying *not* to react." His wife reads this silent treatment as an act of hostility or not caring. It only inflames her frustration. She may then escalate the conflict, increasing the danger that he will end up feeling flooded—and blame her for making him feel *physically* miserable.

"It may be more desirable biologically for women to get issues aired and settled and for men to avoid them," says Dr. Gottman. Couples can improve their chances of harmony greatly by seeking help in learning how to communicate and resolve conflicts in unthreatening ways; also how to deal with their inevitably differing expectations of marriage. Dr. Gottman finds that in happy marriages, for the most part, these gender differences in emotional expression hardly exist. But in unhappy marriages, men are major stonewallers, more easily flooded, and thus more defensive.

THE TROUBLE WITH WIVES

Noel, the high school principal, acknowledges that he takes longer to recover from a marital spat than Elena does. "I build up this righteous indignation, and then at some point it explodes on someone." Having grown up with an abusive father, Noel is always on guard against his own aggressive impulses, fearing they might push him over the line. That is one of the reasons he was very anxious before his first child was born: Could he trust himself to check his short temper around a fussy baby? His son helped him recover his innocence; he still hasn't gotten over the miracle. But why push one's luck?

"I'm gung ho to get pregnant," says Elena, "so I can get back to cultivating my gift for teaching talented music students before I'm too old. Noel is uncertain about being able to provide for a larger family. This whole issue has put a damper on our intimacy," she tells me. "We're not on the same page in the hymnal."

The particulars of Noel and Elena's story are not important here. Couples seldom find themselves on the same page when they approach middle life. Men's and women's developmental schedules, and the issues that color them, are usually out of sync. Neither partner is wrong. And there is no one right answer. It may take some years to resolve itself. That's right, *years.* It is the nature of conflict to feel as if it is resolved, then to feel it tear you apart again. The worst response is avoidance.

"What really concerns me is that it doesn't concern me," Noel says, sounding like a stonewaller who has disconnected emotionally to protect himself. Elena has proposed that they seek therapy. "I don't feel like there's any issue that we need to get therapeutic about," Noel responds. "Maybe I just don't see it."

What we call "primitive peoples" have initiation rituals to facilitate transitions. Advanced Western societies do not. Psychotherapy is increasingly performing this function. Couples therapy can be extremely effective in pointing out the repetitive patterns of resistance, retreat, pursuit, flooding, and so on. The other ritual our societies offer is divorce. Twenty years ago, when I wrote *Passages,* it was the men in their forties who complained, "I've grown, and my wife just hasn't." Now it is likely to be the reverse.

> Women in midlife are often the initiators of divorce today.

Between 1970 and 1990 the divorce rate for women between the ages of 40 and 50 increased by *62 percent.* Increasingly, women who are able to support themselves in a reasonable style are choosing not to remarry after divorce, especially in middle life. As celebrated in the movie *The First Wives Club,* even women who are dumped in midlife do not usually want to go back to the old arrangement. If they are able to get back on their feet financially, they often prefer to preserve their independence.

Sadly, it seems to be divorce that provides the springboard for many women to realize their own aspirations. One study found that by their own self-report, 80 percent of women who divorce say they are better off. Only half of divorced men report the same sense of relief. Most often, they feel "locked out" of love, family, and comfort.

How should men and women talk to each other about the emotionally charged issues of change as they move through a new passage with different needs and priorities? What can they do to avoid feuding and flooding, feuding and flooding, and finally disconnecting emotionally and sexually, or even legally?

> Advice for men: Try *not* to avoid conflict and not to retreat.

Nothing is accomplished by "fleeing" into your fort and leaving the conflict unresolved. And you don't want to "fight" physically with your partner. But you do need to "retaliate" in some physical or symbolic way in order to return to homeostasis. Find the fastest form of physical action: go running, go to the gym, go out and attack the crabgrass or the snow, or simply punch a pillow. Once your stress chemicals wear off and your heart rate comes down, you will be much better able to make a constructive response. The first time an uncomfortable subject comes up, however, you may need to mull it over. Plumb your own feelings. You need to know that your wife's or partner's intention is not to attack you personally. She is probably making an effort to keep your marriage healthy, by keeping the channels of communication and closeness open. Once you stop being defensive and come out of your fort, you will not feel so alone and angry. If you can listen to your wife's concerns rather than accusing her of overreacting or getting hysterical over nothing, she will calm down. Almost guaranteed.

If you stay with this discomfort and work through the problem together, a tremendous burst of creativity can be released.

> Advice for women: Confront him gently and often.

You would be wise to introduce an emotional issue gently and give your husband time to retreat and chew on it, without feeling challenged. Don't follow him into the fort; he'll shoot at you! Retreat for a while before you pick up the subject again. Use fewer words (one study estimates that the average man uses only 1,700 words a day!), and stick to the issue at hand. Resist the "kitchen sink" style of argument, where you dredge up all the old garbage and pile it on.

Reassure him: *I am not challenging you. I respect you. Who has a greater invest-ment in wanting you to feel manly than I do?* The more emotionally charged the issue, the more emotionally neutral you should make your voice. If he starts to withdraw again, lower your voice still further, or back off until an opportunity arises to approach the subject once more. If he changes the subject in the middle of a heated discussion, don't take it personally. Remember, once a man becomes flooded with the stress response, he won't hear anything you're saying anyway.

> The greatest harmony in marriage comes from seeking and finding a creative resolution to a major life passage, together.

PART III

FEARLESS FIFTIES

I find my zenith doth depend upon
A most auspicious star, whose influence
If I now court not, but omit, my fortunes
Will ever after droop.

—Prospero in Shakespeare's *The Tempest*

Chapter Six

PASSAGE TO YOUR SECOND
ADULTHOOD

The defining moment that notifies you of your arrival in the strange new country of Second Adulthood can come at the most unexpected times. For Joe Lovett it happened one day in the gents' at the Rainbow Room. Lovett is an independent film and TV producer in New York with twenty-five years of credits behind him. Naturally trim and athletically built, he works at keeping himself well toned and faithfully pedals a bicycle three hundred miles from Boston to New York for an annual AIDS charity event. How old does he feel?

"Honestly? Probably nineteen." (Well, after his quads stop burning.)

Invited uptown for a TV industry luncheon at the Rainbow Room, Lovett took particular care in selecting his haberdashery. The suit he wore looked hip, a little downtowny but still smooth enough for schmoozing with Midtown moguls. He was smug as Beau Brummel that day. After lunch, he stopped in the posh men's room.

"I was at the sink washing my hands. I glanced in the mirror and thought I looked nice. The attendant gave me a towel, I gave him a dollar. And then, as I walked around behind the attendant to go out, I saw this older, tired-looking man walking toward me. We did this little dance:

I went to the right. He went to the right. I went to the left. He went to the left. I said, 'Oh, excuse me.' "

And then—the defining moment—Lovett realized he was dancing with himself.

Most of us find ourselves at 50 in a strange and uncomfortable time warp. The age we feel may be ten years younger than the age recorded on embarrassingly literal documents such as driver's licenses. But there are certain harsh reminders: President Clinton noticed the perforations in his memory and grumbled about needing notes for the first time, not to mention help for his hearing (the toll of years of rock 'n' roll). He also began to drop idle references into his public remarks about "getting old."

How does a man demonstrate his masculinity in the middle of midlife? There are the obvious ways: He blows his bonus on a sexy sports car. Or starts to tinker with his own chassis. A Los Angeles machinist with a mane of completely white hair now spends two hours a day in the gym so he can say, "I look better than most of the thirty-year-old guys in this place. There may be snow on the roof, but there's fire in the hearth, baby."

Tom Brokaw, the famous NBC *Nightly News* anchorman, hit a defining moment in his fiftieth year while writing an essay "About Men" for *The New York Times*. He started out to update every young man's fantasy, a fling with the older woman—Mrs. Robinson. "Then it hit . . . for an older woman to be interested in me, she'd have to be sixty. If a sixty-year-old woman decides to have a fling with a younger man, I would guess that fifty is well above the threshold."

Many men prove their continued virility on the golf course. "You see guys who have achieved everything in their lives, and yet they're out on the golf course playing and playing, as if their lives depended upon it. Why?" This question used to puzzle one of my interviewees. Now that he has reached fifty, he knows: "They want to achieve something that will make everyone around them say, 'Aren't you great?' They knew they could do it at thirty and they could probably do it at forty. At fifty, at sixty, and at seventy, man, they need to know that they can *still* do it."

Other men hit the great divide at fifty and, though they may have been contentedly married for more than twenty years, they start jumping at every young woman who winks at them. "It's got nothing to do with my wife," they will often say in our interviews. "I still love her, but . . ."

> I want to know I can still do it.

THE SAMSON COMPLEX

"Proving it" may refer to any act that defined his manliness in youth—sinking a putt, hooking a bass, bagging a deer, or bedding a babe, which is why the latter is known as "sport fucking." Spending effort on the "still-dos" may be important in helping a man through the transitional phase—what I refer to as the "Samson Complex." The muting of physical aggressiveness and the losing of hair may scare a man into believing, as Samson did in the Bible story, that these are the only symbols of a man's power and sexual prowess. But unless he also works on becoming a person beyond the person he has already mastered, he will stop growing.

Ideals of manliness are mainly tied to youth. The power of a young man is a muscular, propulsive, hormone-driven, often chaotic force; he uses physical strength and competitive zeal to prove himself over and over again. The illusion, and for some the reality, is that these powers will gain him control over others and his environment. Even when they do, he cannot depend on young-man power to sustain him for a lifetime. Sooner or later he will run into one obvious reality he cannot change: *I am no longer young.*

But he is not willing to be labeled "middle-aged" either, since that is a set of stereotypes that applied to earlier generations, when turning 50 meant being over the hill. Today, a man can take advantage of a whole new stage that has opened up between youth and middle age. I call it "middlescence": adolescence the second time around but with love handles and a lot more options. As a man ages, the source of his power and potency changes dramatically. But we have no terms to describe or celebrate this rite of passage from First to Second Adulthood.

> We need an expanded definition of manliness.

It is widely believed that women are the nurturers of society, while men are the aggressors and defenders. "Masculinity," as depicted in popular culture, is so often egotistical, self-glorifying, violent, or at least uncaring. That was the conventional wisdom with which anthropologist David Gilmore began his cross-cultural study of manhood ideologies in primitive and contemporary societies. His most striking finding shakes that old chestnut:

> Manhood ideologies always include a criterion of selfless generosity, even to the point of sacrifice. Again and again, we find that "real men" are those who give more than they take; they serve others. . . . Manhood therefore is also a nurturing concept.

A man who approaches the second half of life, still valuing his physical strength and the aggressiveness to make things happen, can find a new challenge in developing the more creative, intuitive, nurturant side of himself. If he cultivates this side, he can be even more enduringly effective. The times call for a man who is comfortable with multiple identities—who seeds and cultivates a series of possible selves while remaining open to new ideas, tolerant of ethnic and racial differences, able to work with a team and to move from intense involvement with one project to commitment to the next. As he gets older, he can give more of himself by serving his community of interest. Through work with nonprofit organizations, churches, or independent schools or universities, such men will be the pioneers pointing the way for the twenty-first century.

Let's give this postpatriarchal model a new label: *Protean Man.*

> The god Proteus's power lay in his ability to change his shape from wild boar to wild dragon to fire to flood. What he did find to be difficult and would not do unless seized and chained was to commit himself to one single form.
>
> R. J. Lofton, *The Protean Man*

Let's also be frank: This is an ideal. Many men have little idea of what they want out of the second half of their lives. And until they figure it out, they will be virtually powerless to get it. Men can deny aging much longer than women can. At least through their forties and often later, men can muster strong personal identities and maintain a sense of self-worth simply by engaging their aggressive instincts in a struggle for dominance in the social hierarchy.

But as I noted in *New Passages,* these aggressive instincts are an appetite, like the sexual drive. They build up, a man satisfies them, and they build up again. By the time a man reaches middle life, however, he is not as easily contented merely by throwing himself into the competitive struggle. He feels younger men and women, whose aggressive instincts are still raw and ruthless, right behind him nipping at his heels. His body doesn't bounce back from overwork or physical exertion the way it used to. These are realities of this stage. So many men are desperate just to hang on to what they have, they fight change. This is a terrible mistake.

This is not the end of life. This is the end of First Adulthood. It is time to move on. No gong rings to signal the start of Second Adulthood. Women have a universal signal—menopause—that rings down the curtain on their First Adulthood right around the age of 50. If they accept and master the passage of menopause, they move to the other side of the sound barrier and feel freer than at any time in their lives to follow their own polestar. For men this passage is much more challenging. There is no universal physical marker. There is no generally accepted point in the career cycle when men are expected to say: *I've done my duty, I've proven myself, I'm not going to do the same thing anymore.* But today, there is plenty of time for a man to reinvent himself for a Second Adulthood. With people living so much longer, career counselors and therapists tell me they find more men are ready to seek out the opportunity on the other side of the darkness when they hit one of the closed doors, or exit events, of middle life. (See Appendix A, page 259, for advice from top career counselors.)

SIGNIFICANT EXIT EVENTS
- Death of a parent
- Being divorced—on the receiving end of "Honey, I want out"
- Loss of a self-defining job
- Death of a peer
- Loss of a mentor
- Children leaving home

These are among the irreconcilable losses of life. The tree trunk splits in a hurricane, and one major branch falls off or must be cut down to save the integrity of the tree. But have you ever noticed? When hardy trees and vines suffer such radical distress, the next year they push out a more abundant growth than ever.

MATURE MASCULINITY

Given that the American South was an important incubator for codes of male gallantry, I asked my friends at *The Atlanta Constitution* to invite a diverse group for a roundtable discussion on the new postpatriarchal man in middle life. A lively bunch of seven turned up, men ranging in age from 38 to 58 with several seasons of life behind them. They included a former football star, a veteran newspaperman, a plumber, and a professor. They ranged over the political spectrum from liberal to ultraconservative.

For David Meltz, a libertarian law school professor, it was a night that needed to be marked, so he had arrived early and while having a drink in the lounge had struck up a conversation with a fascinating woman. "I almost died last year," he told our group matter-of-factly. "And tonight is my fifty-first birthday." Sitting in a bar and flirting, even harmlessly, might have seemed out of character for a serious intellectual dressed soberly in a dark suit and tie and settling into a monk's balding pattern. But David Meltz is a much freer soul today than he was in his first fifty years. "When you come back [from death's door], nothing bothers you. Every day is a good day," he told us.

Striding in behind him was a tall, lanky, well-proportioned African-American man. This must be Ray Brown, I thought, the former football star who is still remembered as among the best safeties the Atlanta Falcons ever had. After they traded him to the New Orleans Saints, his professional athletic career petered out. Despite his 47 years, he looked like the sort of man who could go to sleep for six years, wake up, do fifty one-arm push-ups, and again be in perfect shape. He wore an elegant tweed sport coat and a well-trimmed mustache and goatee along with a gold-capped tooth.

"Right now I feel probably thirty, at the peak of being a man emotionally and mentally," Ray said for openers. "It is a time of my life with no problems. My two sons are in college, and I'm going back to younger days and having a lot of fun."

These opening statements did not have the ring of total candor. But a certain amount of posturing was to be expected. "I think we're all a bit nervous about going on the record with some of our deepest feelings," said the law professor. Such talk runs counter to the old ideal of solitary stoic manliness imprinted on this generation of men. Before long, however, the participants were eagerly comparing and endorsing one another's bold choices for how to live in the second half.

Lee May, a former Washington correspondent for the *Los Angeles Times*, did not come across as a hard-boiled newspaperman with the usual jumpy, deadline-driven, competitive intensity. That would have described his other life, when he had jetted between war zones, race riots, and earthquake epicenters and covered the White House. "When you're in your thirties and forties, I suppose there's this testosterone thing that causes you to strive," he acknowledged. Other men nodded. "I loved the heat of the battle. I loved the travel. I loved the aura of being a Washington correspondent." But something had profoundly changed. Although this large, well-built black man had a face wreathed in gray beard, his skin was unmarked by lines. There were a clarity and serenity in his expression, and also in his self-description.

"I'm fifty-four. I feel fifty-four, and I like it. Some days I feel older, some days I feel younger, but on average I feel better than I did fifteen or twenty years ago." Lee May likes being on the verge of that wonderful stage when he will have the license to say at any dinner party he finds boring, including his own, "I'm tired, I'm going upstairs now, good night!" "I also enjoy knowing that I don't have the need to see every woman as a potential conquest," he added. "Those are metaphors for the general sense of freedom that aging gives a person."

Suddenly a much younger man dashed in, a 35-year-old bachelor bond trader in a black-and-white houndstooth-check jacket and cashmere V-neck. He had plenty of hair, hair that grew like ground cover in the sun, and one just knew he had a sexy sports car—the kind of semiotics that can make a man over 50 silently weep.

But the older men didn't flinch. How did they feel about turning 50? I asked the others. David Meltz, the law professor, responded with a comic belligerence: "I take out my AARP card, throw it on the table, and say, 'I'm entitled. I've paid my dues. I'm fifty years old. I'm entitled to my opinion.' "

"But if you think you have all the answers, you become fossilized," countered John Jacobs, a former executive who was downsized. He had seized the moment, at 55, to go back to school and pursue a postgraduate degree.

"Welcoming surprises—to me, that's what prevents a person from becoming stale or old," amended Lee May.

Mike Fisher, a 58-year-old salesman, echoed many men of his age when he said he has become much more tolerant as he's grown older. "Tolerant to different people, different social classes—I have a lower-middle-class background myself." Mike had opened his own liquor store and lost the business. "I'm more accepting of human weaknesses by this age. I've exhibited all of them at one point or another and survived."

Before long, several of the men began to describe the "little deaths" that had allowed them to shed outgrown identities and transform themselves in time to enjoy their fifties as the fullest, richest stage of life.

FORMER PRO FOOTBALL STAR

"I played for ten years, and I was good," was how Ray Brown described his golden years as a pro footballer. He was barely into his midthirties when the shades of sudden obscurity came down and he entered that strange twilight of premature retirement that sports stars seldom anticipate. "It took two years to find out what I wanted to do, and that probably was the hardest time in my life," he said. It was his wife, he says, who cut him the slack to find himself. A college graduate who had stayed home to raise their two children, she struck out to begin a career as a manager of apartment complexes. Eventually, Ray jumped into the construction business and built his own remodeling company. Approaching 50, he was delighted with his marriage and his work, proud of his fathering, and committed to continuing the personal development that had become possible only after his "star self" had faded. He was clear about what had facilitated this development: "The right mate is the key to life."

GEEZER IN GRADUATE SCHOOL

Bo Holland nodded in assent. A handsome, softly featured man with a dimple the size of a thumbprint pressed into his chin, he spoke of his sense of liberation upon turning 50 this year: "I'm just hitting my stride. I learned a great deal from going through a divorce." His first wife, he said, had been spoiled and dependent. When he remarried, he looked for a woman who had her own drive. "My wife at this point," he said, "I worship the ground she walks on. She makes three times what I do, but I contribute in a lot of other ways. She works long hours and has a lot of pressure—I'll cook dinner. It's total role reversal."

That unorthodox role reversal had allowed Bo to discover options he wished he had thought about when he was 30, not 50. Having followed in his father's footsteps, running a small family-owned company, only now did he realize there was life beyond real estate and contracting. With that realization he felt entitled, at last, to take time off from the family business to attend classes and study. He had taken the chance of being called the oldest geezer in graduate school, but it turns out he isn't the least bit ashamed to be writing papers in his midfifties. On the contrary, he is thrilled to be stretching his mind at the same time as his tendons are tightening up. More important, he feels he is staking out an identity of his own for the first time: "I think I passed the midlife crisis safely by going back to school."

GLOBE-TROTTING JOURNALIST
TURNS GARDENER

For years, Lee May's life was like an action-adventure flick. He would parachute into a war zone, look around, and bark, "What's the body count?" "That's a young man's game," he told us. At 50, "I wasn't living hurricanes and mass murders and intrigues in the White House. I was living gardening and gourmet cooking and thinking about making connections with other people." These new passions of his were hard to explain, even to himself. Was he turning soft? Maybe not, but he was certainly getting older, and he was becoming terminally dissatisfied with the journalism he used to find so exciting. He was stuck.

So many men have told me they faced the same dilemma around fifty. They'll say, "I wish I could be a writer or a theatrical producer or work with the volunteer fire department"—whatever their passion happens to be—"but there's the mortgage, the kids aren't finished with college yet, my wife would have to work for some boring corporation to get the health benefits. So I'm stuck." This is the signal to stop and do a life review. Contemplate: *Where is my missing piece? What part of me did I leave behind that desperately wants to find expression? What old wound or musty anger is locked up inside? Can I now let it go?*

It occurred to Lee May that the father he hadn't seen in thirty-nine years must now be pretty old. His mother and stepfather were already gone. He was down to one surviving parent. Certain connections would soon lapse for all eternity, unless . . .

"It was scary to have to find your father's phone number through Information." He dialed the long-distance operator in Meridian, Mississippi. Trembling inside, he introduced himself: "Hello, this is your son. Sonny."

Long silence.

Of course, why should his 80-year-old father recognize his voice? They were as much strangers as two men standing side by side in a public urinal.

"Well, I'm going to be in Meridian," Lee continued bravely, "and I thought I'd stop by and maybe we could have a chat."

"Yeah, come on by."

And that was how the birth of a Second Adulthood began for Lee May.

Sitting on his father's porch, "We talked about things that strangers talk about, trying to break the ice, and that's the weather." The older man said, "I've been having to water a lot."

Lee said, "You know, I've been having to water a lot too, up in Washington."

"Water? Water what?"

"My garden."

The old Alabama man turned to his fancy citified son, flabbergasted. "Your garden? You're a gardener?"

At that moment the ice was broken, Lee told us. "We knew we were not only kin, but we were kindred souls. I could not have made my connection with my father when I was twenty-five or perhaps even thirty. I don't think I could have done it without recrimination even at forty. At age forty-eight, we were just two men. One old, one middle-aged. And what I wanted to do, and apparently what he wanted to do, too, was start from then."

Start from then . . . it was a conscious reprieve that rang true to several of the men. For Lee May, the concept of letting go of the past gave him the courage to decode some of the emotional needs he had ignored.

"I was faced with two hard choices," he recalled for us. "One, stay in the job I was doing and choke, strangle, die psychologically, or quit and face the possibility that we would crumble financially."

Choke, strangle, die, I repeated, those are dire words. How many men feel that way in middle life but stick it out?

"I really do believe that bad work can kill you," Lee said. Other men nodded. Only change would allow Lee to survive. He quit his job with the *Los Angeles Times.* It was four weeks after his wife had left her job.

"Horror. Distress. Fear." Those are the words used by his third wife to describe her shock. A beautiful TV journalist, Lyn May had never lived in a household where nobody had a job. Her formerly decisive husband seemed to be in limbo.

"Our household was an unhappy place," Lee admitted. "But had I stayed at the old job, my unhappiness would have pervaded our relationship." It took several months before Lyn May trusted her husband's instinct. Meanwhile, she jump-started her own career and became a spokesperson for her city in preparation for the 1996 Olympics in Atlanta. Lee May took a year out to research his past and write a book, a personal memoir and tribute to his father. "We had credit card debt, so it was dicey. But we got through it, and now my wife understands that I was right."

Once his earlier life was enclosed between the covers of a published book, this globe-trotting journalist felt free to write about what moves him at this stage—his own backyard. He started a popular column on gardening in *The Atlanta Constitution.* "I'm writing now about what speaks to people's souls—gardening, food, travel. A garden has everything that happens in life—birth, nurturing, growth, love, disappointment, heartbreak, and death." His father had recently passed away, but there was no remorse. Lee repeated his father's saying: "Some people don't want to get old and they don't want to die. You've got to do one or the other."

THE FEARLESS PROFESSOR

"My professional passion is teaching," said David Meltz, a law professor. "The problem is, at the university level, the reward structure is for publishing, not teaching. I'd spent most of my life looking for the position that would allow me to do what I most love." In his late forties, Professor Meltz saw a chance to create that position for himself. Suddenly, he was fearless. He walked into a law school that was about to be shut down, and he told the Board of Bar Examiners, "Give me this school. I'm the only person who can revive this place. You've got two hundred students. I'll teach every damn subject if I have to." They gave it to him, and over the previous four years, as both academic dean and professor of law at John Marshall Law School in Atlanta, he had taken the school from a backwater to the verge of accreditation by the American Bar Association.

The second revelation had come in the middle of the last, rough year. His father had died, and his mother had fallen apart and turned to David to be the pillar holding up her life. Under the strain, his diverticulitis kicked up. He went into the hospital with a perforated colon.

"You need emergency surgery," the doctor said, sitting on his hospital bed.

"Fine, let's prep for the morning," David agreed, thinking he sounded pretty tough.

"The anesthesiologist is ready, the morphine's outside, you're going in right now," the doctor said, handing him a consent waiver to sign. Shocked, the lawyer put on his glasses to study the deal. "If you take time to read it, I'm going home," the surgeon said. "There's a ten percent chance you'll be dead by morning."

There was no negotiating room. David Meltz had to surrender his fate to God and a surgeon he had just met. "I made some deals in that hospital," he told us. "Get me out of here. If you do, I'm going to live. I'm going to live like I haven't lived before. Every day is worthwhile now. I don't worry about death. I have no fear of it, and that's the first time in my life."

Many people are knocked flat at some point in middle life. What's important is not how you get knocked down, David said, it's whether or not you can pick yourself up. An avalanche of two hundred personal messages and prayers from his former and current law school students reached him in the hospital. He was overwhelmed. "That was a testament to what I'd meant to other people," and it stimulated an epiphany. "If I do nothing else, if I'm known as the founding dean of this new law school, I'll be very satisfied." Even though by the calendar he is older and now counting backward from the end, David Meltz finds that since his close brush with death he is not in such a hurry. Time is not running out. He savors every day. "I feel I have more control than I ever did as a younger man, and that gives me a sense of mastery."

His story brings to mind a few lines from the Irish poet Seamus Heaney:

> —to wake and know
> Every time that it's gone and gone for good, the thing
> That nearly broke you—
>
> Is worth it all, . . .

I asked the Atlanta men one last question: How do you define or demonstrate your masculinity at this stage?

"Start fights in bars." That first crack came from the young, ultra-conservative bond trader. He was still in his midthirties, after all, and he wanted the group to know "I'm really competitive. I definitely like what are traditionally considered guy things: sports and airplanes."

Bo Holland, the 50-year-old graduate student, chuckled tolerantly. "I went through that hypermasculinity phase—the athletics and the women." He now has a beautiful, sensual second wife. "Masculinity is more what you accomplish," he said, "like being a good father."

Ray Brown observed that he had been in competition all his life, first as a pro football player and even now in the business world. "But I guess I've refocused what it means to be a man in the nineties," he said. "Guys I used to play ball with may come to the house and catch me doing dishes while my wife is out working. It's a fifty-fifty deal with us. Raising two boys, playing ball with them, trying to set a good example for them, being consistent with them, providing for them, and showing them a good family home, I think that's a very manly thing. The country needs more examples of that from men."

The law school dean had been doodling while we talked. His free association with the words "mature masculinity" summed up much of our discussion:

> Mature masculinity equals self-confidence. Everything else is incubation.

It was late. As the men prepared to leave, there were jokes about the hot time the young bachelor bond trader was probably going to have while the rest went home to their wives and kids. That prompted the most revealing admission of the evening.

"People who are married with kids seem to think that being single and my age in Atlanta is just heaven on earth," said the young bachelor. "But it's changed. If I am driving down Ray's street or Lee's street and I've got some megabombshell blonde in the next seat, and I see Ray out in the front yard playing catch with his sons, or I see Lee working in his garden with his wife, I think, *Lucky them.*"

BEYOND POWER

Power as it is usually defined—being in a position to make things happen—is seldom exercised in the same way by men in middle life as it was when they were younger. Power is a very liquid thing. One never really has it completely. Becoming too possessive about having it—or keeping it—makes a man very vulnerable. The most vulnerable are men whose titles and positions appear to confer princely powers, without which they fear they will be nothing.

He presides from high on the fourteenth floor of the Condé Nast building with windows overlooking Madison Avenue—a prince of publishing. Steve Florio, president and CEO of Condé Nast Publications, leans back at the end of a day that routinely begins at 5:30 A.M. behind a desk the length of a diving board. Florio can fill a doorframe with his meaty shoulders and fill a room with his "Italian guy from the boroughs" bellicosity. He is both charming and intimidating behind his bushy black mustache. He has the power to make people jump. But not forever.

The office next door is occupied by the Big Boss: S. I. Newhouse, Jr., the publishing magnate whose family-owned empire is studded with glossy magazines from *Vogue* to *Vanity Fair* to *The New Yorker* and whose personal fortune is estimated by *Forbes* magazine at $4.3 billion. Newhouse is close to 70. Florio is abutting his fiftieth birthday. One day, a reporter from *Advertising Age* asked Florio a deliberately provocative question: "You guys look good right now—up 103 percent over last year—but the word on the street is that Newhouse and Florio are probably both going to retire in the next five years. So what are the prospects for the company when you're both gone?"

"Mr. Newhouse has no intention of retiring," replied his number two.

Retire! The boss virtually bounced off the walls upon hearing about the interview. His own father, the son of a Russian immigrant, had bought the business in 1959, built the empire, and run it practically up to the last days on his deathbed. Newhouse Jr., like other sons of powerful fathers who emerge late from the filial shadow, is still building. He slips into the office before the sun has made up its mind what to do that day and religiously ducks out to the gym after lunch. To him, the prospect of retirement is a living death.

Florio was equally chilled by the prospect. "I can't imagine not doing this," he told me, "can't imagine it." Whenever retirement is mentioned in front of his wife, she will say, "I have lived with this man for twenty-five years. If you took his job away from him, he would die quickly."

But Florio is nobody's fool. "As CEO of a major company," he says, "in the cold light of dawn you realize that you're like a major-league baseball player. At some point the chairman is going to say, 'Bring in the left-hander.'" He has been in management positions in publishing for twenty years. As president of Condé Nast he is in his fourth year and counting. Presidents and editors are not "eased out" of this company. "It's more like a cannon shot," Florio says with a smirk. "One day you find yourself over on Lexington Avenue. I've seen guys who didn't anticipate it . . ." He leaves the thought agape.

Does he have a Plan B?

"The fantasy is that I won't stop. I'll start my own publishing business." But of one thing he is sure—what he is *not* going to do.

Florio's defining moment occurred in the Florida Keys. He was down fishing with his son over Christmas vacation, the two of them feeling exhilarated as they returned from an early-morning expedition in their little twenty-two-foot runabout. The sun was eclipsed for some time as they tried to pass an enormous yacht. It looked easily 150 feet long, Florio calculated, and was probably worth a cool fifteen million.

"C'mon, Pop, get closer," his 19-year-old son begged. "I want to see it."

A man not much older than Florio was seated on the transom. All by himself on this huge boat, he was being served his morning coffee by men in uniform. Spotting Florio and his boy, the man leapt toward the railing and called down, "How'd you guys do this morning? What do you do for a living? What's going on in New York now?" The yacht owner kept up the conversation with some desperation until Florio's fingers began aching from holding on to his wheel. Finally the man confessed his frustration: "I retired when I sold my company last year. Now I sit on this goddamned boat all day long."

The man was no more than 52—handcuffed to a fifteen-million-dollar boat. A lot of people would say "I wish I had that problem." But to Florio, it was a rich man's version of the little old lady in Queens with her elbows propped on a pillow on the windowsill, condemned to spending the rest of her life watching the world go by.

Florio looks up at a print of a big sailboat on the wall of his office and waxes philosophical. "My generation, baby boomers who came of age in the sixties, were going to be young forever. Now you have a whole generation of men waiting in line to deal with their own mortality. We've all seen the specter of downsizing. At the end of the line is the great beyond. You talk to any fifty-year-old guy who says he doesn't worry about that, and he's lying to you."

If this is potentially a major life crisis for men as powerful as Steve Florio, imagine the predicament faced by middle-level employees or blue-collar workers. These men often describe themselves to me as "dinosaurs," especially if they are in businesses related to information technology. They know they are in danger of being replaced at any time by two 30-year-old "skirts"—women with twice as many degrees at half the salary—or worse, by twentysomething nerds who are perfectly happy graduating from a college dorm to a cot in the office where they are willing to work ninety hours a week and beg, borrow, or commit investor fraud in order to finance their first initial public offering before they're 30.

"I've seen so many of these guys," says Florio, referring to men of his age who are junked prematurely. Today, they can expect to live at least another thirty or so years. What, I asked Florio, do you think they will do?

"I think a lot of them will die of a broken heart."

――――――――――――――

Restructurings, takeovers, mergers, executive shake-ups, sudden sell-offs of whole corporate divisions, all mean, as observed by the chairman of a Wall Street bond fund, that "You just can't count on stability anymore." Donald Marron, CEO of PaineWebber, agrees that high achievers have a very hard time anticipating change and managing it so they can avoid winding up with a broken heart. "It's their ego—they can't believe they won't win the competition if they just stay in the game and play hard enough."

Marron likens the dynamic to the competition at the U.S. Open tennis tournament. From 128 players, the field is whittled to eight finalists, known as the "round of eight." When a man makes the round of eight, he knows he is in the winner's circle, while those outside the circle are convinced they are losers.

"It's the toughest kind of competition," Marron says of the round of eight. "It's not enough just to be good at what you do. Everybody at that level is good at what they do. It takes other talents to win—intangibles such as determination, experience, competitive focus, tough-mindedness, and staying power. And a little luck. Some have those talents, some don't."

Winning throughout a long career requires change—more precisely, a change of gears. Having managed men for many years, Marron knows they will face at least a couple of traumatic career experiences. "One is in the late thirties, early forties—when you and others begin to sense whether or not you will make the 'round of eight.' And if so, do you have what it takes to be the best of the best? The other traumatic period comes in the fifties, when the successful man wants to find a new challenge or additional purpose in life beyond mere winning."

What percentage of the high-achieving men he manages are able to make that more difficult passage in their fifties? I asked.

"Not many."

What distinguishes them?

"They continue to take risks. But these men don't see what they're doing as risky," he says, qualifying his answer. "They're not looking over the edge at the fall they might take. They see risks as opportunities. And they're always ready to seize the next opportunity. If it fails, they say, 'Well, that opportunity didn't work out. What's next?' "

BARRY DILLER'S SEARCH FOR SELF

Barry Diller is such a specimen. A West Coast wunderkind, his stance had always been that of the outlaw. He chose not to go to college and cultivated powerful mentors starting in his teens. "He never seemed to be a kid, always a tough guy," observes a fellow Beverly Hills rich kid who grew up with Diller in the film business. "He was prematurely bald in his midtwenties and looked pretty menacing." He invented ABC's *Movie of the Week* in his twenties and at 32 became one of the youngest movie studio chiefs in Hollywood history. "He was so amazingly aggressive and self-confident," says his colleague, "his swagger seduced Charlie Bluhdorn" (then the powerful head of Gulf & Western and owner of Paramount, who fostered Diller's career). Diller says, "Since I was forty, I have been trying to kill the concept of a mentor."

By his forties, Diller was revolutionizing television. He launched a brand-new national network for Rupert Murdoch, Fox TV, and created enormous value for the media magnate. He was proud of finding a voice that was edgy and risky, with shows such as *The Simpsons* and *Married . . . with Children*. He was also running the fledgling Fox movie studio for Murdoch, feeling flush and powerful, like the Hollywood moguls he had always emulated.

Diller had just turned 50 when Murdoch came out to Hollywood in early 1992, itchy to run the movie studio that Diller had come to believe was his own. At a board meeting Diller argued strenuously against another board member's point of view. He was confident that he had won the argument hands down. Murdoch changed the subject; he simply ignored Diller.

Diller walked out of the meeting shattered. "It wasn't my store. I acted like it was, but it wasn't mine."

He later reconstructed that moment of epiphany for me: "I may act like a principal—and look like the elephant in the room—but in the parent company of Fox I didn't count. Rupert was treating me like a boy. God! For me, who's so controlled, it was humiliating." Diller then told me something he had never revealed: as a boy he was physically tortured by his older brother. The humiliation of again being treated like a powerless little boy, even at 50, hugely successful though he was, threw into question the very foundation of his "self." So a few days later he confronted Murdoch: "I think I have to be a principal in this company. It's important to me." Murdoch came back and told him flatly, "The truth is, there is only one principal in this company. It can't be done."

That left Diller with a classic existential burden. He had forced the issue: to be or not to be. Would he now act or admit to himself that he was too weak to act? In April 1992, Barry Diller resigned as chief executive of Fox Inc. And so began the process of a long, painful, but gutsy self-examination.

Most people would think that a top executive in the entertainment business who cashes in and walks away at the age of 50 with more than a million dollars for every year of his life would have very little to worry about. But being stripped of the "false self" and forced to look inside to find the real self can be just as harrowing a passage for a heavy hitter as for an average batter. I asked to meet with Diller every six months or so to record his inner experience of this long passage.

At first, he was in free fall. His constant, terrifying thought was: *What if nothing happens? What if the only thing I'm capable of being is an employee, and I've topped out?* "It took me months to be clear. You either are, or you're not. The only reality is to be a person who has standing of one's own—that's where self forms." He was caught up in a common struggle between allowing himself to continue to be defined and controlled by others and staying the course to fuller self-realization. The stakes are high at his level, the traps many and treacherous. "I'm in the middle of it now," he told me. "I was thinking today, how did it happen that all this stuff has been stirred up? Then I thought, you schmuck, *you* stirred it up."

Six months after he resigned from Fox, he told me, "You actually have to take action to develop a 'self' of your own. It's not a pose, not a negotiation, it's not something you make up." But he did not yet look comfortable in his own skin. Everything about his physical language looked blunt: a bull neck, thick skin, handsome features set deep in a shiny skull that resembles a cannonball, menacing lines flaring across a ridged forehead. But beneath the tough exterior was a sensitive soul searching for more subtle forms of power. It helped that he could laugh at himself.

In a follow-up interview a year and a half after his resignation from Fox, Diller said, "I'm sure I've got a hell of lot more 'self' than I had last year. Real self, as against made-up stuff. I mean, I lose it, I gain it, I lose some, I gain a little more. Each day the rebound loss is a little less. More sticks."

By then he had notched one rung higher toward being the principal. He had taken over QVC, the first cable company to offer round-the-clock electronic shopping. He was in love with cruising for new opportunities along the information superhighway and planned to create his own entertainment powerhouse. But he was also bored with being stuck in a drive-by suburb of Philadelphia and out of the Hollywood loop.

When I interviewed Diller in his vast suite in the Waldorf Towers in April 1993, a year after he had left Fox, he looked quite happy in his own self-operated kingdom. "I have my own voice mail, I just punch this number in to get my messages. I have my own fax modem. I love to be alone." His famously described companion, an IBM PowerBook, stood with its milky blue face open on the antique secretaire. The other dominant picture in the living room was the high-definition TV screen, featuring his twenty-four-hour shopping network, but with the sound of QVC's relentless pitchmen turned off. What had he learned about preserving real self as opposed to the made-up self? I asked. Diller had arrived at an important insight: "I'd been CEO of corporations for eighteen years," he said, reviewing his record of creative ideas and killer deals, all done as a corporate executive for somebody else's company. "In the end, you decide what really belongs to you. It's not your accomplishments. It's your *ability* to accomplish. And the quality of being afraid or not being afraid."

As that conversation wound down, I asked Diller if he ever thought about death.

"No!" He was emphatic. He glanced at his watch and blurted, "Gotta go!"

Next Diller tried to buy his own movie studio, Paramount. He fell into the common trap of overreaching. After losing the six-month high-profile battle to take over Paramount, Diller sounded exactly like one of the eternal risk takers described earlier by Don Marron. His first comments after the failure were "They won. We lost. Next!"

But "self" is more than what one does, Diller had discovered by the time we next met in his suite in April 1994. "It's the sense that you are entitled to your own opinions and beliefs and that you are entitled to act on them. It has nothing to do with other people's opinions. If you don't have self, you may get some sharp applause, but you come home and close the door, and then what? It goes down the drain. There's no stopper in the tub. Why is there no stopper? How do you make that passage?"

Two moments of revelation in the previous year had eased the passage. He had stood up for his father as best man at the 81-year-old's second wedding. Diller had dared to ask a close relative if his memory of being physically tortured from the age of three to seven by his now-deceased older brother was accurate. His relative squeezed his hand to confirm the terrible truth. "It was a real moment," he said.

The second revelation occurred to him during the long, bruising, very high profile battle for Paramount: What would he have done without the consistently intelligent and discreet counsel of his longtime companion, the elegant fashion designer Diane von Furstenberg? He trusted her utterly. As a child he had trusted no one, no one at all, so this transformation of personality in middle life was quite unexpected. Now the lifelong bachelor, the outlaw, began yearning for a continuity of intimacy. He had no children. But he had been close to Diane's children for almost two decades.

"It seems perfectly plausible to me that if there were no children in one's life, there would be no point," he mused. "So I'm crafting a family with Diane and her children and one or two other people. I have obligations and responsibilities to them." He and Diane were house hunting together.

In 1995, Diller resurfaced as chairman of a small broadcasting company that then acquired the Home Shopping Network. He was also shopping for a wealthy partner in hopes of turning HSN into a new powerhouse network. Despite being offered the leadership of some of the largest media and entertainment companies, including Universal, he had made a no-turning-back choice: He would never again work for somebody else. After two more years of struggling to breathe life into the elusive business of electronic retailing, he had turned his business around. Diller told me in a follow-up interview in his temporary offices on Manhattan's West Side, "My company is not chopped liver [$600 million in annual sales], but it is not a big media communications company—and I would like it to be." Leaning back in his chair in an empty boardroom with his meaty hands clasped over the top of his head, he mused, "In men who have lost prowess in their career, you see the hunger in their eyes, or the sadness. They haven't translated the power into influence." It was still just as essential for Barry Diller *to count*.

He had even asked a psychiatrist, "Can one change those essentials?" Very rarely, was the answer.

In the fall of 1997 Diller was on the comeback, big time, with a plan to build and run a TV empire of his own. He had made a deal with his old friend Edgar Bronfman, Jr., scion of Seagram Company, to acquire a major portion of its Universal Television operations. That gave Diller the giant cable network USA Networks, Inc., a subsidiary of Universal, to develop on his own. Overnight, he strode back into the arena of fierce TV contests as a significant player—chairman and chief executive officer of the newly named entity.

Now, at last, he had created the conditions to be able to immerse himself again in television programming, a passion to which he had longed to return since leaving Fox.

It had taken him six years, but it had been worth every step and stumble of the passage. Diller was more than his old "self." And he had accomplished that redefinition on his own terms.

PROSPERO'S PASSAGE

We tend to think about the stresses in our lives as unique to our times or to ourselves, but the heart of the problem has always been there. When I saw the New York Shakespeare Festival's production of *The Tempest* in 1994, I found myself thinking, *How contemporary, how absolutely applicable to the crises men face today*. As usual, Shakespeare had spotted the dilemma in a much earlier form. *The Tempest* was a confirmation of the universality of this great passage in men's lives.

The bard's last play is concerned with possibilities for regeneration. He depicts one man's life story as a journey through time as well as space, initiated by a tempest and a shipwreck that "represent the violence, confusion, and even terror of passing from one stage of life to the next, the feeling of being estranged from a familiar world and sense of self without another to hang on to."* The heart of the work is the tempest itself.

Prospero, Shakespeare's central character, starts off in *The Tempest* bitter and rivalrous with his brother, robbed of his political power and isolated on an island, where he fools himself into thinking he is omnipotent and plots to wreak vengeance on his enemies. He uses "magic" tricks the way young men do to compete with older and wiser rivals. Prospero is no longer young, but he is not old either—scholars usually suggest he is in his late forties—but like many men he fears that aging means he will lose his potency.

Like many men today who enjoyed comfortably powerful positions but who have been—or fear being—prematurely overthrown or junked, Prospero had been caught completely by surprise when his brother and friend pushed him out of power, and he had turned bitter. When we first meet him, he is a tyrannical parent and a loveless man. But having lost all his external status, he is forced to look inward, and ultimately, to change. Prospero was indeed the prime duke, but he loved the liberal arts and was dedicated to improving his mind—we might call him a dilettante. Having left the day-to-day business of government to his brother, Prospero seethes, "*He* did believe *he* was the duke."

In those words I heard Barry Diller's bitter cry when Rupert Murdoch invaded the realm he believed was his, the Fox movie studio he was running: "I was just an *employee.*" That shipwreck launched Diller on a tempestuous passage.

Prospero, like Diller and many other men, is murderously competitive. When Providence sweeps his treacherous brother and confederates onto his island in another tempest, Prospero re-creates for them his own nearly fatal voyage. Were this a Greek tragedy, he would have taken his tidy revenge by repeating the wrongs done to him and become ensnared in a vicious cycle of successive family revenges.

Real power, as Shakespeare depicts it in this, his ultimate statement, is not inherited, not a mere matter of princely birth nor of political "magic" tricks.

---

* Kahn, Coppelia. *Man's Estate: Masculine Identity in Shakespeare.* University of California Press, 1981.

> Real power is developed from within; it is an extension of
> self-knowledge.

The force of it is then felt, recognized, and respected by others. That
is Prospero's profound if painful discovery. Only when he accepts the
need for compassion and forgiveness and grows into his own age does he
become a "good parent" who is able to let go of his daughter, give up revenge, and redefine himself as man rather than magician. Having become
almost whole in his humanity, he takes back his kingdom while making
way for the next generation to come into its own.

The brilliant British theater director Peter Brook believes this character is Shakespeare's "complete and final statement; it deals with the whole
condition of man." Unlock this puzzle, and a world of understanding
may lie before you.

Denial of our own aging is hardly new. The dilemmas are greatly exaggerated today by the fact that we are taking so much longer to grow up
and so much longer to grow old. But the basic problem existed back in
the seventeenth century. Shakespeare does not tie up the loose ends. The
play—like Prospero's story, like life—is unfinished. The most profound
questions are left unanswered: What does it mean to need magic? Did
Prospero ever need it, and if so, why? And though he talks a good deal
about renouncing it, does he in fact give it up?

What is the lesson?

WELCOME TO THE AGE OF INFLUENCE

Men need to define power less narrowly as they move on in Second
Adulthood—not only as a position where you can "make 'em jump" but
as a broader, more subtle alchemy: the ability to influence the next generation. Influence is a more subtle, indirect form of power, but it can be
a far more effective way to shape events or motivate people to do what
you want them to do. And it is the only way when you no longer have the
authority to make people jump.

> Power never lasts. But influence can outlast your mortal life.

This does not apply just to business. How do you steer your adolescent children away from drugs, get your twentysomething daughter to avoid a disastrous marriage, or convince your 30-year-old son that he would be happier if he got a life instead of writing code twenty-four hours a day? Try to order them around, and you've lost the battle. The only hope you have is to try to exert influence—to inspire them with another vision of what their life could be—and throw in a little bribe here and there to sweeten the deal.

Drawing upon his experience and greater patience, the older man must learn new strategies for exercising power, particularly over younger people. My own husband, Clay Felker, had to alter drastically his modus operandi when he shifted from being an autocratic editor to being a university instructor, working with young-adult graduate students. "You have to learn to lead younger people in a Socratic fashion, asking them questions and making them think things through, not by giving orders but by convincing people to do things because it is in their best interest," he has learned. "You can't always win them over, but you know if you give them orders you can never win."

After seventeen years as a senator, Bill Bradley traded in the power of political office in 1996 for more indirect forms of influence. Deaths close to him had prompted the thought: *Maybe there won't be a tomorrow.* He was frustrated by the ambiguity of Washingtonspeak: "I wanted to sum up my position at the midpassage of my life." So he wrote an autobiography to clarify his thinking and, on the proceeds, began traveling around the country to restate the premises of the civil rights movement. He found himself, at 50, in what he calls "the teachable moment."

In cross-cultural studies, remember, "real" men are those who give more than they take; who serve or nurture others. Mature manhood ideologies always include a criterion of selfless generosity. As baby boomers reach the peak and start their Second Adulthood, having lived through some of the most prosperous and healthy of historical periods, most will be able to see themselves as reasonably successful. "This is a comfortable time to live for most people," observes the president of one of America's finest universities, Lee C. Bollinger at the University of Michigan. "They view this as a time to make money, pad their 401(k)s, not worry about the poor." But more and more men who enjoy success by their fifties do not feel that this is enough.

Ted Turner stunned those who complain of "compassion fatigue" when the highly political tycoon and founder of Cable News Network suddenly announced a $1 billion gift to benefit U.N. programs. His role model, he said, is George Soros, the international currency trader who escaped the Nazis as a Jewish adolescent and has become one of America's premier philanthropists. Soros immediately put another $500 million on the international table to become the leading philanthropist in Russia. Thus Soros and Turner have established a new status position— global benefactor—for men who have already proven themselves winners within the "round of eight."

But raining megabucks on one's pet causes is not the only way to give back. Peter Drucker, the guru of management theory, spells out a different sort of life design that could infuse a man's Second Adulthood with meaning:

> What we need most are men who are willing to be social entrepreneurs—men who will try out new local approaches to the crises in education, in health care, in race relations, social innovators who will find out what governments can do, and then make them do it.

Bill Gates, the boy wonder of the business world, is still young enough to believe that the human brain and computers are equivalent—and that eventually computers will be able to mimic human thought and emotions. But IQ and intelligence are not as all-important as we once thought. Even more valuable is knowing how to make good choices. That is wisdom. If it comes at all, wisdom comes only with years of experience, with failures transmuted into successes, and with the understanding that there is a greater power beyond oneself. This recognition, and the help of a higher power that comes with it, must often wait until the Influential Sixties. But before we examine that next stage, let's look at some everyday men in their fifties who have run up against common obstacles in work and love and used them to help themselves grow.

Chapter Seven

REDIRECT YOUR LIFE BEFORE
THE HAMMER FALLS

Most men follow their "program" and expect to be rewarded when they get close to the top; they don't think about reinventing themselves unless or until they are hit over the head with a hammer. The hammer doesn't fall until the late forties or fifties, when a man may find himself "excessed" in a merger or downsized, or when he may be divorced and "abandoned" by a wife who wants to find herself, or when he runs into his first health crisis.

Robin Holt, who directs career counseling and corporate services at Alumnae Resources in San Francisco, has watched the male model change drastically in just the last decade. With all the upheaval in the workplace, men are now facing the same issues that have historically confronted women. "The male model was to get on the ladder, climb the hierarchy, play by the rules, do what's expected, ascend as far as he could toward the peak, and then he would be safe and entitled," Holt summarizes. "Our model for women was that they would change jobs often and leave the workplace for long periods of time. We thought that was a female model. Now men, too, make frequent and dramatic job changes and may be out of work or choose to take a period as 'Mr. Mom.' "

Seven million American workers lost their jobs in corporate restructurings between 1991 and 1995, according to the Bureau of Labor Statistics. Downsizing has had a disproportionate effect on men in middle life. In today's marketplace, driven by the information revolution, there is a distinct bias in favor of youth. The average software-engineering qualification becomes obsolete in about five years, according to an American survey by *The Economist*. As a result, a student fresh out of college is likely to be seen as more valuable to a company than a 40- or 50-year-old, and certainly cheaper. Many of the new businesses spawned by the Internet are headed by men and women in their midtwenties.

Become an entrepreneur! coax some career coaches. But that shift does not come easily to a man long accustomed to the structure and support of belonging to a corporate "family." Of one hundred thousand downsized workers around the United States being tracked by Edward Molt, former director of the Entrepreneurship Center at the Wharton School of Business, only about 12.5 percent are now self-employed. But most of those became contract workers. An even more rarified 3 percent of downsized employees actually became entrepreneurs who have launched their own businesses and hired employees, intending to grow.

The haunting question is: What happened to all the rest?

Major American companies such as IBM and Packard Bell are still cutting down their workforces in large numbers, then rehiring many of their former employees as temporary contract workers, stripped of most benefits and swimming around the big tuna like interchangeable pilot fish. With the shredding of the old corporate safety net, many men realize the need to self-fund their retirement.

THE DARK NIGHT OF JOE O'DELL

"It's really hard for me to change," Joe O'Dell told me. "I do the same things, same way, every day."

Joe started as a cleanup boy in a food company lab. He was eighteen, a high school graduate in the muscular city of Chicago, and after seven years with the same company he worked his way up to research technician. He was content to stay in the food business for the rest of his days. But he could go no further in his company without a college degree. So he and his wife went to the library and pored over a map of California, looking for community college towns that would be welcoming and cheap. They decided to pick up and move to the Bay Area with their two children. That was the boldest change Joe O'Dell ever made in his life.

"When you're younger, the world hasn't beaten you down yet, you're still pretty optimistic that you're going to make a million before you're thirty-five," Joe remembers. "I had a lot more confidence then."

By his midforties, Joe O'Dell believed he was set for life. After struggling through eight years of night school while holding down his day job, at last he had attained a secure white-collar status. The blue-collar life with its unpredictable layoffs was behind him—or so he believed. Having earned the more prestigious title of food technologist, he worked in a laboratory doing quality control. He wanted to work there until his seventies, God willing.

The early signs of aging—getting glasses, feeling a threadbare patch on the back of his head, noticing a padlock on his leg muscles after unusual exertion—did not particularly bother him. The real shock came with the birth of his first grandchild—*Hey, I'm not a kid anymore!*—but it was muted by his joy in bending over to kiss that sweet, innocent face and seeing in it his better self. And then, while not looking, Joe felt the blow of mortality on the back of his neck. A decade before our interview, his precious granddaughter had slipped out of life as abruptly as she had come into it—a sudden crib death.

His perspective on life was profoundly altered by that terrible life accident. It coincided with the start of his passage into Second Adulthood. "When I was younger, the whole objective was to make a lot of money," Joe says. "Closing in on my fifties, that became less and less important." He found a job that made him feel more valued; it was in a private company, but he had checked out the owner and believed he was solid. Joe looked forward to spending more time with his wife.

Four years after making the job change, Joe and his wife were loading their car for a vacation in the mountains surrounding Lake Tahoe. First, they would stop to lay flowers at the grave of their granddaughter, and then, to salve the memory of her birthday, Joe would lose himself in the splendor of crossing the Donner Pass in his secondhand Corvette.

The phone rang inside the house. "Don't answer it," his wife warned. "It could be about your job. I want to enjoy myself."

Just like a woman, always anticipating some crisis. Joe didn't pay much attention to gossip around the water cooler. There had been mutterings about how his company was not paying some of its bills, but he knew he was indispensable. He and his boss were the only two technical people in the whole company, and Joe did 99 percent of the lab work, often pushing for twelve hours straight to test a new product on deadline. He hadn't taken a full week's vacation in his four years there. Heck, he only needed to be away on a three-day weekend and his boss would track him down to ask him something. He went to the phone.

"Joe?"

"Yeah?"

"How you doin'?"

It was his boss, of course, and Joe was annoyed: My first day off, and here he is again, looking for something in the lab. Joe said, "What's goin' on?"

"I got to tell you something."

"Doug, tell me."

"We're laying you off. You and fifteen other people. Today."

"Shit, you've got to be kidding me."

"No." Long pause. "Are you going to be all right?"

"No! I'm not going to be all right!" Joe thought about his second granddaughter: she had survived, and to help out, Joe had taken her in as full guardian. He thought about the second mortgage he had taken recently to put in a swimming pool.

"Is there anything I can do?" Joe asked, the rasp of desperation creeping into his voice.

"Nothing . . . they're going to be letting me go in about four months."

"What if I take a cut in pay?"

"Joe, it doesn't make any difference."

"What if I give up my benefits?"

"It's already done. The checks are made out, and it's a done deal."

The whole transaction was quintessentially male. Whatever defense mechanism is hardwired into males, it often overprotects them from spotting the potential for disaster. And Joe's male boss, probably struggling with his own feelings of loss and betrayal, had no idea how to soften the blow.

Five years later, I met the Joe O'Dell of 53 in his suburban California community for an interview. A big-shouldered man, he was dressed like a boy athlete in shorts and a basketball T-shirt, but with lots of loose meat over good biceps. His face was sober and flat, the plates behind his skin having slid down and left little welts where his cheeks used to be. His hair was tinted brown, a protective coloring. But beneath the macho exterior, Joe O'Dell had become a much more sensitive, self-aware man.

"I was out of work for eighteen months" is how he began describing himself. "It stripped me of everything—my pride, my manhood. Nearly wrecked my marriage. I just let myself go, and it started a downward spiral.

"I was in shock, then I went into anger: How could they do this to me? I never even took a vacation! I dropped all my friends. I was always athletic and a casual wine drinker. But I started drinking more. Stopped exercising. I'd get cravings. I'd just jump in the car and go over and get a couple of Whoppers and french fries and a milk shake. I think I ate because I was upset. Then I drank even more. Being depressed, a lot of free time on my hands . . . I just hung around the house and moped."

He sold his Corvette, started working nights in a convenience store for five dollars an hour, and when an assessor came over to sniff around his house in hope of a foreclosure, Joe broke down and cried. "After the first year, I just stopped reading the ads in the paper. My wife kept saying, 'Don't worry, things will work out.' But as time went on, I assured myself I would never get another job."

DESTRUCTIVE DEFENSES

Most men over 50 in corporate life have been conditioned to be good corporate citizens, to go with the flow, to be chameleons, and to choose their mates and build their lives around externalized values and material accomplishments. To be suddenly rendered obsolescent feels like a personal betrayal. It is natural to feel numb for a while, to deny what has happened. Being downsized—cut down to size—is often as stunning as a knockout punch. It is a life accident, and as with most life accidents, it may take two years to internalize the new reality and move ahead.

Joe O'Dell used many of the classic destructive defenses that appeal to men in crisis. First, he dropped all his friends and retreated into his "fort." The more disconnected a man becomes from others, the more cut off he becomes from himself. As his power drains away, it is replaced by dread. Since dread is an intolerable state, he begins to shut down, to feel nothing; all his remaining relationships go flat. Social isolation is a killer of growth.

A man who uses drinking to medicate his anxiety or sadness, as Joe did, invites many self-destructive effects. Alcohol is fundamentally a depressant, so it plunges him even further into despair—*I will never get another job*—and eventually he stops looking.

Drinking, of course, can plant the seeds of a destructive illness: alcoholism. But more commonly, it leaches through his last defense as a man: chronic drinking is a precursor to premature male sexual slowdown. By then, one of the only ways to get a good feeling about himself is to medicate himself with high-fat foods, such as hamburgers and milk shakes, which boost feel-good brain chemicals, but only temporarily, and then leave their sludge in the circulatory system. The blood and oxygen supply to a man's heart and gonads is further compromised, and there is a greater drag on his metabolism, so everything slows down.

Joe O'Dell's blues would probably not qualify as a textbook case of clinical depression. His case is a more common garden-variety midlife slump, the kind that is usually stimulated by a loss or exit event at this time of life. Left ignored or untreated, this malaise can progress into chronic low-grade depression. And more commonly, this is happening to men.

> Men over 45 are the new at-risk population for significant problems with anxiety and depression.

Depression manifests itself differently in men than in women. Women show their feelings more readily—by crying—and use food to insulate themselves. Men are much more likely to cover over their feelings with destructive actions: drinking and drug abuse.

> Disguised depression is one of the greatest vulnerabilities that men have.

As I see it, men who experience low-grade depression in the transition from First to Second Adulthood may be unable to mourn for their lost idealized self. Or their lost dream. But if they are encouraged to stay with the mourning process, they will come out much farther ahead on the other side of this critical passage.

THE COMEBACK OF JOE O'DELL

Joe's family finally dragged him out of social isolation. His wife went out and took a second part-time job, on top of her full-time position. "I was really impressed," said Joe. "It was like I had given up and she didn't." They kept their house. I then asked Joe a key question for men in middle life:

> Did you ever think: "I can't do this all by myself. I need to reach out and build a team"?

No, he hadn't thought of it, he admitted, but that is what had happened in spite of himself. His adult son had seen that Joe was dangerously depressed and had come up with the idea that they start a little business aerating people's lawns.

"I don't have the strength or the ambition to start all over again," Joe protested.

His son wouldn't hear no. "We can use your little pickup, and I'll rent the aerator."

"But I'm lousy at selling myself," Joe said. "I just can't go from door to door."

"I can do that." His son reminded Joe that he had been in telemarketing before he, too, was laid off. He assigned his father to do the heavy lifting of the machines: a clever strategy, because it got Joe back into disciplining his powerful but slackened physical plant. He was 50. He was sore at night. But he was alive again.

"Outside in the sunshine, talking to people, it was therapeutic," Joe can appreciate now. After a few months of going out every day with his son, working side by side, shoulder to shoulder up against the world, the relationship between the two men was transformed. "I saw another side of him that I never saw before," Joe tries to explain. "My son turns out now to be my best friend."

With the elixir of friendship and wifely love, the support of a team, and physical labor with a decent reward at the end of the day, Joe revived the confidence to put himself back into play. He reconnected with friends and former colleagues and customers. Within a short time he had a job even better than the one he had lost. "My wife and I got closer, because I was forced to open up when I was depressed. I desperately needed someone to talk to."

Joe had crossed a harrowing divide between his First and Second Adulthoods and survived, but he was still not aware of the momentous changes he had made. He was very aware of the huge amount of pain he had inflicted upon himself and others, some of which might have been avoided. "If I'd read this book you're writing before it all happened to me, I might have anticipated the change," he said. "At least I wouldn't have dropped all my friends and built a wall around myself and gone into drinking and depression. It could have ruined my marriage with a wonderful woman."

THEY'LL NEVER FIRE ME

Privileged, well-educated professional men of a certain age speak of the barriers to retaining their positions and their dignity. "Those of us who are most senior, and presumed to be the most expensive, are disproportionately penalized in the downsizing phenomenon," as a former executive at Digital Equipment Corporation described it. "Companies have called these programs 'open windows.' Those of us on the other side of fifty who had to walk out an open window found it quite a fall. After a year and half or so of going through your severance pay, you find it's taking more than twice as long to get a job interview, let alone a real opportunity. Sure, you can get a job selling VCRs at a chain store, but don't try to come back in as a senior manager."

The editor of *Worth* magazine, John Koten, whose readers are among the richest men in America, recognizes that the problem is not solved by mere wealth. "A lot of men live their lives according to a program. If someone comes along and talks about changing the program, it threatens them: if you mess with my program, you threaten *me.*"

Derrick Davies* offers a classic case of doublethink. Tall, lean, direct, dynamic, Ivy League smooth, and nearing 50, he figured he was sitting pretty in a position that had been created for him as a divisional director for a major communications organization. Elise,* his second wife, was a sophisticated marketing consultant in New York. She saw the shadow on the wall before the hammer fell.

"Der," she hinted, "does it look to you as though your organization is in a slide?" No response. The more she hinted, the more definite Derrick became that he was absolutely indispensable. "I had been hotly recruited for this position, and I had a lot of visibility in the trade press," he said. "I was all puffed up. Elise, well, women in general, operate on a different level of signals and vibrations. But I didn't want to hear or see the signs."

Turning 50 a few years before had caught him by surprise, like a mugging. He had set out for a dinner with friends in a celebratory mood, thinking "My fortieth was great, I never felt smarter or better, so fifty can't be that bad." Then my friends gave me a big birthday card":

> To Derrick, 1941 to 1991.

"I stared at those dates—it looked like a gravestone. I didn't get out from under that weight for six months." (It was more like a good year and a half, as Elise remembers that painful period.) Derrick felt betrayed by time. He had always been a dutiful son to his demanding parents. He was still doing the "shoulds." A new inner dialogue began yanking him around like a dog with a bone: *Look how I've been wasting my life. Should I start*

---

*A pseudonym.

over again? What about those dreams you postponed? Where is the Renaissance man you
left back in college who was going to drink down the world in great gulps and play concert
piano and write novels and make passionate love to dangerous women?

His was a second marriage. The courtship leading up to it had been
rampant and wonderful. Maybe it was an attempt to re-create the abandon he had felt with Elise that prompted him to start another affair—
this time one that was "wildly inappropriate"—during the turbulent
passage into his fifties.

"That affair was like being on a roller coaster, speeding down an increasingly steep mountainside," he said. "For the moment you're speeding,
it's ecstasy, it's eternity. Speed obliterates the dimension of time. After a
while you lose touch with everything except what is in the moment." All
his rationality and responsibility fell away. But Derrick also sensed that if
something didn't pull him out of this nosedive, he was a dead man.

He told his wife before he destroyed all that he truly valued. "Elise was
the only thing strong enough to pull me out of it," he realized. Understanding that he was "out of his mind," Elise put aside her own hurt and
helped him regain his emotional bearings.

"It's one thing to be in touch with your inner child," Derrick quips in
retrospect, "but when your inner child is actually driving the car, you're in
trouble."

Having rendered himself more dependent on his wife than he liked to
admit, he dug in his heels when she warned him that his job was tenuous
and he should develop a fallback plan. They were together at his organization's annual meeting when a board member announced that the major
program of Derrick's division would have to be eliminated. On the car
trip home the couple had a terrific fight.

"Stop fooling yourself," Elise said, frustrated that her gentle hints
over the past year had been ignored. "My guess is that they'll eliminate
your position in the next six months—which means you've *got to act now.*"

"That pissed me off," Derrick admits. "I resisted because it meant I
had to change."

The greater a man's uncertainty, the more rigidly he gets his back up
against change. There may not be anything he can do about the outer obstacle that is in his way, but he can work at removing the usual inner obstacle: rigidity, a black-and-white thinking style that makes it difficult to
look at the big picture in a different way. The anxiety level can rise so
high that a man becomes paralyzed in passivity or inaction.

> If I change my life, what will people think of me?
> If I leave my job, won't everybody assume I was fired?
> If I go back to school, will that look as if I'm regressing?

In fact, men who survive the inevitable "exit events" of middle life and go on to thrive in their Second Adulthood usually do some or all of those things. And when they emerge on the other side of the passage, other men envy them and wonder how on earth they did it.

THE REBIRTH

Derrick woke up in the middle of the night six months after the fight with his wife and poked her. "What's the difference between a fifty-five-year-old man and a tuna?"

"What?" she said.

"There is no difference. We both get canned."

It had felt like waiting for an accident to happen. "Women are more reflective and look at the big picture," he said. "Men just look for a road." Exactly as his wife had predicted, the president and vice president of his company called him in for a meeting. He needed only to look at the faux condolence in their faces to make an educated guess: "It's over, right?"

Yes, they said, his division would have to be eliminated. They convinced him to fly to Chicago and "clean out the place." After he had fired his whole staff, they pulled the trigger on him. But Derrick was ready. "If this had happened to me without the six months of getting my act together, the résumé, making the contacts, learning everything I could about the digital revolution, I would have been bereft," he says. "I would have felt like 'Nobody knows me, nobody cares, my contacts will fold in a few weeks, and I'm never going to be able to make a living again.' "

Despite his resentment over his wife's "harping" at him, Derrick had taken her professional advice: he had found a career coach. She startled Derrick with her first questions: "How long do you need to keep driving along the same track? Let's talk about your values. What makes you feel good? Do you really want to be a PR man for a big outfit forever? Or is that what your parents or somebody else wanted you to be?" She worked with him to explore different tracks and to test which ones were viable. She also asked how much time he spent with other people. How many real friends did he have? Like most executives, he had to admit he was guarded: he really had only one friend as confidante, and that, of course, was his wife.

"Expand your relationships," the career coach urged. "Whenever you anticipate a major change in the company—a merger or a buyout or down-sizing—*triple* the amount of time you spend with others. It's important to cultivate business relationships and to deepen your personal relationships."

"That's just what my wife said," Derrick admitted. But he still didn't grasp the answer to the basic question he faced:

> Who gives a man permission to change? He gives it to himself.

"If Derrick had continued to refuse to see this termination coming," says his wife, Elise, "he would have gone through more grieving." Based on her own professional experience with men, she suspects, "He might have gone into depression—so many men who are pushed off their perch do. That's six months. To get a network started takes another six months. Then it takes another six months to find work. An eighteen-month process is standard—unless you have thought about the realities in ad-vance and begun to develop a Plan B."

Derrick added to his team an employment attorney, to protect himself from being stripped of benefits. To work on buoying his self-confidence during the transition and letting loose his more creative aspects, he found a therapist. He and Elise joked about his "all-girl team." But it was work-ing. And Elise was very optimistic: "I see this rebirth happening for my husband which is going to be incredible."

During the play of light and dark that prescribed his moods during the months of preparing to shed his old corporate identity, Derrick started playing the piano again—not as a dilettante but as a serious stu-dent. He searched up his music teacher from college days, now retired, and persuaded her to help him fill the empty horizon ahead with the closest thing to the sacred, which for him is the music of Bach and Mozart. He pulled out the manuscripts of two unfinished novels written in his salad days. He decided to make a fresh start on a third novel. An empty horizon is also an open sky.

"What's going on for me now is the desire to stake a claim to those things I wanted to do as a young man," Derrick told me one night over dinner. His dark eyes sparkled. A red print bow tie added a touch of insouciance to his sober black suit. He was one of those men who had never been young, having had what he described as an unstable mother and a stern taskmaster for a father. Youth, for him, had been merely a brief prelude to serious, responsible, wage-earning adult life. "I never felt empowered to attempt my dreams," he realized. "Now I've reached a point where I can say—thanks to Elise and some therapy and a few years going by—I may never be a concert pianist, but I'm going to play the piano as well as I possibly can. And I'm going to write until I can't hold a pen anymore."

Derrick had plunged into learning about the Internet and was devising a service business of his own linked to it. While methodically networking, he was also giving himself the time and mental space to allow for inner experiences that might contribute to his spiritual growth. Making this momentous passage consciously had given him a whole new perspective on what makes a man today. He sounded off: "In this environment, the men who will be successful will trust their own intuition and be smart enough to listen to the women around them. Early human societies were matriarchal. The modern world makes it clear that the patriarchy isn't really getting the job done. We will require a different kind of male. It doesn't mean a guy is necessarily going to be any less of a guy, in sexual terms or strength, but the way he relates to the world will be different."

I asked Derrick to be totally honest: If he had it to live over again, did he think he could have accepted his wife's initial intuition and changed direction *preemptively*?

"No," he said without hesitation. "I wouldn't have been able to integrate the idea of changing and act on it, because it was totally counter to the way I thought."

THE WINDOW OF OPPORTUNITY

"For a male executive in his fifties, the odds are stacked against him in vying for a salaried position," says Robin Holt, the director of job counseling at San Francisco's Alumnae Resources Career Center. "The reality is, he can't just slug his way through anymore. He is likely to be laid off or at least told to change what he does. It opens a little window—but a big opportunity—to find why he may not have been satisfied by his work but was unable to admit it."

Men in middle life are flocking to unconventional placement agencies such as Alumnae Resources, which is a "membership" career center, to take self-assessment classes. When counselors encourage them to talk about how their values may have changed and then ask them to consider their new needs, the men's jaws drop: *It's okay to talk about my needs?* Like Derrick, many say their top value in work was a big paycheck. To their own surprise, what is now likely to come out of their mouths will reflect other, more subjective values:

- I want to believe in what I do.
- I want to make a contribution.
- I want to spend more time with my family.
- I need challenge.
- I need intimacy—more safe, trusting relationships.
- I want a chance to be more creative.
- I want a chance to see what I can do on my own.
- I need to be recognized—to have others see something that I did is great.

The emphasis on mastering the wiles and weaponry of corporate or political warfare then shifts to figuring out how to utilize one's internal powers and emotional reactions. An important choice needs to be made.

> Are you ready to commit yourself consciously to growth and new learning?

This is one of the most crucial decisions one makes in life. M. Scott Peck, the inspirational author of *The Road Less Traveled*, notes that there is no evidence that this choice is made in childhood. Indeed, it can be made at any point in life. "I have known people whose critical moments of making that choice seemed to come in their thirties, forties, fifties, or sixties, or even in the month or two preceding their death," Peck writes. It's not simply a matter of how much experience you have in life, but what you learn from it and what you do with it. Before you set off on the passage to the Age of Mastery, ask yourself three questions:

- What kind of man must I become to make this passage?
- What needs to change?
- What coaching and assistance do I need?

MIDLIFE MONEY REALITIES

Since your career voyage is likely to be interrupted—involuntarily if not voluntarily—how do you keep yourself from sinking financially? John Jacobs, a former Porsche executive who was unceremoniously fired at 51, is not going to be burned again. In preparation for a serial career, he says, "I've taken some classes and sharpened my skills and built my résumé so that I can do many jobs—I don't necessarily need a company to say that I can do it." He's remade himself as a Protean Man, ready to move on before a merger or restructuring catches him again.

The other precaution is to knock out every bit of debt that one possibly can. Several men in the Atlanta group spoke of the liberating act of cutting up their credit cards. "There's a lot of power and independence in getting free of debt and the habit of debt," says Jacobs, "to know that if push really came to shove, I could just live on the beach and rent beach chairs."

Suppose you have always wanted to be a writer. Imagine that next week you will sign a contract to write your first book—with an advance of only $10,000. Or say you've always longed to be a painter, but you gave up that dream for a more practical career in commercial art. Imagine that you had a commission to do a major portrait.

> What would you be prepared to give up in your material life to try making your dream come true?

Asking yourself this question will help you to assess your resources: What accustomed furnishings of your former life—suits and ties, an expensive leased car, country club membership—no longer seem essential?

How could you simplify? Then project forward: How would your life structure have to change to accommodate your commitment to live out your old dream?

Many men are irrationally fearful of any loss of status. They fear if they no longer have a title and a secure salary, they are going to lose their wives. They worry they will lose the adoration of their children or disappoint their parents, if they still have parents alive. They fret about the loss of social status within their circle of friends. The truth is, no one benefits much from living with a hollow man who goes through the motions of successful living but for whom not even the ingredients of an affluent life can bring him to a boil. A wife with an understanding heart would usually prefer living with a man who is excited about getting up in the morning. Adult children want to see their fathers stay healthy. And parents of the middle lifer are likely to be cheered to see a son still growing—it's testimony to their own example.

What's more, your neighbor or golf partner is probably going to be struggling with the same fears and contradictions. Except for a privileged few, you are not alone.

WHAT COULD SPOOK JOHN WAYNE?

Twelve colonels sit ramrod straight around a table in the Executive Dining Room in the Pentagon. Having agreed to participate in one of my group interviews, each of them has dutifully filled out a life history questionnaire, and now they are probably reconsidering why they have come, since the subject of our discussion is exactly the reality they do not want to face: turning 50 and hitting mandatory retirement.

Colonel Mike Nelson-Palmer, our host, describes how the military started "deranking" men and getting rid of a lot of senior officers in the 1990s. "The 'service train' keeps moving," he says. "Either you're on it or you're not." For these men, having to give up power purely because of arbitrary age limits is an imminent reality.

"Having given your adult life to the service, do you feel let down?" I ask the participants.

A tall, strapping, silver-haired man—the very vision of a senior commander who could stand up to any test—speaks first. "I love getting up every day and putting on this uniform. For all my life I have never thought of doing anything else," enthuses the colonel (I will call him Wayne, after the most idealized military man in the movies, John Wayne). An active-duty army colonel with twenty-seven years of service, Wayne has a soldier's way of walking. Had this been a dress occasion, his chest would have been plastered with purple Legion of Merit medals. But he, like the others, did not make general. "I'm extremely apprehensive about getting out," Wayne admits. "I did sacrifice a lot of time from my family to foster my career." Now there is the gap of intimacy to overcome.

His wife, feeling neglected when the colonel went off to the Persian Gulf War and elected to stay for a sixteen-month tour of duty overseas, had turned a cold shoulder when he came home. Within the last year he had experienced two common, wrenching exit events. His father had died, mute to the end about his feelings for his children. A few months after his father's death, Wayne drove his daughter to college. "When she turned and walked away and didn't look back, the bottom dropped out."

Others nodded in recognition. "I see this period coming up as the most difficult time for me, emotionally," Wayne went on. "It's more than control, you have a huge comfort system in the military." He grimaces. "I joke about it, but, uh, I guess I'm afraid to go out and earn a living."

Afraid? Not a word military men often use. Wayne has been close to death several times—in Vietnam, and on an airfield in Saudi Arabia where he and his soldiers had no cover when pieces of a Scud missile hit. Colonel Nelson-Palmer, who is facing the same cutoff, makes a remark that prompts all twelve colonels to nod around the breakfast table this morning in the Pentagon: "Wayne is more terrified of leaving the military than of being under a Scud missile."

GIVE UP "I'M THE BIG SHOT"

Let's say you are accustomed to being a big shot like the colonel. Once you lose your high-profile position, you will have to stop waiting for others to come to you. Most younger people in your field, or the students you might teach, don't know who you are or what you have accomplished in your life. Or if they do know, they will dismiss it as passé in order to make themselves feel important. So you will probably have to learn a whole new modus vivendi: Reaching out. Starting over. Becoming an amateur again—a learner.

It is not possible to enjoy the liberation of being a learner again as long as a man still masquerades as the big shot who has everything under control. When former bigwigs meet each other at the club, they say, "Hey, Harry, how's it going? You lucky devil."

"Oh, it's wonderful," says Harry. "Paris last week, Russia next month, going on a safari this spring."

Fred, who is still working sixty hours a week, thinks, "By God, Harry's got it all together." Then he runs into Jerry, a former senior executive given the "open window." "Hey, Jerry, how's it feel being a man of leisure?"

"It's faaan*tastic*," Jerry lies. "You should try it."

These men never tell one another the truth. They won't let slip that facade of being in command, because for most of their adult lives they have been the person who made the decisions. The idea of admitting to another man, "I'm really not sure about anything at this stage," is out of the question. If they talk to anybody, it will probably be to a woman therapist or career coach. Indeed, women have been developing a whole new lucrative cottage industry as counselors for men trying to get across this passage.

"You can't get from one side of the pond to the other without some interim steps on the rocks," the big shots are told by Anne Weinstock, a frank and very effective career counselor in Wilton, Connecticut. She sees the cream of the commuters who used to work in New York City and live in Fairfield County and are "between careers." A large percentage of these highly successful men are on their second marriage. The new wife is much younger, very attractive, often a trophy wife. It is quite clear to Weinstock that such a woman likes the big house in Greenwich, the country club, and the limousines to the airport. "If that lifestyle is not going to continue, she's out of there."

Weinstock would tell a man like Jerry, "Welcome to the real world. You are going to be calling people and giving your name and they'll say, 'Who? What company are you with?' You're not going to be able to say, 'I'm a vice president at Humana.'" That is an important realization. Now, she will say, let's take off all the constraints. "Forget about what you are equipped to do. Forget about the fact that you've been a financial person for your entire life. If you want to sing opera, if you want to be a veterinarian, if you want to play shortstop—I don't care whether you have the skills for it or not, what would you really love to do and where would you do it?"

The idea is to develop themes and try to formulate a new dream. Men are given a writing journal to jot down their fantasies. The successful transitioners, says Weinstock, are the men who are honest with themselves and who have an open, trusting relationship with their spouse. "A lot of them don't tell their wives what they're feeling. And the wife just goes right on shopping. She's out there buying clothes, planning trips, and saying, 'All I know is it's February, and that's when we go to Saint Bart's. What's the problem?' "

Starting over demands hard work, humility, and sacrifice. Humility, because you will be an amateur again, not the expert, for a while. You will make stupid mistakes and feel foolish. If you go back to college or graduate school, you will be unaccustomed to the academic grind. But you will be stretching and growing a "new self," and that is the greatest payoff of all.

BUILDING A TEAM

First, build your tower of dreams in the sky—that's the hard part. Then you can start constructing a foundation to support it. But you may very well need some help. Professional allies such as a career counselor, a good doctor, a therapist, a spiritual guru can help you see that you are not a wimp. A new law of natural selection is operating: men are living longer but being replaced earlier. It is time to revise your maps and charts. And it is healthy to do so. You are not crazy. You are not old. And you are not a failure. Don't waste precious time running yourself down or entertaining revenge fantasies. It is better to put your effort into redirecting your life, assembling a new team to replace people you are losing, and possibly seeking out support in the spiritual realm.

> Create a new network of connectivity.

Okay, you may be saying, *that's fine for these guys who already have the world by the tail. But I feel overwhelmed. I don't know where to start thinking about a new dream. I can't even get my taxes filed on time. It just makes me feel like a screwup.*

Ask yourself some questions:

- Are there ways in which you are limiting yourself?
- Don't you think you have more potential than you acknowledge?
- Do you worry that you shouldn't succeed more than your father? Or your brother? Or your wife?

The Protean Man concept, described as a healthy approach to identity for men in their forties, becomes an even more effective armor in the fifties and beyond, when dominance in certain roles will have to be relinquished. The middle passage begins in earnest when you ask: *Who am I apart from my personal history and the roles I have played?* If you are already cultivating multiple or possible selves, you have a built-in resilience against the inevitable injuries to ego as you shift from doing what you know to pursuing a passion for what you don't yet know.

Paul B. Baltes and Peter Graf, two of the principals participating in the MacArthur Foundation Research Network on Successful Midlife Development (MIDMAC), have confirmed in longitudinal studies the importance of having a whole "system of selves" in order to maintain self-esteem and a sense of personal control as one ages and changes.

> Most humans have rather differing expectations of who they are, who they were, who they would like to be, who else they could be, and who they would not want to be at all. Because we have a system of selves, it is possible that when one self is challenged by an injury (e.g., being an athlete), for example, another self (e.g., being a lover of music) is there to take its place.

A second important principle in remaining open to multiple directions for refreshment in Second Adulthood is the willingness to alter your goals and adjust your aspirations. If it looks impossible to become a rock star or a concert pianist at 50, it may be rewarding in other ways to reduce your aspirations and work with young performers, or to raise money to support the arts in your community. As Baltes and Graf point out, older adults tend to become more flexible in tailoring their goals to real-life circumstances, rather than holding tenaciously to unattainable goals. This strength allows older men to create new life scenarios.

The process of discovering the multiple selves upon which you can call in Second Adulthood is basic to cultivating your capacity for resilience. If you make it over this hump, you will have a tremendous storage tank of resilience to meet and master the next passage or life accident.

OPENING THE SPIRITUAL DIMENSION

As men move beyond the first half, the prodding of the soul often leads them on a spiritual search. The universal question is: *Why am I here?*

Outplacement counselors tell me that men over 50 who have lost their jobs are generally very practical. "Save the counseling stuff for somebody else that needs it more than I do," they'll say. "I just want the meat and potatoes here. Who do you know? Do you think I'm overweight?"

But even for a man who is psychologically healthy to start with, the "counseling stuff" may be critical in helping him to gain mastery over this passage. Whenever a life accident smashes our sense of control, any unresolved emotional pain from the past will be called up in some form. For example: *My dad always told me I wouldn't amount to anything, so I'm not surprised my boss fired me first.*

Our relationship with an employer is symbolically very close to our relationship with earlier authority figures, especially parents. And that sort of historical baggage can magnify the immediate crisis, often making it seem insurmountable—or deserved. Good short-term crisis therapy can help a man link the way he feels about the current crisis with the historical antecedents in his life and help him to understand why he is so wigged out. Once he sees the link, he can say: *Oh, this isn't my father doing this to me—this is just Company X. I still feel the pain of what happened in my family, but you know what? I'm a big boy now, and I can go on and do something different.*

Dee Soder, a New York psychologist, is a pioneer in the burgeoning field of executive coaching. She started her company, CEO Perspective Group, ten years ago as men began to wake up to the fact that they are living longer and will want, or need, to continue actively working into their sixties or seventies. But how, and at what? She counts among her clients members of Congress, ambassadors, senior executives, lawyers, and doctors.

Frequently, men come into her office shell-shocked, claiming that they have been fired with no warning. But when they trace back the salient events together, she can almost always point out signs that they should have noticed six months before. "But they usually have ignored the signs. They kept thinking that hard work would pay off. And they generally don't pick up on the more subtle cues. They're too busy charging ahead and focusing on results."

Men do not always take into account subjective factors beyond competency. A recent survey by a large law firm found that 68 percent of factors involved in getting a promotion or keeping a job are *subjective.* Yet according to Dr. Soder, men, more often than executive women, are in denial that demotion or downsizing could ever happen to them. "That's where you get the wives, the significant others, the girlfriends, their female friends at work, and occasionally some of their male friends who are more in tune, who can be valuable in hinting, 'Gee, don't you think . . .' "

"That's what my wife told me" is a classic statement that Dee Soder hears from many of the executives in transition she counsels. But often they can't accept the insights from a wife because they don't think she can be objective. Also, they don't want to feel dependent upon wife-as-mother, just as they resisted their own mothers' protective warnings.

Yet sometimes we have to rely on another person's belief in us until our own belief kicks in. A wife, too, can give a man the license to change.

"One of the things that my loss of employment did for me personally was to make me value—no, cherish—my wife of twenty-two years," says Bob Graham. The first son of a blue-collar Irish Catholic family to go to college, he made it as a publishing executive only to become a casualty of the contracting corporate world, not once but twice, at 43 and again at 52. "Every time I had a job crisis, my wife knew how devastated I was, and she came through splendidly." A year and a half after he was fired for the second time, he was no longer ashamed of his battle scars. At 53, Graham projected all the bonhomie of a good salesman but one seasoned with insights from his ten years as an outplacement consultant who has helped other men across the fearsome passage of job loss.

"Call me Bob," he began as we sat down for coffee. He had driven into New York from Westport, Connecticut, where his executive search business is now thriving. But more important, after twenty years as a lapsed Catholic, his time in the dark wood led to a resurgence of faith. He leaned over the restaurant table, eager to explain.

"A big career often cannibalizes who we really are. It takes little pieces out of us. We men compartmentalize our lives—education/marriage/career—and unless there's an intercept, we tend not to be introspective. We're more action-prone."

During the rough passage after he was fired for the second time, he found an enormous source of fulfillment and self-worth in becoming a founding member of a local chapter of A Better Chance, a national non-profit organization that provides secondary school education for talented minority students. By extending himself into the community, he developed a new circle of friends, most of whom turned out to attend the same Protestant church. Bob went to see the pastor. "I've never met a member of your congregation I didn't like or respect," he said. "I think it's a sign. I was raised a Catholic, but I don't want to spend the rest of my life alienated. I feel like I'm open to God's grace." The pastor invited him to come to a Sunday service and check it out.

"So here I am, fifty-two years old, holding on to the hand of my Jewish wife while I cross the threshold of a Protestant church." Bob chuckled as he recalled the nervous moment. "Now I attend every Sunday with no thought of 'I have to go.' I'm taking barnacles off. This kind of discovery just comes to you if you're open."

Remember the downsized Digital executive who was quoted earlier saying "Those of us on the other side of fifty who had to walk out an open window found it quite a fall"? Bob Graham was able to see the window as an opening that allowed him to recover some of the lost, best parts of himself. "I have a greater sense of wholeness today," he said, "but I wouldn't have had it if I hadn't lost my job. I had to get hit by a two-by-four to get a heightened perspective." He still has fire in the belly, he says, but it's okay that he is not the president of a company; it's okay that another man has a bigger house or smarter kids or a prettier wife. Bob is more honest about the masks and poses he used to hide behind, and that helps him coach other men in similar predicaments.

"Now is a time in life to be more tolerant of others and accepting of ourselves," he tells his male clients. He especially encourages them to reach out and make more friends. Friends are a crucial part of the team a man needs for support as he deals with a job dislocation. Even if a man does not have the wake-up call of job dislocation, he will need to expand his friendship base in middle life.

FIND YOUR PASSION AND PURSUE IT

The event that acts as a wake-up call for men over 50 need not be job loss. As mentioned earlier, many other exit events commonly occur after age 50. And if you are a man who has the benefit of some success behind you, it is not necessary to wait until a loss or setback blows up in your face.

> If you are really smart, you will precipitate a change of direction before you hit a crisis.

In this way you will outwit the culture. You will be in the vanguard, because now there is another reason beyond adapting to the new adult life cycle—a culturewide shake-up of the whole social and economic landscape—that is prompting men to alter their game plans.

The key to a vital Second Adulthood is to find your passion and pursue it with full heart and mind. Once having given yourself permission to change, how do you search for the passion that will enliven your second half?

Dave Meltz, the law school professor in the Atlanta group, found clarity when he had to surrender his will to a surgeon at the point of near death. He dropped out of the publish-or-perish competition to return to doing what he most loves—teaching—and created a position for himself where he is indispensable as both dean and professor in a fledgling law school. He now lives his first love: nurturing his students.

Lee May, the Atlanta journalist who took a moratorium year to search his past, discovered that his passion in middle life was for nurturing his garden and sharing his love of plants and food with a devoted circle of readers.

In earlier life history surveys I did of thousands of professional men who were an average age of 52, drawn from all over the United States, those who looked back and reflected on the first half of their adult lives were often rewarded by feeling "aware of progress in important parts of my life." A generation ago, these same men might have felt on a decline after 50. Today, they can appreciate the progress they have made *and are still making.* Many of them say they are not as angry, driven, or selfish as when they were younger. And that makes it easier to rediscover what excites their passion.

Understand that finding your passion doesn't happen on demand. Men are used to getting answers right away. But this problem is not about getting the answer quickly. Take the "Time Flies Test": Think back to when you were a teenager or even younger. What was it that you used to do when time flew and you didn't even know it? In that activity there is probably a kernel of an idea that might enliven your life. Don't worry about whether or not it seems practical at the beginning. Just try to get down the essence of what you love about that activity. Then chew on it, dream about it, argue about it with your spouse, inquire about it with your friends.

> It is the *search process* that keeps hope alive.

It will also keep your immune system boosted. Men who remain focused on what they have lost in career status often drift into chronic low-grade depression, maybe without noticing it. Eventually they turn up with cancer or heart disease. Scientific studies of the immune system strongly implicate our feelings as culprits in rendering us susceptible to such diseases. In a fascinating human study at UCLA, Margaret Kemeny, a Ph.D. psychoimmunologist, found that the effect of strong feeling states—happiness, anger, or even active sadness—produced an increase in the number and activity of "killer cells" that help fight off disease. And this increase in effective functioning of the immune system would happen *within twenty minutes* of the subject's change of mood. It was the *absence* of emotion that depressed the immune system and predisposed a person to disease.

Be patient. This search process may take a year or two—even a decade—but it is something you need to start thinking about as you approach the end of your First Adulthood. By the time you hit 50, you need to make it your goal every day, like brushing your teeth or deciding whether or not to wear a raincoat.

> What is my passion?
> How do I find it?
> How do I *live* it?

Chapter Eight

LOVE AND WAR WITH WIVES, FATHERS, CHILDREN

As men grow older, they need more emotional nourishment. In earlier stages, when ordinarily the focus is on achieving success and status in their careers, men may feel no pressing need to nourish their relationships with others. In their fifties to midsixties something changes. Men are often surprised to find themselves mellowing, warming up, and wanting richer, more complex relationships with their wives, children, friends, and selected family members.

"Oh, you just want men to be more soft" was the tease of the famous TV interviewer Charlie Rose.

No, I said, I just want us all to be more whole.

When men begin to enjoy landscaping their homes, take up a musical instrument they once loved, reach out to repair a frayed relationship, or reach inward to reflect on their own lives or their connection to the spiritual realm, it is obvious that a major reorganization of their personalities is in progress. Anthropological studies tell us that as they age, men continue to identify with being male, rather than becoming feminized or androgynous, but their earlier need to prove themselves by sexual and aggressive conquests subsides dramatically. They also become freer to express themselves creatively, to experience their emotions, to appreciate their surroundings aesthetically, and to be more artistic, tender, and nurturing.

Theories of adult development, on the other hand, having been mostly constructed by men—from Freud and Jung through Erikson and Levinson—have concentrated on achieving the full individuation of the "self," which is based on *separation* from others. The emphasis is on power and control. Very little importance is placed on building *mutual* relationships with mates, men and women friends, coworkers, adult children, and members of the community. Only in the final stage of a man's life do Erikson and his fellow theorists give their blessing to generativity, the process by which a man becomes paternal and creative in a new sense, feeling a voluntary obligation to guide new generations and to mentor younger associates.

Yet it is their experience of relationships that can make grown men cry—when their fathers die without uttering the words "I love you," when their wives "abandon" them, when they "give away" a beloved daughter in marriage to another man. Just as women do, men have a primary need for human closeness. They, too, were once infants whose experience of being merged with mother in a timeless mutuality was the closest they came to bliss. But cultural norms call for boys to make an emotionally violent break from the mother and, in the process, to learn how to disconnect from the whole feeling world of relationships.

FROM COMPETING TO CONNECTING

A very different approach to men's psychological development has been worked out since 1981 by psychiatrist Stephen Bergman and his wife, Janet Surrey, who conduct workshops and research at the Stone Center at Wellesley College in Massachusetts. They point out that disconnecting is learning how *not to listen,* how *not to register the feelings* inside oneself or expressed by others, how to "turn off" in order to remain in control and get the job done. In place of the old either-or dichotomy, they emphasize "the healing power of mutual relationships, with men and women both." The goal of development is not to increase one's solitary power and control but to increase one's ability to build and enlarge *mutually enhancing* relationships. "As the quality of relationships grows, the individual grows . . . the more connected, the more powerful," writes Dr. Bergman.

> The important shift for men in middle life is from competing to connecting.

That observation is a result of my seven-year study for *New Passages.** Connecting means being open to both giving *and* receiving—from the heart, not just from the head. It means being willing simply to listen to and empathize with a spouse, not always trying to fix whatever may be wrong; being able to show a male friend how much you care and being able to accept his affection; developing an ear actually to hear the feelings being expressed beneath the words used by an adult child or an employee to express their needs or frustrations. Connecting to nature, to music, to the spiritual dimension, tuning in to his own subtle intuitions—these are all ways in which a man can enrich and deepen his inner life and render himself less and less dependent on external valuation.

Men who allow this natural shift of emphasis to occur also become more valuable as leaders or managers. Traditional top-down, military-style management practice worked very well for the John Wayne generation, but it is not a style that fosters the *networks of connectivity* necessary to get the job done in a global, multicultural, service-oriented marketplace. Managers today have to be teachers and nurturers, able to help determine what kind of people, knowledge, and skills are required to do the next project and to hire, nurture, and eventually replace those people with the next team. The best professors, too, are nurturers, prized not so much for teaching their subject but for being hands-on professional guides and gurus whom students can emulate.

The men in my Atlanta discussion group, like those in the previously described San Francisco and Memphis groups, emphasized their need to be more involved fathers and more attuned mates, and to find some way to be useful and valued in society. They talked, in particular, about the importance of connecting at a deeper level with their wives. Ray Brown,

---

* A life history survey was answered by 7,800 adult women and men. I conducted close to five hundred personal interviews and studied eight hundred "pacesetter" men and women in the middle-life years.

the pro footballer who later started his own company, came to a realization that may seem obvious but isn't to many men: "When you get caught up in the business world, trying to make it, you stray away. You don't really show your wife that she's important in your life." He overheard the wife of a friend making a fervent complaint: *You never do the things that you used to do when you were courting me.*

"That hit home with me," says Ray. "For the past five years I've tried to do little things that we used to do when we didn't have the kids. That makes my wife feel like she's very special. Those are our crowning moments. I guess with our boys away in college, there's a part of her missing. So I have to compensate for the boys myself. It feels good."

But connecting emotionally may also feel strange and even frightening to a man who has been taught to associate manliness with being a fierce, solitary competitor. And as a wife comes into her own, he may feel overshadowed.

GENDER CROSSOVER: COMFORT OR CRISIS?

A half-dozen couples were enjoying their decaf coffee after a New York dinner party on a weeknight. The women, all in their fifties, included a lawyer, an interior designer, a real estate broker, a cartoonist, a professional caterer, and a yoga instructor. At 11:15 P.M., the women all began fidgeting, looking at their watches, and mumbling polite exit lines: "I'm afraid I have an early meeting." "I'm flying to Washington in the morning to see a client." "I have to finish reading my brief before court tomorrow." The men, ranging from their midfifties to midsixties, were relaxed and drawing stimulation from their conversations. They were in no hurry. Why the difference?

The women are all working full-time and their careers are still growing. Their husbands are all slowing down or retired.

Partners at the same developmental stage are often out of sync. When healthy, educated women reach their fifties today, they generally feel a great release of energy—what my own mentor, Margaret Mead, dubbed "postmenopausal zest." They are likely to say, "Hey, I have thirty or forty years ahead of me! Let's go!" Men facing the same passage, if they view it as a loss of power or potency, become threatened that they are less needed by women. This imbalance has created one of the newest and most challenging passages for married men and women in middle life today: the Gender Crossover.

This is an upheaval that didn't occur when men were assured of being rewarded for loyalty in middle life and retired with a comfortable pension, while the postmenopausal wife was expected to turn off her mental engines and coast into the golden years as grandma and volunteer nurse to elderly family members.

The new realities, as mentioned earlier, are these: Men continue to drop out of the workforce earlier and earlier, while women are working later and later. Hard evidence of the Gender Crossover comes from the latest unpublished figures by the U.S. Bureau of Labor Statistics:

> Two thirds of men aged 55 to 64 do some paid work. But their participation in the labor force has not increased at all in the last ten years.

Conversely, women's participation in the workforce in their middle years (55 to 64) has increased steadily and strongly over the same period.

> Half of women aged 55 to 64 now do some paid work.

In 1996, when the American job market began a robust expansion, men over 55, often retired or semiretired, began to show signs of reentering the workforce. But among women over 55, the increase in jobholders was 50 percent higher than among men of the same age group.

So the fiftyish wife is now in takeoff position, starting her own new business, or going to graduate school, or rushing around the world to save refugees. Perhaps her husband has chosen to retire early or has been "given a package," or he sees his career contracting. Now he wants his wife to slow down and keep him company, but her engines are just revving up. Through nobody's design, there is a disruption in the balance of power in the relationship. The stage is set for a clash.

If a couple approach this natural crossover openly and make the most of their expanded repertoires of behaviors, the tensions of holding on to rigid male-female distinctions can relax. Their partnership can become more exciting and dynamic. The Gender Crossover escalates into a crisis only when the man does not feel sufficiently strong and capable or has bought into the myths of manhood dictating that the man must always be dominant in all spheres. He will then have difficulty watching his wife discover her own strengths and capabilities. The story of the coach and the nurse, while the details may differ from your experience, is probably a familiar one.

COACHING THE COACH

At 24, Coach* was one tough hombre. A promising competitive boxer in public high school, he was in perpetual training: running circles around his working-class neighborhood, up and down hills, lifting homemade weights; he was solid as a side of beef. His part-time job as an assistant high school football coach was a side bet. What his heart was set on was making the U.S. boxing team.

When he didn't make the team, it hurt so badly that he stopped working out, stopped running, although he continued to eat a training table diet. Going heavy on the meat and potatoes, he said, "made me feel like I'm an athlete, I'm a competitor." He married a nurse in training, and right from the start she was on his case: "When you stop working out, you're not burning those calories."

"Eileen,* you don't understand the mentality of an athlete," he said dismissively.

"No, you're right, I was only on the women's varsity tennis team, so I really don't understand."

But in those days, Coach always had the last word. He was the undisputed breadwinner—his wife had stopped working before the birth of their second child—and he threw himself heart and soul into being a football coach. He was always in a hurry: to get to practice, to move up

_____

*A pseudonym.

from high school to college level, which he accomplished in his midthirties. He was also in a hurry when he made love. Coach prided himself on being as fast as a racing car: zero to a hundred in less than a minute. His wife was a good sport about it all. She always said, "His job is his mistress, and that's fine with me."

Suddenly he was nearing the fifty-yard line in his own life. Racing against younger jocks to enhance his reputation, he aspired to coach a professional team. He was close, he was being wooed, when the first health crisis interrupted: he passed out on the sidelines during a tense game for the conference title. "Fat chance they'll hire me now," he thought. Sensing that the bottom was about to drop out of his dream, he boxed up the whole question of heart disease and pushed it out of sight. Both his children were away at school. But his wife got on his case: he needed a follow-up by the cardiologist, more tests, maybe surgery.

"You'll just have to make the appointments for me," he told his wife.

"But you've been diagnosed with an illness that is life-threatening," she reminded him.

"I don't have time for that stuff now, I'm focused on building this damn team so we'll be ready for the Bowl on January first."

Being a nurse, Eileen knew how to read an angiogram. On the map of her husband's heart the major blood vessels looked like narrow dirt roads; one good storm, and they could be impassable. "I'm scared," she told him.

"You're just going to have to do the worrying for the both of us," Coach insisted and tuned out.

She wanted to tell him he was in denial. She wanted to say, "You know what? Denial is *not* a river in Egypt." Instead, Coach disconnected from his body while his wife took it on as her responsibility: she made sure he was scheduled for angioplasty.

The day before the procedure, Coach heard back from the general manager of his suitor in the NFL: "We really wanted to hire you, but the owner isn't sure you can handle it. Hey, I'm sorry." With impressive fraud he expressed amazement, then phoned his doctor to say that he was coming over to sound off. "Wait a minute, Doc, I'm not that bad!" he protested. "Can't you clean up my report so I can get this job?"

After examining Coach, the doctor announced, "I'm going to put you right in the hospital. Your head's about to blow off."

"No."

The doctor addressed him as if talking to one mentally disturbed: "Now, just a moment, your blood pressure is one-eighty over one-twenty—"

Coach was up against his own death by dull formula, and defiance sprang up inside him. He snatched his body from the edge and propelled it toward the door, calling back to the doctor what seemed at that moment the overpoweringly clear and present danger: "I haven't been laid yet by a Scorpio stewardess with a water bed!"

While driving across a bridge, he thought how nice it would be to drive straight up into the hills and get out and run, run with the reckless nonchalance he had in his twenties, run so hard his blood would leap, burst through its walls, flood free and warm. . . . *Please, God, let me have a heart attack, right here, right now,* he thought, *and get it all over with.* He fantasized about lying on the hospital bed, the grainy, impersonal sheets, the whispers and tears. His wife would stop criticizing him. His sons would appreciate him. His players would stop by and mumble, *What you did for us, Coach, when you was sick yourself, that took a lot of balls.* It would be an *exhibition* heart attack, like an exhibition game. Then he would get up and walk away, still every bit a man.

His wife made sure Coach showed up at the hospital the next morning. The clogged arteries in his heart were reopened. Eventually the health crisis passed, but so had the couple's golden opportunity for discovering how they might work together in a mutual relationship. Had Coach and his wife experienced the healing power of *staying connected* through crisis, restoring his health while uncovering a new level of closeness, they might not have gone in opposing directions in midlife.

"My thoughts turned to survival," Eileen admitted. "I was only a part-time nurse, I relied totally on him and his benefits, and if anything should happen to him, our children and I would be left with nothing." Should she go back to work full-time? Given the couple's traditional values, it was a torturous decision. Eileen worked in the burn unit of a children's hospital. "My supervisor had been hounding me for years to go full-time," Eileen recalled. "I told her, 'Gosh, I probably can't learn. I'm too nervous now.' I didn't realize that at my age I could learn to start an IV on a small baby. It was amazing to me to see that women can make up for lost time."

Coach gave his blessing, and Eileen went back to school to upgrade her skills. To her surprise, it wasn't scary, it was exhilarating. She received her baccalaureate degree by mail and her career immediately took off.

The whole family was amazed. And once she started working as a full-time intensive care nurse, there was an even greater surprise: she was now making more money than her husband. Every year, progressively, she received a raise. As a college coach, her husband was lucky if he got a raise every two years. Neither of them mentioned this major alteration in the balance of power between them. One day, one moment crystallized the gulf in their perceptions of one another.

It was Sunday, and the big game was over. Coach missed his wife. She hadn't been home for sixteen hours. He went over to the hospital to take her doughnuts and pick up the checkbook. "Your wife is very busy specialing a child with third-degree burns," he was told. When he saw Eileen on her own playing field, he could hardly believe his eyes. She was surrounded by high-tech survival equipment and bent over a charred five-year-old boy with plastic foliage sprouting from his nose and chest. While Eileen intently read the numbers off a huge ventilator and a cardiac monitor, beeps and whistles and alarms kept up a terrifying symphony of the battle between life and death.

He had never before seen his wife as separate from himself, as a professional in her own right, and he could not find the words to say "I am extremely impressed with your level of knowledge and competency." So he made a bad attempt at a joke.

"Well," smirked Coach, "I guess you really can save a life all by yourself!"

"What do you think I do in here?" Eileen shot back. "Sit and rock babies?"

More of the emollient of intimacy that smoothes over troubles in any marriage dried up. As Eileen gained higher status through her late-blooming career, she felt a surge of energy. Simultaneously, Coach felt as though he was winding down. He simply had to come out on top. So he took a second job, as a real estate agent in the off-season, and once again he emerged as the top earner in the household. That left very little time in their lives for talking intimately—or for talking at all. Coach eats and works, eats and works. By the time he comes home in midevening, Eileen sighs, "He's exhausted, he's not ready to hop in the sack."

By now, Coach is 52 years old and almost a hundred pounds overweight. It would appear that he is so angry at himself for "failing" his manhood ideal, he is locked into macho habits that have become self-destructive. Despite the fact that rationally he supported his wife in her return to full-time work, on some irrational level he seems to be punishing her for no longer making him the center of her attention. Coach's way of coping with the Gender Crossover is to sheathe his anger in fat and deny his wife intimacy and sex.

WITHHOLDING SEX

The departure of children can and often does revive a couple's love life—if they are not locked into an unresolved power struggle. But when a husband or wife is filled with anger or resentment, the departure of children only magnifies the problems in their relationship. Since women in midlife today are generally becoming more focused on their own personal growth and goals, men should not count on their wives to continue to place their own needs and desires second. Their wives are entering a momentous passage, too, with menopause as the indelible marker. Moving into the Age of Mastery, then, demands that any marriage be renegotiated. Both partners need more room to shuck off the shells of confining roles they have by now outgrown, to stretch and grow. The arena where this renegotiation usually takes place is not some lawyer's office—it is in the bedroom. It is not about words; it is about sex and desire.

A man like Coach is responding to perceived assaults to his masculine predominance. Sometimes these feelings are expressed, but more often they are not. Resentment builds. Not wanting sex is a natural outcome of anger and resentment in a relationship. It can also be an effective (if often unconscious) way for the partner who feels powerless or upstaged in the relationship to wield his or her own power: negative withholding power.

Withholding sex used to be the weapon of last resort for wives who felt their needs ignored over the years. Now experienced sex therapists say they have seen the tide turn. "In my practice, ninety-five percent of the complaints about loss of sexual desire in a couple come from the man," says Bernie Zilbergeld, Ph.D., a sex therapist with a quarter century of experience and author of an excellent book, *The New Male Sexuality*. "But men are really good at pushing it away for ten or twenty years. The biggest change is, now the wives are complaining."

It all starts with unresolved anger at the partner. What better way to get back at one's partner than by not offering sexual attention or closeness, thereby invalidating her desirability?

> Loss of sexual desire most often results from problems or power struggles in a couple's relationship.

For nearly one third of average couples who both work full-time, American women's salaries now exceed their husbands'. African-American males usually trail black women professionals by midlife. Even the best-adjusted couples of any race admit they have to work extra hard to keep their relationships on an even keel when the woman brings home the bigger paycheck.

This trend appears to be growing. Even in an economy that has steadily recovered from recession and is as robust as the American economy is, the man in the average middle-class family may not have fully recovered his status. The median earnings of full-time male workers *fell* in 1996, despite the fact that unemployment dropped to its lowest level in a quarter century.

Equity in earning power is even more exaggerated among the most successful couples. The top 5 percent of working women have enjoyed a heady *one-third increase* in their earnings over the past two decades. The fattest increases have been gained by well-educated women married to higher-earning husbands. These smart, usually professional women are carrying on working right though middle life, gaining status and extending their earning power. How do they respond to the instability or premature termination of their husbands' careers?

> - Professional men in the United States have median weekly earnings of $857. Among men in the Age of Mastery—45 to 54 years old—*half* are now earning above the median for full-time salaried male professionals.
> - For women classified as professionals, the median earnings are $647 a week. Among women in the Age of Mastery— 45 to 54 years old—almost *one third* are now earning above the median income for full-time salaried professional women.
>
>   *Source:* Unpublished 1996 data from U.S. Bureau of Labor Statistics.

THE SAFETY NET WIFE

It would be a mistake to count on a wife's selfless support as a man makes his way through a bumpy passage in middle life. Women, too, are responding to entering this new stage of life. Once unleashed, the aspirations of women in their fifties today are virtually boundless. As they move beyond the full-time caregiver role, they may guard their newfound independence fiercely. The fact that most men's lives are changing at this time, by design or by circumstance, has profound consequences for their partners.

"I used to be embarrassed that my husband was not the big shot he used to be," confessed an exceptionally gifted New York psychotherapist. "He was the globe-trotting financier. I was the dumpy little social worker, dabbling part-time while the kids were growing up." In his fifties, the financier cashed out. The "dumpy little social worker" earned her Ph.D. in psychology and launched a private practice, counseling mostly the casualties of corporate ups and downs (as she had done for her husband all those years, gratis). Suddenly she was the star in the family. It was her work that was the most compelling and most lucrative.

"It was a shift in my reality as well as his," she told me. "Maybe it was mythical, but I'd always thought of him as the giant on the white horse. My sense of security and my standing in the world were tied to his career status. Some friendships eroded as a result of the change in our living circumstances. I couldn't afford to compete at the old level, and I really didn't want to. We were part of the first wave of downshifting."

With so many formerly high-flying men now finding themselves a little lost in middle life, many working wives are experiencing a hard landing. This is the stage when children need college tuition at the same time as parents may face health crises. If the once-successful husband is now unemployed—or underemployed—who is expected to hold the family up financially? The wife becomes the safety net. Even if a woman is making a very good income, she often feels angry, even abandoned: Whatever happened to the husband she expected to be powerful and protective?

"What I say has a lot of validity because I'm *living it*, not just helping people through it," says the psychotherapist, who admits to having intestinal distress as well as emotional upheavals alternating between anxiety and anger. "The biggest challenge for me, and for the women I counsel, is to separate out the myths of the child in me, who grew up believing that the prince was going to come, from the real facts of what's happening in a husband's life. Some of us emasculate our husbands for disappointing us. That only creates more problems for the man in coping with the chore that he has. But it's also very normal and natural. As adaptable as we are, the smartest, most success-oriented women, when you ask them to tell you their deepest personal feelings, they still feel like they should have a husband who is more successful than they, who they can lean on for emotional and financial security."

Even if the woman is earning a sizable income, there is likely to be some resentment if she is expected to pay the bills. Most professional wives I have interviewed don't object to paying for the family vacation, sharing school fees, or buying the Christmas presents one year. But the idea that they should take on the daily operating expenses or shell out for the down payment on the new house is in conflict with the role they were taught was theirs. The higher the husband's earnings, the less likely he is to share housework and child care. He feels entitled to being taken care of on the home front. Does he lose that entitlement when he is no longer working full-time? Suppose the wife feels that she is now working harder than he is? *And* earning more? She comes home from a Saturday spent in the office and finds her husband "gone fishing," no groceries in the house. He may feel such a degree of hostile dependency on his wife that he sees any request to help around the house as "challenging me." There is bound to be friction. When roles reverse, who is responsible for what?

An increasing number of men in all social classes are having trouble accepting their wives' success, according to mental health professionals. The most obvious forms of retaliation are physical abuse and emotional undermining, but many use the subtler forms of drinking, overeating, or having a get-even affair. Ron Levant, a Boston psychologist and coauthor of the book *Masculinity Reconstructed,* counsels many such men and their wives. If her career requires a sacrifice from him, suggests Levant, "she's got to say, 'I adore you; how can we make up for it?' " She should also acknowledge, in private and in public, that she couldn't have succeeded without his full support.

But the man in this position may be accurate in sensing that he is in some peril. Women who work and can support a reasonably pleasant lifestyle are increasingly jettisoning the older man who has lost his position, his motivation, and his masculine confidence. Statistically, it is women between 40 and 54 who have been swelling the ranks of the divorced more rapidly than any other age-group since 1970. Many of these divorcées are radically different from the classic dumped middle-aged wife without skills or status. One of the unremarked revolutions of the last two decades has been the increase in professional women who find divorce a springboard and *choose* to remain single. Thus, a man who loses his job in middle life and who may never get back onto the same footing with his career—or chooses not to try—stands to lose his marriage as well if the couple does not find help getting through this transition. This can be a devastating loss.

"Men are secretly very needy and dependent," the noted psychiatrist and author John Munder Ross told me. "They have greater separation anxiety than we like to acknowledge." The anxiety over separation refers to all of men's maternal and paternal figures, but most significantly it concerns the maternal figure. Munder Ross pointed to the respected Judith Wallerstein divorce studies: "Not one of her male subjects left his marriage without having a woman waiting in the wings. You could interpret that as, oh, sure, he finds a young thing, uses her to restore his virility, and she breaks up the marriage. But the other way to look at it is that he needs a maternal female figure to depend on."

If only couples knew enough to be prepared for a crossover in middle life. When a man's career status changes, it opens a little window—but a big opportunity—to find out how his needs and values may have shifted. For a while, at least, he may not be top dog. He may well need to rely on his partner's income-producing activities to spell him for a period of reassessment and exploration.

In interviews for this book and for *New Passages*, all of the professional men over 50 said that their spouses are their primary source of intimacy and comfort. All of them. They often acknowledge in interviews, "My wife has helped me to discover aspects of myself I never knew were there." A natural crossover between men and women may have been an evolutionary design. It can open up a marriage and allow both partners to stretch beyond their earlier domestic roles, becoming more interesting to each other as well as more broadly valuable to society.

MAKING THE CROSSOVER WORK

You may recall Lee May, the newspaperman in the Atlanta group. When Lee was wrestling with his midlife passage, he put his marriage at risk. His reconciliation with his father and the year he took at home to write a memoir freed up his aesthetic side and led him to his passion: writing about gardens and food. When that crossover took place, he was out of work for a year. His wife, Lyn, was prompted by financial necessity to make her own career more meaningful. She found a "home" on the executive staff of her city's Olympic Games Committee and was soon swept up in a five-year "forced march." The crossover eventually strengthened their marriage.

Marilyn Puder-York, Ph.D., a New York psychologist and executive coach who has been counseling professional couples for twenty years, believes it is crucial for couples in Gender Crossover to find support— whether through religion, therapy, or the help of their friends or extended family. (See Appendix B, page 263, for couples therapy resources.) "You really need *practical* spiritual refreshment that fits your own philosophy of life," she advises. Tell yourself, for example: *There is a reason for this; there is a valuable lesson here if I can search it out.* "This makes you feel less a victim and more like a person with a mission," she says. "It can turn what feels like a disaster into a potential opportunity for growth."

I told her about a friend of mine whose second husband has an extremely successful father in the real estate business. When the father retired and sold most of his properties, he made $10 million. That became the benchmark for his son, who was also in real estate. He had a string of properties just like Dad, but he took his company public and fell prey to a hostile takeover. All at once he was out scrambling for a job, any job, to keep up with alimony payments to his first wife and hold the respect of his new second wife. But the make-do job did not pay the bills. He wrestled with himself: Should he swallow his pride and go to his father to ask for a bailout?

His new wife, a professional woman, worked with a good therapist until she felt comfortable offering to help him. She would pay to keep his children in private school and keep up the mortgage payments on the house. She preferred to take that role temporarily and free him to quit the make-do job and look for a solid career direction with a future. It was the only chance she could give him to get back on his feet and eventually to resume responsibility for the lion's share of their budget. Most important, he would not have to go to his parents and ask for money like a little boy. "Because that way," predicted the wife, "he's not going to grow."

"That's a wise wife and an evolved woman," said Dr. Puder-York. And, indeed, after nearly a year of active searching, that husband did find an exciting job with a future and their marriage was revived. There are other, sadder stories, however, where the husband never rises to his previous level of success or prominence. One of the hardest lessons for women is to face realistically the market forces that may impede a man who was assumed to be on the fast track. It may not be a motivation problem. The husband could be knocking himself out and still not find the right niche, and it's not his fault. The job market has changed.

BRAIN-SEX CHANGES

There is also a physiological basis to what has been described as the Gender Crossover. It is an evolutionary reality far more fundamental than recent cultural trends: what I have called the "Sexual Diamond." For the first ten years of life males and females are more alike than different. We become radically differentiated at puberty and arrive at the farthest reaches of our oppositeness in our late thirties to early forties—the most distant poles of the Sexual Diamond.

But in the fifties and sixties men and women move closer together again and take on many characteristics of our gender opposite. As men show greater interest in nurturing and being nurtured, in expressing themselves artistically and appreciating their surroundings, women across cultures age psychologically in the opposite direction, becoming more focused, aggressive, managerial, and political.

This shift may be less noticeable among contemporary women entering the Age of Mastery. Many have worked throughout most of their lives, along with marrying and mothering, and thus have never lived the extreme gender-role divisions that were standard among previous generations. In a recent study of "Gender Identity Crossover" conducted for MIDMAC by Margie Lachman, Ph.D., at Brandeis University, the male subjects showed a more striking personality shift in middle age than did the women in the study—all of whom continued to work and to parent concurrently.

Now there is intriguing evidence from neuroscience that the actual *physical* structure of the brain changes in both males and females in middle and later life. Dr. Marion Diamond, director of the Lawrence Hall of Science at the University of California at Berkeley, has been studying and measuring these changes for nearly fifty years.

"Looking at the right and left hemispheres of the brain in rats, when they are young, the male shows a significantly larger right hemisphere," she says. "As the male ages, the right brain decreases in size and his overall brain structure becomes more like that of a female." Dr. Diamond proposes a question: "Could these cerebral changes be partially responsible for the decline in aggression seen in the older male? It has been reported that the older human male has more domestic qualities."

In the female, the two hemispheres of the brain are fairly equal in size from birth through to middle adulthood. "That makes sense to us as scientists," says Dr. Diamond, "because the basic function of the female is to reproduce and to take care of the young. She needs to pass information and intuitions between the right and left sides of her brain very rapidly; she is the scanner of emotional as well as physical danger." But as females age, the opposite change in brain structure takes place from that in men: their right brain hemisphere increases in size and becomes the dominant one. "I think that this explains why women become more focused as they get older," suggests Dr. Diamond. "Women lose their inhibitory fibers."

MELLOWING OUT

At least one change in brain chemistry as we age promotes greater harmony between couples: the branch of the nervous system that is responsible for restoring calm (the parasympathetic branch) becomes less effective, so older people are less resilient to stress. Those with good survival instincts begin consciously "mellowing out." This is noticeable in healthy marriages: the partners are not so quick to confront; each becomes more accepting of the limitations of the other. Tolerance and tenderness replace some of the bickering and competitiveness that may have characterized the Gender Crossover.

Beyond marriage, smart men make an effort to simplify their lives, streamline logistics, and, most especially, to weed out of their datebooks as much as possible people who are pains in the neck. It becomes more and more important to spend time with good friends, favorite relatives, adult children, and grandchildren.

EMPTY HEART

Over and over again, I hear admissions of muffled anguish from men whose children are preparing to leave the nest. A computer programmer described being overwhelmed by emotions he had never felt before with such intensity: "I feel like I have a hole in my heart."

President Clinton memorably expressed some of those emotions when, in the autumn of 1997, he and Hillary joined parents across the country in a familiar rite of passage: taking their child to some distant place to start her freshman year of college. The most powerful man in the world admitted his sense of utter powerlessness as a parent at this stage: "There's nothing I can do now," he told reporters mournfully. Nothing but what all parents finally have to do: let go. The President comforted himself by getting a dog.

The "empty-nest syndrome" has always been associated with mothers. But it is probably fair to say that fathers belonging to the current generation in middle life never had enough time with their children. They were too busy competing and scoring. By the time Dad is ready to clear his calendar to make room for his children because he now needs them, they have usually left home (or are so intent on proving he is irrelevant, he may wish they would go!). It may seem as if the chance has passed, but it is never too late to make an effort to reconnect with a child. Not to do so can haunt a man for the rest of his life: research on midlife parenting shows that a man's view of himself is profoundly affected by perceptions of his adult children's success or failure. Any disappointment is compounded by a father's memories that he was not sufficiently involved in, or a positive role model for, his children.

Dr. Ed Phillips is a catch-up dad. "My fifteen-year-old son is talking about going away to prep school in New England," he said during a Miami men's group interview. A busy obstetrician-gynecologist, his patients over the years enjoyed far more of his tender mercies than his son did. "Now I'm losing my buddy. Who will watch the Panthers win the Stanley Cup with me? Being a parent has come to mean a great deal to me—it makes me feel ten feet tall—and I don't want to lose that."

Dr. Phillips also feels the loss of professional prestige and intimacy with his patients. He chose to be a solo practitioner just as the new managed care environment brought wrenching changes. "Now solo practice is becoming like the house call—nearly extinct." At an age when his own family is naturally breaking up, he is also losing patients he has known for sixteen years, families who are expecting perhaps their third child but who must pull away from Dr. Phillips and accept the obstetrician offered by their insurance companies. He feels prematurely old.

His wife, who is nearing menopause, is going through a crisis of confidence as well. The challenge, Phillips recognizes, is to find room to grow close to his wife again, to get back to sharing their emotions. "The fear of intimacy is sometimes the fear of getting too deep into yourself. It's a mirror. I'm afraid to look for the old jock image of myself and find out, 'Hey, you're really not that good.' " But Phillips remarks with some pleasure that he and his wife are eyeing each other again. "That's exciting. There will be room in the house when the kids go. Women used to teach us about sensitivity. Now they're teaching us how to age gracefully."

MR. MOM

If you have any doubt that men are in the process of a dramatic transformation, consider how many men in this book have expressed the wish in middle life to try playing "Mr. Mom." And among divorced couples there is a strong countertrend to the cliché of "deadbeat dads."

> The fastest-growing family structure in America today is the devoted single dad.

A generation ago, only I percent of families with children under 18 were headed by single fathers; today, fathers head 5 percent of families. This historic change was heralded in the fall 1997 TV season by no fewer than five new sitcoms featuring custodial fathers. Man as caregiver commands a new respect. He is also likely to have a considerable economic advantage over the single mother. But money doesn't always make up for the social isolation experienced by some single or noncustodial fathers.

Roger,* a research scientist who lived in his head until he hit 50 and left his empty marriage, suddenly noticed the sharp, chronic pain of separation from his two children. Massachusetts law gave him the right to demand joint physical custody, as it does in most states by now. "I saw my former wife as the gatekeeper. She could padlock my children's hearts, and I might never get back in. I used to have nightmares that I'd go to pick them up and the locks would be changed."

He wrestled with common revenge fantasies. Why not just make a clean break? Move from the establishment East Coast to southern California and start over again? Get a condo, dye his hair, look for a young bud, and let the kids visit when it was convenient? It would be so much cleaner and easier emotionally. And he wouldn't have to face the failure of his marriage in front of his offspring.

On reflection, he finally made the decision to stay involved in the lives of his children. "Settling for joint legal custody meant a painful surrender," Roger confessed. "I was giving up my rights as a full-time father at a time when I felt wronged. But I forced myself to think long term— what would be best for the kids?" It meant sticking around the same neighborhood so he can see them several times a week and perform fatherly tasks, like driving his daughter to the dentist, watching his son's soccer game, or doing homework with them over the weekend.

Take-out fathering, it might be called. It is not ideal. As Roger found, "It's tough to keep dropping in and out of their lives and trying to win them over again. Hard to learn how to hug and expose myself emotionally." But in retrospect, he is aware that the necessity of fathering became the centerpiece of his life. "It grounded me." Otherwise, he might have done a lot of silly or self-destructive things to make up for the dull ache of emotional hollowness. And after seven years of being consistently in-

---

*A pseudonym.

volved in the details of his children's lives, he says proudly, "They really like to see me—and now I'll never lose them."

FATHER HUNGER

One of the most consistent themes in the men's group discussions was their hunger for the missing father in their own lives. This need may not surface consciously until middle life. "What we're doing in men's groups like this is looking for the fathering we didn't have," said one of the walking wounded who attended a session in Minneapolis.

Father hunger is particularly sharp among men who have lost close contact with their children as the result of divorce. Often, the relationship with their own fathers was distant, mechanical, or downright intimidating, and they have reproduced much the same pattern with their own children. The longer they allow the relationship with their children to lapse, the more difficult they will find it to break that pattern, to feel comfortable hugging and laughing and crying together.

Men who are willing to revisit their father hunger can most readily heal themselves by connecting with a child or children. And once that happens, they become the delighted beneficiaries of a reward that women take for granted: becoming the object of unconditional love in the eyes of a child. Does this mean you have to give up "guy things" like working on your car or watching sports on Sunday afternoon? No. It isn't the quantity of time, or even its quality, that really matters. A recent study in the *Journal of the American Medical Association* shows that doing lots of activities together is not the crucial variable in the relationship between parent and child; rather, it is a *sense of connectedness.* I can confirm that observation from my group interviews with men. In one discussion after another, it was the men who described being intimately involved with their children who felt more manly, more indispensable, more emotionally grounded. That learning process often allows men to be more open with their partners, friends, and male colleagues.

> Men actually learn to connect through being close to their children.

LETTING GO OF A GROWING SON

As a father senses the shadow of middle age gathering over him, he watches enviously his son's surging growth into a headstrong young adult with all the great "firsts" of life ahead of him. The father cannot help contrasting his own narrowing chances for success and his comparatively static capacities with the big dreams and brash chances his child is willing to take. And how different and inscrutable it is for the older man to imagine his son's ease in love—not girlfriends seen from afar, as objects to pursue, but young women who start out as peers, playmates, and pals and become real partners.

> Predictably, the midlife father starts acting to keep his growing son in his place.

Walter Anderson, the editor of *Parade* magazine, was the abused child of a violent alcoholic. He spent almost five years as a marine sergeant in Vietnam. He covered the streets of New York City as an investigative reporter. Tough. He has seen more than his share of horror and tragedy in the world. And in his thirties he believed he had wisdom. In hindsight, he knows it was arrogance.

Did he find the passage to his middle life traumatic in any way? I asked. "No," said Anderson at first, "my life may be the exception to the rule." We sat together as he reviewed his life aloud until, about twenty minutes later, he stopped short.

"I didn't realize, yes, there is something traumatic that happened. It's funny how I suppressed it up until this moment. This was in my late forties—my children began to become adults. The recognition of letting my son go—to realize that he's not mine, that he's his own person—and to see my daughter become an adult was more traumatic for me than I realized." His smooth forehead became corrugated with the memory. "It was wrenching."

In his struggle to hold on to his control over his son, Anderson would talk to him as if he were a child, throwing questions at him he knew the boy couldn't answer. This only drove a dangerous wedge between them. Anderson found that his role as father had to change after his youngest child left home. Recognizing that this change is taking place and refor-mulating a view of oneself in relation to one's transformed world is es-sential to a man's well-being. It also opens up possibilities for a new kind of friendship with a man's adult children. But there was more to Ander-son's midlife passage than he had admitted to himself. It involved the loss of his surrogate father at the same time that his son was growing away.

"I've never told anyone this," he said. "I had so much trauma in my life when I was young, the death of my own father was a relief. But I had a friend—my closest and dearest friend for years. Bill was my fishing buddy. Just a local magician. He was much older than I was . . ." Ander-son's voice thickened. "I don't mean to get emotional when I talk about this. I never realized how close we were. We talked about everything. We had such great fun together. Right before I turned fifty, just before Christmas Eve, he got pancreatic cancer and died."

For three years Anderson, an avid fisherman, couldn't go fishing. He couldn't talk about his friend's death. Never mentioned it even to his wife. But in private he talked to his friend. He kept up the conversation for three years, talking to keep his friend alive.

"When my actual father died, there was no unfinished business be-tween us," he continued. "When Bill died, I was almost fifty years old and I wouldn't admit to myself that my friend died. In a sense, I pre-tended that he didn't die. I didn't realize how traumatic that was to me." He paused. Perspiration beaded on his forehead. "That was *my father's death.*" The sheen of relief settled onto his face.

At the same time, I suggested, you were going through the painful stages of letting go of your son. It's really reciprocal, isn't it?

Anderson nodded. "A friend of mine, Irving Wallace, the late author, said something very wise: 'A boy cannot become a man until his father dies, either literally or symbolically.' I understand that now."

Like most men, Walter Anderson reacted strongly against the chal-lenge of a growing son. But a man in midlife who loses his own father at the same time is likely to feel even more uncertain of his own potency. Writes John Munder Ross, "If he has failed to establish his sense of 'pa-ternality' and hasn't put together the forces of femininity and violence within himself, then he may enter the fray, often with disastrous conse-quences: tyranny, incest, heart attacks, unwise affairs, and more. If he's a matured man, he savors his sons' and daughters' powers and vicariously revitalizes himself by taking in their youth."

At the age of 52, Walter Anderson took his 26-year-old son down to Florida to go fishing. And for the first time, standing shoulder to shoulder with his manly son and enjoying the banter of fishing buddies, he was able to talk about his friend Bill. The dam of sadness broke, and Anderson felt ferried to another place in his life.

"In the last year, I've come to realize that my son knows things that I don't know and that I can learn from *him*. In many ways I'm more involved in my son's life than I ever was before, because now we're friends. If you would have asked me four or five years ago if this change was possible, I would have said I don't really think so."

HOW MANY MEN FRIENDS CAN YOU COUNT?

Another powerful source of emotional sustenance comes from men reaching out to be close to other men. Women have been getting together with women for the last thirty years, and the effect has been truly revolutionary. Now it is men's time to band together.

A career army officer who joined the men's discussion I held at the Pentagon was trying to prepare himself for forced retirement. "God is my anchor," he said. "Next is my wife. But close friends are absolutely essential." The officer had dutifully filled out a life history questionnaire, but he was stopped by this query:

> How many close friends do you have; that is, friends in whom you can confide almost anything?

"I was shocked to realize I have not developed a single friend at that level since college," he admitted.

"My best friends are women," says Bob Graham, the 53-year-old corporate refugee described earlier who subsequently founded his own executive search firm. "I don't have to compete with my women friends, put on bravado, play games—I can be myself." But like the army colonel, like most men, he hadn't made any effort to cultivate new male friendships since college. And he realized he was bereft of men who knew and cared about him enough to endorse his efforts to change.

"When you're growing up, you've got your dad, the coach, the Scout leader, the priest or pastor. Christ, you get to be age forty-five or fifty-five, and they're dropping like flies. Dad is the first of the parents to go, historically. Your mentors in business, if they're alive, are in Florida. Your kids are leaving you. Who do you have to turn to?" He strongly urges men to reach out and consciously try to make new male friends.

> "When you make a new man friend after 45, hang on to him—it's a rare find."

The hunger of men for connection with other men has been growing exponentially throughout the 1990s, seeding informal men's groups all over America. Some are support groups instituted by companies. Others have sprung up among sophisticated urbanites, usually men in their forties to sixties. These informal groups meet in coffee shops, bars, church basements, or in homes (where men send their wives or significant others out and prove they can fix pasta all by themselves).

———

Dr. Robert Schuller, the Christian leader who preaches from the world-famous Crystal Cathedral in southern California and reaches an audience of 2 million with his weekly television program, *The Hour of Power,* has an increasingly active men's ministry. Several times a year he invites men from all over the country to gather strength from bonding with one another. The men-only rule was waived to allow me to attend one of these Christian Men's Conferences, in May 1996, and I was deeply moved by what I saw and heard.

In contrast to the showy men who attend big cigar-smoking bashes, these are more traditional men. Some three hundred of them had brought their pain and problems to a three-day conference to hear inspirational speakers and find permission to be human, tell their stories, hug strangers, and find safe friendships with other men. Almost all the attendees were white professional men. Roughly half were in pre–middle age. The other half, silver-headed, sat in the sunny serenity of the cathedral with notepads perched on bare, Bermuda-shorted knees, men at a stage where they cannot afford to make any more major mistakes.

What kind of pain do they bring? I asked a volunteer host. "Broken relationships. Putting work before wife and family. Kids who hardly know them as fathers," said the African-American volunteer. "Men so often focus their identities on who they know, the credentials they have, the trophies they've won. And on the inside, they're hollow." The conference theme was "Leadership from the Inside Out." During lunch break, I joined a table of ten men and asked what messages had come through to them most strongly from the morning's speakers.

"The willingness to let down your barriers," said David Stricker, a handsome 64-year-old community activist from Minnetonka, Minnesota. "Especially for those of us who are seasoned and in our second half of life, when you let down your guard and admit there is a lot more to life than what we've locked ourselves into, it's amazingly freeing." David's deep brown eyes sparkled and he looked very virile in his denim work shirt and khakis.

The men talked about what it felt like to hug other men, strangers, for the first time.

"My family's a very warm, hugging family, and I have four children," said David. "But huggin' another guy is not my thing—until now!"

"It's even stranger for Earl and I, because he's my father-in-law!" admitted a 36-year-old man named Andrew Vasile.

"Yeah, but I found out my son-in-law is more than just a wonderful, great Italian stallion," responded Earl Ellsworth. Everyone chuckled. Earl was a 60-year-old, macho-appearing man of solid heft, his silver hair combed back in a neatly trimmed mane. There were deep pouches of pain beneath his eyes. He looked directly at me as he opened up: "I lost a son to AIDS about a year ago. I think that helped me get my life in order and reflect on my mortality. As I said to these guys, I had some little indentations on my butt. I found out it was God's toe that had been kicking me for many years, but I didn't feel it until recently."

The rest of the men introduced themselves and talked about why they had come to a men's conference. Suddenly it occurred to me that we had been talking for a good thirty minutes and nobody, not one of these ten substantial men, had mentioned what he did for a living.

"We're not here for competition," affirmed Andrew Vasile. "It's not about who's going to come out on top. So it doesn't matter if I'm a janitor or president of a big corporation. I'm here for the same reasons that everybody else is here—for camaraderie." Andrew's mother was dying. "To watch my mother go from a complete person to a woman lying in a hospital bed, slowly dying, it makes you look at your own life. This type of gathering teaches me to react differently and *not* to take it out on my wife and family."

"I see this as getting our batteries recharged," offered Ellsworth. "We need that recharging, no matter how strongly we might be committed to Christ. This gives us an environment that's totally open, nonjudgmental. Basically, we come in here with no clothes on. And nobody is going to be critical of us for three whole days."

"On the contrary," said Walt Smith, a 60-year-old practicing CPA from Wisconsin who was raised a traditional Catholic. "When you don't have to keep up the macho image, you find out you can talk to another man just like you can talk to a woman. That is, you can be open and discuss your problems, hopes, and dreams."

THE NEST IS EMPTY—ARE YOU READY FOR LOVE IN THE MORNING?

Remember the coach described earlier who denied his heart problems and felt so overshadowed by his wife, the late-blooming nurse, that he took a second job and spends most of his waking hours working or eating? When I interviewed his wife, Eileen, a petite Irish American woman with a touch of glamour in her strawberry blond–tinted hair, she was reasonably self-assured but resigned. Being on the brink of 50, she was going through menopause, but that wasn't the problem as she saw it; she was symptom-free.

"I feel terrific," she says. "All except for, well, the marriage thing."

"Do you crave emotional intimacy with your husband?" I ask her.

"Sometimes, yeah."

"How about sexual intimacy?"

"I think I've shelved it. It just doesn't seem possible at this time." Eileen looks down, suddenly at a loss for words. "I just don't know what to say. I can put all the blame on me, but I don't think it's all my problem."

Several nurses in her department have been divorced around her age. Inevitably, a younger woman is in the wings. To deal with their hurt and anger, the nurses often joke, "He must be going through male menopause." Eileen wonders about Coach.

I ask if her husband's sexual potency has changed over the decade of his forties.

"Probably. Yes, I think so," she replies. "He went from speeding in our twenties to stalling out at forty and zip at fifty."

Did that bother him?

"Probably. He never says anything like 'This really upsets me, what are we going to do about it?' I would not go to him and say, 'We don't have sex because you're too heavy.' I don't want to hurt this man and make him feel less of a human being."

Her sentiments are properly empathetic, but she is also paralyzed.

How important does she think it is to a man to be potent?

"I really don't know," she confesses. "I haven't lived in a man's body." Eileen then expressed a wish that I have heard, in variations, from many wives of men in Second Adulthood: "I am looking forward to the time when we have no children living in this house. When the two of us can run around naked if we want to, where if we want to make love, we don't have to worry about someone popping in on us. I'm looking forward to traveling, to enjoying my husband and his body—whatever size it may be. My only hope is that he will change, so he can last long enough to enjoy it."

Change would have to begin with the couple acknowledging problems in their relationship. But beyond their ongoing struggle with the Gender Crossover, there are surely physical issues standing in the way of Eileen's dream of postnesting intimacy with the coach. Even as a health professional, she was unaware that men's testosterone levels drop with age and that those levels can be measured by a simple blood test. She was surprised to hear that obesity and cholesterol levels are related to sexual function. It came as a revelation to her that a great deal of male middle-life sexual slowdown can be prevented or corrected simply by making disciplined changes in one's lifestyle. And beyond that, there are very effective new treatments.

Men who are prepared, not scared, will be able to protect their health and prolong their potency, probably indefinitely. Let's meet some of them.

PART IV

WHO'S AFRAID OF MALE MENOPAUSE?

Would get up at night,
go to the mirror and ask:
Who's here?

Would turn, sink to his knees
and stare at snow falling blameless
in the night air.

Would cry:
Heaven, look down!
See? No one is here.

Would take off his clothes and say:
My flesh is a grave with nothing inside.

Would lean to the mirror:
You there, you, wake me,
tell me none of what I've said is true.

—Mark Strand: "About a Man"
from *The Late Hour*

Chapter Nine

THE MALE SEXUAL LIFE CYCLE

I will be the first one to use the 's' word," Danny offered bravely in the Memphis men's group discussion. "Your sexual ability—at what point does that trail off?"

Throats cleared, half smiles quivered.

"Can I address the sex question?" It was Tad, the 42-year-old who had recently become a father for the third time. "One day, I remember I was on a plane, and it struck me that sex was no longer the obsession. Is it an age thing? Male hormones? Having a two-year-old at home?"

Other participants averted their eyes. They all professed to be married to women they love who had excited and delighted them in the past. Yet sex with their wives had become more dutiful than spontaneous; it was delivered weekly rather like the Sunday paper.

Maybe it's a time thing, another man suggests.

"Time is a killer, that's true," Tad said with a nod. "But my wife and I always had a very passionate relationship, even when I was working ninety to ninety-five hours a week starting out. I love her and treasure her," he avowed. "But I hate to admit it—I do not have the same burning desire every day. Today, *she* is the complainer."

Had they talked over this strange change in sexual ardor with their wives, a doctor, male buddies, anyone? Heads shook "no." That brought forth a startling admission from Rick, the downsized Yuppie whose wife was now earning five times as much as he in his fledgling efforts as an entrepreneur: "I think there's been a lessening of sexual desire on *both* our parts. We're good at talking to each other, but that subject we haven't touched. It's sitting there on the coffee table, and we walk around it a lot."

MAGICAL EXPECTATIONS

The specter of "male menopause" has become the latest, greatest anxiety of baby boomers faced with middle age—and younger. The male midlife potency crisis is now a concern that covers several passages. It starts earlier than previously thought. One of the pioneers, psychiatrist Domeena Renshaw, who has run a sexual dysfunction clinic in the Chicago area for twenty-four years, confirms the evidence of my surveys and interviews:

> The major change in the last five years has been the increasing youthfulness of men complaining to doctors of impotence.

Over and over again in the group interviews, married men in their late thirties and early forties would admit their sex lives were seriously anemic—like those of the Memphis men. On their confidential questionnaires they were even more frank: the usual frequency of sex for these robust, successful men was once or twice a month! Is this male menopause? Hardly. But it's no great surprise, either.

> The most common complaint of married couples today is a lack of sexual desire.

That observation, from San Francisco psychologist and author Lonnie Barbach, Ph.D., at the University of California Medical School, is echoed by professionals around the country. In the late thirties and early forties, a loss of sexual desire most often stems from problems in the relationship: unresolved anger or power struggles between the two partners, excess stress, one partner feeling unimportant or repeatedly unheard, fear of intimacy, or distraction and fatigue as a result of putting everything else before intimacy.

But beneath the apparent lack of desire may be a cave-in of sexual confidence and a black hole of ignorance. Most men I have interviewed admit they don't know very much about how "that thang" down there works. They just expect it to work as consistently as an oil rocker. And expectation has everything to do with the cause of impotency. There is also a common generational hang-up: a great many boomer men, performance-conscious in every way and obsessed with remaining young, are already overreacting to normal, age-related changes. They may be tyrannized by fables of Herculean sexual prowess. Wilt Chamberlain, the former Los Angeles Lakers basketball giant, claimed he had had sex with 20,000 women during his basketball career. Six or seven women every day of his life? Is it humanly possible?

"It's just a macho thing," says Dr. Peter Bruno, a Park Avenue internist who takes care of the New York Knicks basketball players. "The language in locker rooms, even professional locker rooms, is like being back in high school. Talking about sexual prowess, exaggeration goes on."

Magazines devoted to men may add to their self-doubts with headlines such as "Be Better Than Her Last Lover." The body image ideal is now set as impossibly high for men as the Barbie Doll fantasy that has frustrated women: rock-hard abs, vein-bulging arms, cleavage, year-round tan, fly-rod flexibility, unflagging energy, and perpetual virility—puhleeze! So what's a poor guy to think if he has had sex with only twenty women— one thousandth of Wilt's claimed record—and now he's married, a time-starved workadaddy who's not aroused anymore at the drop of a bra?

> The problem for these premidlife men is inflated expectations.

The power, the myth, the status attained by a man who convincingly portrays himself among other men as a raging stud are so important, the last thing a man will mention is "You know what happened to me last night? I couldn't get it up." To make such an admission in the company of other males would be as unlikely as a bunch of Houston space programmers talking about the missiles they *couldn't* lift off.

An anthropology professor at UCLA, Anna Simons, spent a year and a half watching and listening to Green Berets to discover how these professional soldiers bond and thus develop trust. First off, they didn't get to know one another intimately—no late-night debates about politics or religion—because, perhaps subconsciously, they sensed that the revelation of strong differences would only drive them apart. The Green Berets couldn't brag about how intelligently they performed their jobs or how tough they were physically, because on those tests their measure was being taken by their buddies every day. The one subject they could boast about without the risk of being proven wrong was their sexual prowess: *"Met this girl last night, took her home, and made it five times."*

"Talking about sex is an incomparable way for soldiers to prove they can compete," Professor Simons concluded. (But if women are around, they shut up.)

For boomer men anxious about holding on to their "alpha male" dominance in the face of increasingly "ballsy" women, the expectation level is higher than ever for a man in his forties or fifties: perpetual virility at the level of his 25-year-old self. "The number of men who will have normal age-related changes, which they or their spouses overreact to, is high today—and that creates a more significant potency problem for them," says Dr. Michael Perelman, a New York psychologist who is acting codirector of the Human Sexuality Program at New York Hospital–Cornell Medical School. Referring to himself as a "sex detective," he describes a classic scenario that he sees and hears of happening all the time:

> You are a 45-year-old man. You are out on your fifth date with a very attractive woman, and you have every expectation of pleasurable intimate relations. After a great dinner you end up in bed together, only you're exhausted from work. You may have had three or four glasses of wine instead of one. You both take off your clothes with eager anticipation and—nothing comes up. She gets a concerned look on her brow. You're thinking, Oh shit, I wonder if anything is going to happen.

> The chances are, if you're a 45-year-old boomer male, there is nothing wrong with you.

"This is a function of age-related changes, fatigue, and a few too many drinks," says Dr. Perelman. "Even if the two of them are smart enough to pass it off with 'Let's try again in the morning,' if the man is preoccupied with how he failed the night before, rather than understanding that it's a perfectly normal age-related change that he shouldn't be the least bit concerned about, he will fail again. And a cycle may ensue leading to impotency."

As founder of the Loyola Sex Therapy Clinic outside Chicago, one of the most respected and oldest in the country, Dr. Renshaw is surprised that her clinic is now attracting Yuppie couples, fortyish and getting younger. Many couples have a "double desire disorder": he doesn't feel like sex anymore, and neither does she. Why?

"The men under fifty who have erection problems are usually reacting to a psychological or interpersonal problem—job loss, fatigue, divorce—and that's not male menopause," says Dr. Renshaw. "The average couple is so overextended, S-E-X is number twenty-four on the to-do list. Even in the 1990s," she adds, "sexual ignorance is one of the major risk factors for impotence."

Before we turn our attention to male menopause, it will help to get a perspective on the normal male sexual life cycle.

THE MALE SEXUAL LIFE CYCLE

RACING CAR SEX
Ages 15–30

Young men are in a hurry. Typically, they race the sexual act as if they were competing in the Indy 500—*See how I can accelerate from zero to a hundred miles an hour in thirty seconds!*—at which point they screech to a halt, roll over fully spent, and fall asleep. It's instant gratification and fast crash. It's

THE MALE SEXUAL CYCLE

| AGE 20 | 30 | 40 | 50 | 60 | 70 |

RACING CAR SEX   DUTIFUL SEX   MASTERS SEX   S U R F I N G   S E X   SNUGGLING SEX

narcissistic. It can be very exciting for the man but may be unsatisfying to his partner. Women take longer to arouse and are generally more pleasured by the tenderness, touching, and affection in prolonged sexual intimacy than they are impressed by racing car sex.

The biggest problem for young men is slowing down their response to sexual desire so they can be more in control. Psychological stress is the primary cause of any impotence problems in this age group.

DUTIFUL SEX
Ages 30–40

The thirties today are crunch time. Many of the tasks that were customarily engaged in during the twenties are today postponed and become telescoped in the thirties. A surge in career competition usually seizes men's attention at the same time as the urge to mate and put down roots becomes paramount among their female peers. Sex becomes powerfully linked to procreation.

A man often feels displaced by the firstborn in his family. If he and his wife have any problems conceiving on their desired production schedule and submit to fertility treatments, sex can become more of a regimen than a passion. In an era where modern technology invades the home at all hours, delivering the tensions of the workplace, there is scarcely any refuge for real intimacy. Dual-career couples with young children are burdened with sharing, or handing off, child care. And children are omnivores: they eat up time and physical and emotional energy. Given all these simultaneous, exhausting demands, is it any wonder that sensuality in the thirties is often buried under efficiency and the lust for a good night's sleep?

MASTER'S TOURNAMENT SEX
Ages 40–55

The forties are usually the virtuoso peak of a man's sexual life cycle. True, his peak hormone and energy level is reached at 30, but it is not until his forties that his sexual responses slow enough for him to control, choreo-graph, prolong, and savor each erotic encounter. As long as he keeps him-self healthy and fit, a man in his forties to midfifties has a whole repertory of moves that can make him truly masterful in sexual play.

In past life history surveys of men in Second Adulthood, I have asked, "How much did you think about or engage in sex in your *twenties?*" Men usually recall engaging in or fantasizing about sex anywhere from twelve to twenty-four hours a day. "And *after 45*, how often do you engage in fantasizing or sex?" The usual answer is one hour a day. If that change is understood to be normal, no particular psychic whammy comes with it.

Physical changes do start occurring. Testosterone levels begin drop-ping gradually, normally by about 1 percent a year after age 40. A pro-tein called Sex Hormone Binding Globulin (SHBG) begins binding up more of the available testosterone. The penis begins growing sluggish: the spongy chambers that fill up with blood to produce an erection start to clog with dense connective tissue. Arteries that act as the hoses pump-ing in blood to produce the erection also begin to narrow. Changes in diet and disciplined exercising, however, can counteract these natural age-related changes.

Men in this age range who develop minor potency problems usually do not have any obvious disease, according to urologists, they are just not as "good" as when they were twenty. However, men with a diagnosis of heart disease may exhibit signs of moderate impotence. Smoking, heavy alcohol intake, hypertension, and diabetes all foster earlier and more se-rious potency problems. Depression can lead to total impotence. Five percent of men are completely impotent in their forties.

SURFING SEX
Ages 55–70

Sexual drive in older men is more dependent on fantasy, general health and energy, and a sense of well-being. Married men and their wives often enjoy a resurgence in desire when their children move out—along with the freedom to have sex in the afternoon, in the kitchen, anytime, anywhere.

It is normal for a man, after 50, occasionally to have a partial erection. There is a noticeable delay between one sex act and sufficient arousal to perform again. If he scores himself only on speed and performance in comparison to his younger, friskier self, the "performer penis" will eventually fail him. Foreplay—direct stimulation of the penis—can reassure him and bring him a better erection. But if he doesn't know that partial erections are part of being over 50, then he may panic and withdraw from his partner.

A clever man will educate himself to graduate from adolescent "racing car sex" to "surfing sex." The surfer won't exhaust all his sexual energy in a frenetic effort to reach full erection and orgasm timed on a stopwatch. Instead, he will ride the waves of erotic love, gliding up with the swells of pleasure when sexual energy is high and down with ebbs of intensity, when stroking and intimacy can be enjoyed. After a brief rest, he and his partner ride up on the next pleasure wave and down in the rest cycle, when they just lie there holding each other and whispering endearments, until they feel the next wave of sexual energy starting to lift them toward Eros again. He will learn the ways his partner likes to be pleasured, with hands or tongue, in between their couplings. He will enjoy receiving pleasure from his partner's touch. With this change in technique, an older man can be the true captain of the sexual experience, prolonging the act to the point where he and his partner's bodies are so attuned to each other and so saturated with sexual energy, they can experience a flood of orgasm.

Two major studies on the incidence of impotence suggest that the big jump occurs around age 60. However, almost 40 percent of men age 65 and over are functioning just fine, enjoying sex a few times a week, according to an academic study, *The 1993 Janus Report*. Fifteen percent of men, however, are completely impotent by age 70.

SNUGGLING SEX
70 Plus

Although the concern about flagging potency is concentrated among men between the ages of 45 and 60, at the bona fide sex clinics I have observed in Chicago, Dallas, San Francisco, and New York, men in their seventies, eighties, and even nineties are now strolling in to say their sex lives aren't all they should be and they would like some help.

"The age spectrum is widening," observes Dr. J. Francois Eid, an assistant professor of urology at New York Hospital–Cornell Medical Center, who sees almost eighty patients a day for erectile dysfunction. Dr. Eid notes that the younger ones (under 40) usually have more of a psychological problem, while those over 55 usually have a root physical cause.

Illness will inhibit sexual interest. If a man or his partner doesn't feel well, sexual contact usually falls off. But touching and tenderness are more important than ever during periods of ill health or invasive treatments such as surgery, chemotherapy, or radiation. Snuggling is always possible. More imaginative couples can learn techniques of massage, reflexology, or therapeutic touch, all of which feel good and have scientifically proven beneficial effects on health and mood as well as promoting better sleep.

THE UNSPEAKABLE PASSAGE

When does male menopause kick in?

"The old zest starts going in your fifties; there's no question about it," grumbled my friend Fitzgerald. "Men will often run after other women at that age, but the point is that the same cycle starts all over again."

Are we talking simply about getting older? Yes, but also about a larger challenge to a man's vitality and virility, an identifiable phenomenon that begins in many men's lives usually in their fifties or sixties. It is a normal process without a proper name. ("Menopause" refers to a pause and eventual cessation of fertility hormones in women and thus cannot accurately refer to men; nonetheless, "male menopause" is a shorthand label in popular use.) With men, the issue is not fertility. A healthy proportion of men continue to produce enough upwardly mobile sperm to sire children into their late age. But most men in middle life do experience some lapses in virility and vitality.

This might be called the "male middle-life pause"—or MANopause for short—a five- to twelve-year period during which men go through

hormonal fluctuations coupled with accelerated physical and psychological changes. Dr. Tom Lue, an internationally renowned researcher and
professor of the Department of Urology at the University of California
at San Francisco, refers to the syndrome as "male middle-life slowdown."
He notes that almost all parts of the male body and metabolism slow
down during the midfifties to the late sixties—an accelerated slide—before they stabilize and a normal rate of attrition resumes. Dr. Lue's private practice has been overwhelmed in the last several years by more than
three thousand men seeking help for male middle- and later-life impotence.

MANopause is more gradual and elusive than female menopause.
Common symptoms are irritability, a feeling of sluggishness, and mild
to moderate mood swings. The most familiar psychological effect is a
slump in a man's overall sense of well-being. Physically, a man may notice
a decrease in muscle mass and strength. Hormonally, he won't notice anything, unless he goes to a urologist and asks to have his testosterone levels measured. Surprisingly, a lot of otherwise educated men don't believe
they have hormones—those are something women have—so how could
they have anything equivalent to menopause?

But the greatest fear, the phobic event that may become a self-
fulfilling prophecy, is intermittent problems in gaining and sustaining an
erection. How many men in the general population are affected?

Moderate impotence was recently found to be much more widespread
and less benign a problem than previously thought, according to the most
comprehensive study of male sexuality since the *Kinsey Report,* the Massachusetts Male Health Study. This community-based survey of aging and
sex conducted in 1987 to 1989 among a normal population of healthy,
aging men, produced startling results. Projecting from that study:

> 52 percent of healthy American men between ages 40 and 70
> can expect to experience some degree of impotence.

A rough estimate by the National Institutes of Health (NIH) is that
20 million American men suffer from some degree of impotence, although Dr. Leroy Nyberg, Jr., director of urology programs at NIH, believes that is just the tip of the iceberg. When ignored or denied, this

sexual freeze extends more deeply into every aspect of a man's life than was previously thought. "Impotence is a highly prevalent health problem which has a profound impact on the quality of life of many men," concluded Dr. John McKinlay and the Massachusetts researchers. It can be an underlying cause of depression, divorce, even suicide.

The most predictive factor is age. Important hormones—not just testosterone but human growth hormone and DHEA (Dehydroepiandrosterone)—decline gradually in direct proportion with advancing age. Dr. Richard Spark, a Harvard Medical School endocrinologist, describes other changes with aging: "Blood flows less briskly to the genitals, and nerves that carry signals to allow erections have less velocity. Meanwhile, the hormonal system chugs along at an adequate if not ideal pace." The combined effect of simultaneous slowdowns is what produces a more halting sexual response. But aging alone does not foretell a droop in mood or manhood. Let me state an important fact up front:

> Forty percent of normal, healthy males remain completely potent at age 70.

Underneath the whole "male menopause" syndrome may be a man who feels he is losing control. The more uncertain a man feels about having control over his life, the harder the middle-life male slowdown may hit him. Losing his job or being passed over for an expected promotion in midlife, for instance, is tantamount to falling off the top of the heap in the chimpanzee hierarchy. Empirical evidence from both humans and animals demonstrates that defeat decreases testosterone. Therefore, a sudden loss of self-respect and dominance reduces male sex hormones, which may further dampen a man's sex drive.

Bob Graham, the former outplacement counselor, told me that many of the men who consulted him after being downsized confided that their libido was flagging. "And when they did try to have sex, they were so uptight they'd be impotent," he added. "At least half of the men I counseled took a vacation from sex while they were out of a job."

Thus the midlife male potency crisis has a cluster of causes—age, hormone levels, psychological mind-set—but more and more it is recognized as being mediated—or exaggerated—by a man's *physical condition.*

Basically, anything that dulls the nerves, weakens the muscles, or impedes the flow of blood and oxygen to the penis is a natural enemy of *Homo erectus.*

"Anywhere from fifty to eighty-five percent of patients have a real physical cause for their sexual difficulties," claims Dr. Myron Murdock, director of the Impotence Institute of America in Maryland and instructor of urology at George Washington University Medical School. His estimate is considered exaggerated by some other experts. But even he acknowledges, "Of course, any male with sexual difficulties will have a secondary psychological impact—they go hand in hand."

The idea of a male equivalent to menopause broke into the national consciousness in the spring of 1996 through an episode of *Coach,* then one of America's top ten TV sitcoms. A middle-aged coach by the name of Hayden Fox is shown feeling generally lousy and, worst of all, uninterested in sex with his wife. Not even the bouquet of beautiful budding cheerleaders around him can arouse his interest. His wife suggests that he might be going through something like male menopause. The coach recoils. The term horrifies him: menopause is *woman stuff.* Finally his wife persuades him to see an endocrinologist—a specialist in hormones— who diagnoses the coach as having a low testosterone level and recommends a testosterone patch. When the coach returns home, chagrined, his wife tells him he is really terrific. He has made a breakthrough. He is a *pioneer.* All the coach can think of is: "Ohmigod, they're going to start calling it *Hayden Fox disease!*"

In fact, "male menopause" is a contemporary label for a dread as old as the Bible. King David reached a point where neither the familiar charms of Bathsheba nor those of his many other wives and countless concubines could arouse him. His people, like people today, equated sexual potency with power. His advisers brought him a young virgin to relight his fires. She cherished the king, the Bible tells us, "but the king was not intimate with her." So King David (knowing nothing about testosterone patches) suffered an ignominious overthrow by subjects who saw him as a weak, impotent leader.

Like TV sitcoms, most physicians and researchers home in on sexual pathology and cast the whole issue for men in terms of impotence. It is such a repugnant word, it is not even allowed within the lexicon of curses men use on one another. (Nobody says, "Your old man's impotent.") The preferred term today is "erectile dysfunction," or ED for short. Yet the near-universal nature of the male midlife experience need not be fraught with secrecy, shame, and denial. Younger men seem eager to learn about it, and even some men in middle life were willing to talk with me about it.

MEN BEHAVING INTELLIGENTLY

In an attempt to start an informed conversation, an extraordinary colloquium on "Sex, Health, and the Midlife Man" was held at Rockefeller University in New York in June 1996. Medical professionals, anthropologists, and sociologists discussed basic questions to which answers are still unknown: Do men over 50 suffer an inevitable decline in sexual desire? What is the "normal" level of testosterone for a man in midlife?

A panel of celebrities—men I called "civilian heroes"—volunteered to take the part of the average post-45 man and describe the kind of changes in attitude and behavior they experience in this stage of life. As moderator, I started off by asking the panel, "How do you think it was for your father at this stage of life? What did he expect to enjoy in terms of sexual vitality?"

Michael Lafavore, the executive editor of *Men's Health* magazine since its successful debut in 1988, spoke up about a mystery in his own family: "My dad sort of went through this passage in a blaze of anger. He was facing a lot of the questions about his life that we all face, and he certainly didn't have anybody to talk to. Didn't have any friends. Wasn't about to talk this over with my mother. So it consumed him for a while. He spent ten years in a terrible rage, and then all the fire just went out. He became this gentle little old man. I have no idea what happened. It is very puzzling to me."

This is how it used to be for most women, whose mothers were usually in the dark about the health and sexual impact of menopause and who thus rarely spoke about the subject with their daughters.

Len Berman, a well-known sportscaster at WNBC-TV, reflected the humorous brush-off the subject usually warrants from men: "I am not sure these issues [of sex] were thought about or discussed in my father's house. The only sign of getting older probably was that earlier trip to the bathroom in the morning—which we call the six A.M. passage."

Terry Anderson, the former AP correspondent who was held hostage in Beirut for nearly seven years and lived to write and lecture about it, had a very different perspective: "My dad, classically, went through that zone you are talking about between forty-five and fifty. He was a truck driver and had emphysema. When he retired at sixty-two, on a medical retirement, he bloomed. My mom was dead. He was dating. He unfortunately died when he was seventy-two, but in those last ten years of his life he was enjoying himself. He skipped middle age entirely and went back to his youth."

Anderson had the unusual perspective of a man whose life had been stopped at 38 and suspended for seven years. He had consciously started a Second Adulthood when he came back, inviting new risks to get his juices flowing again. I asked him how often he thought men in their mid-forties consciously reintroduce risk and challenge to ward off the sexual blahs?

"I think a lot do," he said. "But women seem to be able to switch roles a little more easily than men. I think you do reach a point where, whether you are successful or not, you say, 'Is this all there is?' "

Dr. Robert Goldman, president of the National Academy of Sports Medicine, described the cycle that may be kicked off in men who hit the psychological impasse Terry related. "That makes them depressed. They try to break out of the cycle by going for large toys, like boats and fancy cars, almost a sexual extension of the man, or chasing after inappropriate women. This is a sublimation because they are not kicking out the appropriate hormones any longer. They don't feel good, because their body is not producing what it used to. It is very common. There is one spike at forty, because the number forty wigs out a lot of men, and then in the fifties it happens again. If they live through that passage, they are okay for a period of time."

Mr. Anderson then made an important and accurate point that often gets lost when people talk about middle-aged men's sexual activity:

> You may slow down a bit, but you are an awful lot better at it. You are more cooperative.

Finally, I asked the celebrity men, "In the course of a normal physical checkup, how often will your physician ask any questions about your sexual health or functioning?"

Mr. Anderson: "Never."

Mr. Berman: "Never."

Mr. Lafavore: "Never."

Dr. Goldman: "I don't think most doctors are any more comfortable talking about it than most male patients."

In a Gallup survey released at the conference, fewer than 43 percent of physicians reported asking their patients about sexual problems. And only one out of twenty men affected by potency problems or lack of sexual desire seeks medical help. When I did a national survey with a thousand-plus working-class men and their wives (members of a readers panel selected by *Family Circle* magazine to approximate a representative national sample), I learned that 85 percent of the women believe that men go through a menopausal passage in middle age. And 50 percent of the men agreed! But do men sit around the neighborhood tavern or the firehouse discussing it with other men? No, horrors! They don't talk about it even with their doctors. Why should they, when the response reported to me by a Texas man is so common?

The retired and normally tough-skinned Texas airline pilot finally worked up the courage to tell his doctor that his libido had collapsed: "You could put me in a room with a hundred naked dancing girls, and nothing would happen." The doctor said, "What do you expect? You're fifty-five years old. It doesn't last forever."

This is as ignorant and sadly prevalent a response as the one many doctors give women when they report strange sensations they believe signal the advent of menopause: "Oh, no, you're too young." It has been only in the past few years that women have educated themselves about the health and quality-of-life issues around menopause and dragged their physicians into the twenty-first century to deal with it. Now men must do the same.

MIND OVER MANLINESS

Until very recently, the American medical profession largely ignored the syndrome of male menopause and its serious consequences for physical and mental health in older men as well as the impact on their wives and families. As a result, current data on what is normal, what sort of sexual drive and proficiency a man should expect after 40, are seriously lacking. In the absence of a holistic approach, fly-by-night male health clinics are explicitly advertising "breakthrough treatments" that sound magical: "quick, nonsurgical, and guaranteed success in virtually every case."

Among themselves, many urologists refer to the problem as "just putting some lead back into the pencil." Almost universally male, urologists of the Lead Pencil School may tell patients that their potency problems can be cured with a few office visits, a shot, and soon by popping a pill.

Dr. Irwin Goldstein, who directs a high-profile urology clinic in the Boston University Medical Center, insists, "Really, it's all hydraulics." Hydraulics is what makes elevators go up. A man's confidence in his potency is a little more complex than getting to the twenty-second floor.

Technology-oriented, male-dominated medicine often refuses to acknowledge the mindbody connection. "We can get most of these men erections," asserts Dr. Kenneth Goldberg, a pioneering urologist who runs a Male Health Institute at Baylor Medical Center in Dallas. "But too often it doesn't make a difference in restoring their confidence so they can function sexually on their own. The vast majority of these guys just can't accept that it's their mind-set that's doing this to them. They're looking for the quick fix."

It is much easier to prevent male menopausal impotence than to correct it. The early phase of stuttering potency can become psychologically toxic if ignored. The longer a man waits before he seeks treatment or makes healthy changes in his lifestyle, say urologists, the harder it is to help him regain his sexual vitality. And once a man develops the *habit of impotence*, it is extremely hard to break.

But today, a man who is ready to adjust his mind-set and willing to do the physical conditioning essential to maintaining the drive and performance of his sexual engine can look forward to extending his potency well into the late afternoon of life. The next chapter looks at how.

Chapter Ten

SECRETS OF PERPETUAL VIRILITY

I t's ironic: the macho image of the Marlboro Man made smoking synonymous with being an indefatigable stud. In fact, by the time he hits middle life the Marlboro Man would be lucky if he could "bend one in," as Groucho Marx put it. Smoking is devastating to potency. It is probably the leading cause of male sexual dysfunction, according to the experts who study or treat this malady every day. Riding hard in the saddle isn't great for the gonads, either. And we know from the real-life male models who posed as the Marlboro Man that the price of this pseudomacho pose was often lung cancer and premature death. Anything that causes constriction of the blood vessels and thus reduces the supply of oxygen and blood is going to make it very difficult for a man to be sexually potent.

> Sexual desire and activity are a barometer of a man's general health.

The past few years have seen a surge of interest in preserving perpetual virility. And a whole new impotence industry is galloping to the rescue. Once men are convinced that there are effective ways to delay or reverse MANopause, it is hoped that millions of silent sufferers will come out of the woodwork to seek help with the unspeakable passage.

WOULD YOU RATHER HAVE STEAK AND A SMOKE THAN BE A SEXUAL ATHLETE?

Most men have no idea that so many factors of physical health can handicap their younger sexual athleticism. The current trend is toward medicalizing male menopause and reducing sex to a mechanistic problem of increasing blood flow. Trends aside, studies have shown that certain psychological states common to men in middle life are also strongly associated with potency problems. Here is a list of the major risk factors for mid- and later-life sexual malfunction.

SMOKING

Smoking damages the tiny blood vessels in the penis that must enlarge to accept the substantial inrush of blood during the course of an erection.

DIET/HEART DISEASE/HIGH CHOLESTEROL

The Massachusetts study produced the first firm evidence that cholesterol level is related to sexual function. High levels of HDL ("good" cholesterol) were significantly associated with reduced chances of impotence.

"It's not just your heart that gets more blood flow when you make a serious, positive change in your diet," points out Dr. Dean Ornish, the famous San Francisco physician whose books and courses on natural treatment have revolutionized the approach to heart disease. Lowering fat and cholesterol intake, he says, counteracts many risk factors for male menopause. "The blood supply for the penis gets compromised as men age, for the same reason [arterial clogging] that applies to the heart."

PRESCRIPTION DRUGS

Taking medication for heart disease *doubles* the risk of impotence. A man may have to try four or five different medicines before he finds the one that controls his blood pressure but does not impede his ability to have erections. Most antidepressants also reduce sexual efficacy.

Cardiac patients who are taking beta-blockers are among the most lethargic, depressed, and impotent of men, according to Dr. Ornish. "Just getting them off some of these medications and getting them to change their diet," says Dr. Ornish, "often improves their libido and their sexual function." But he doesn't think improvement will last unless the emotional and spiritual components of a man's midlife slowdown are addressed as well.

ALCOHOL

A couple of drinks actually relax the muscles and reduce anxiety and usually excite a better erection. But chronic use of alcohol can murder potency. "When we look at the tissue from patients with chronic alcoholism, the nerve inside the penis is killed," says Dr. Lue. "It's almost impossible to revive. It usually takes ten or fifteen years of chronic heavy alcohol use to kill the nerve."

COCAINE

Like alcohol, in small doses cocaine may encourage erection. But used chronically, cocaine is the most detrimental drug of all to male potency.

DIABETES

As many as 60 percent of diabetic men may have erection problems at some point.

HIGH STRESS/DEPRESSION/ANGER

Stress is often the final straw. Signs of aging and the advent of "male menopause" alone are stressful. "Stress results from any situation that requires a major adjustment of one's behavior," explains the father of the "relaxation response," Dr. Herbert Benson, chair of the Mind/Body Medical Institute at Harvard Medical School. "The male 'menopause' is a mark of behavioral adjustment—and therefore stressful. Psychologically, three changes occur: increased depression, increased anger, and hostility."

Fifty to 90 percent of all depressed men experience decreased interest in sex, as consistently documented by clinical surveys. Men who lose dominance in midlife, or perceive themselves as losing status, will have a parallel decline in testosterone. This often leads to hostility and expressions of anger. And anger, whether expressed outwardly or directed inward, is strongly associated with impotence.

> Vast improvement in mid- and later-life sexual vitality can be created by making changes in an unhealthy lifestyle and taking a more positive psychological approach to aging.

If a man gives up smoking, cuts way back on his fat intake, and has the discipline to do regular aerobic activity to improve his vascular system, he will almost certainly bring his potency back up to par. Just walking fast for a full half hour a day six days a week is usually adequate. And the improvement will do wonders for his overall sense of well-being. (See earlier chapters for a full discussion of dealing with the loss of power or position and detecting disguised depression.)

MAGIC BULLETS

Selling perpetual virility in a vial or a pill is already a megabusiness in the United States—a $700 million market in 1996. We have come a long way from monkey glands, ice baths, pumps, and the surgically implanted corkscrews. Since 1995, to cope with the legions of boomer men entering the age of male menopause, drug companies have mined new research to offer more varied and effective treatments, which are already working in up to 70 percent of cases. But there aren't that many cases, since men haven't wanted to disclose a problem for which they thought there was no solution.

The great expectation is the new "potency pill"—a magic bullet—
that is being heavily marketed as a simple, socially acceptable way to enable men to perform sexually on command. Just pop a pill twenty
minutes before the appointed moment of passion, promise product
managers, and wait for the tingle to turn into a durable hard-on. The
promise is almost certainly greater than the reality. But the untapped
market is so enticing, three drug companies are racing to bring their ver-
sions to the market as early as 1998.

Pfizer's product is on the fast track, with FDA approval anticipated in
the spring of 1998 and the drug's launch planned before summer. **Viagra** is the bullish name. It works directly on the tissue of the penis,
blocking the enzyme that ordinarily neutralizes an erection. By potenti-
ating the relaxation effect, it allows blood to flow more readily into the
penis and stay trapped in an erection that could last for several hours. But
mercifully, unlike injections, Viagra will not produce arousal without
sexual stimulation.

The best testimony to Viagra is the story of how it was accidentally
discovered. It was being tested on coronary patients in England. When
investigators asked the men, "Is your heart doing better?" they said "no."
Investigators then asked to have the medicine returned. The men refused.
"Why, if it doesn't work for your heart, won't you give back the medicine?" they were asked. Most of the men said, "It works great for my sex
life."

Pfizer, having done about twenty clinical trials on Viagra involving
4,500 men, cleverly has ongoing trials involving many urologists around
the country, which ensures their product broad acceptance and use.
Pfizer's research has not yet been through peer review. Side effects noted
in the trials are headaches, hot flashes, indigestion, nasal congestion, res-
piratory tract infections, and flu syndrome, but company spokesmen say
none was statistically significant. Some of the men on Viagra have had
blurred vision for a short time, according to Dr. Lue, who is one of the
investigators. One can already hear the Jay Leno joke: "I tried this new
potency pill, and the flag flew all night long. I woke up this morning, and
I couldn't see a thing. Guess it's true—love is blind." The marketers certainly aren't. Pfizer estimates that 30 million men in the United States
have some degree of erectile dysfunction, mostly untreated.

If so, there is plenty of market to go around for Viagra's competitors.
Vasomax, the trade name of another oral potency medication, is being

tested by a small Texas firm, Zonagen. It, too, relaxes smooth-muscle tissue but may have fewer side effects. Tap Pharmaceuticals, a subsidiary of Abbott Laboratories, is also testing a potency pill based on the chemical apomorphine, which works primarily on the brain.

The "potency pill" is a mixed blessing. It heralds a new world of chemical machismo that can boost male confidence and make aging more attractive. It will also enable many men to cop out on taking better care of their health. Men don't go to doctors nearly as often as women do, and when they do go they seldom ask questions; nor, as previously documented, are they routinely asked about their sexual health. One of the benefits of male midlife slowdown is that it may motivate a man to have a good physical. But if he can walk into certain doctors' offices or fly-by-night clinics and ask for a "potency pill," it may never be discovered that his impotence is a result of depression, or high cholesterol, diabetes, high blood pressure, or that he has evidence of prostate cancer, which is quite curable when detected early.

And expectations will inevitably fall short of the actuality. "I have to believe the pill will not work in men who have damaged penile tissue from smoking, high cholesterol, or who have severely impaired blood flow from atherosclerosis or diabetes or smoking," says a skeptical Dr. Goldberg. No matter what magic bullets the drug companies try to sell men, Dr. Goldberg, Dr. Lue, and Dr. Ornish are all adamant about the real magic: prevention.

> Prevention—through exercise, good nutrition and other healthy habits, and cultivating intimacy with a mate and more friends—is the key to minimizing the adverse effects of aging and stress on male potency.

WHEN SUNDAY-AFTERNOON FOOTBALL IS BETTER THAN SEX

Men who do have adequate libido but are having difficulty with sexual functioning are more likely to complain because they have the desire, but no performance. If you would rather watch Sunday-afternoon football than have a fantasy date with Cindy Crawford, you should ask yourself some questions.

> First question: Are you really suffering from impotence?

The old Masters and Johnson adage—"Use it or lose it"—is just as pertinent to men as to postmenopausal women. Regular sexual activity keeps the testosterone circulating, along with sending fresh supplies of blood and oxygen to the sexual batteries. (Would a man leave his sports car idle for more than a year and expect the engine to turn over?) "Using it" also maintains sexual confidence, which is especially important for any man who has been through a devastating experience with divorce or widowhood.

Widower's impotence is usually caused by some combination of psychological block ("I would feel terrible about betraying my wife's memory"), physical deterioration, and underuse. A man suffering from this type of impotence should try to build a relationship with a new woman before attempting sex. "If he's rusty," says Dr. Renshaw, "I tell him to begin rebuilding his confidence by masturbating."

> *The Morning Flag-flying Test:* If he tries to make love to his wife or companion and fails, but when he's alone and wakes up and masturbates he reaches orgasm, he is not impotent.

> Second question: Could it be a hormone deficiency?

Is your hair or beard growth diminishing? Do you notice mood changes? Are you more snappish than usual when reminded to take out the garbage? Men with abnormally low testosterone levels reported feeling more irritable and angry in a 1995 study at the University of California at Los Angeles. Once their hormone levels were brought up to normal, their moods improved considerably.

> *Best Test:* Get your hormone levels measured: testosterone, free testosterone, and DHEA. These are relatively simple blood tests

that any lab can perform, although the results are only as informative as the doctor reading them.

But only a small proportion of impotence problems are due solely to testosterone deficiency; experts range wildly in their estimates, from 2 percent to 30 percent.

FREE TESTOSTERONE!

Most of us think we know all about testosterone: It's that mean, lean T-bone sex hormone that makes guys hairy, horny, aggressive, and obstinate about never asking for help. It turns out that testosterone is much more fickle than we thought. Its highs and lows are extremely sensitive to a man's successes or failures in competition with other males. The consequences of a man's aggressive behavior affect his testosterone levels, and his rising or falling testosterone levels then affect how aggressive or conciliatory he is in the next encounter.

This circular process is set in motion at puberty, as described in a review of current studies in the book *The Psychobiology of Aggression*. When a boy's blood tanks up with testosterone during puberty, this fiery fuel will interact with whatever pattern he has already established for responding to provocative situations. And whether he decks a bully, is pushed around, or runs away from a confrontation, the outcome will affect his testosterone levels in the future. A highly aggressive boy entering puberty not only is likely to have his belligerence boosted by a surge of testosterone, but if his bullishness is successful, it will lead to a further rise in testosterone. This will enhance his feelings of self-esteem and make him even more willing to challenge other males in turf and status battles.

Simply put, victory increases testosterone; defeat decreases it. The book's author, John Archer, Ph.D., professor of psychology at the University of Central Lancashire, England, suggests that the correlation between testosterone and aggression may have arisen, at least in part, because men who are successful in aggressive encounters enjoy as a result both raised testosterone levels and reinforcement for their behavior, leading them to be even readier to act aggressively in future competitive encounters.

Fortunately for the world, the scientific evidence points to a decline in both testosterone and aggressiveness with age in men. For example, in a study of middle-aged professional men, lower testosterone levels were related to higher marital satisfaction and better relationships with the men's adolescent children.

We know that testosterone is the hormone of sexual desire in both men and women. One might ask then if the age-dependent decline in testosterone in men is cause for intervention and hormone therapy, the same way women are treated. It is a controversial issue, and properly so. Replacement of male sex hormones is effective in only a small percentage of men, and even then it poses more dangers than giving female sex hormones to women.

How much testosterone is "normal" for a man of 45, of 60, of 75? No one really knows. The only number the experts agree upon is that below 350 nanograms per deciliter (a nanogram is one billionth of a gram) is low. (The broad range of "normal" runs from 350 up to 1,200 nanograms.) As men age, the real culprit is a binding protein that fences in more and more testosterone. Young men have twice as much *available* testosterone as older men. So it is important to measure a man's *free* testosterone level.

Erectile dysfunction is not just about a decline in the male hormone testosterone. In fact, the Massachusetts study of normal healthy aging men found *no* correlation between impotence and testosterone (whether free, bound, or total). Other studies estimate that among patients with impotence problems who are treated only with testosterone, *only about 9 percent of them will achieve a better erection.* Startling proof came out of an imaginative study done in Scotland on men who were painfully aware they did not produce enough testosterone to get anything like an erection: the evidence was right beneath their eyes in their abnormally small testicles. Dr. John Bancroft first verified that his subjects had the sex drive of a drowned cat and that, even at night, they made no boners. But when he showed sexy movies or soft-porn videos to these same defeated men—Presto!—they sprang up with erections, although the effect didn't last very long.

"We have known all along that testosterone is not essential for erections," says Dr. Lue. In addition to fantasy, general health, and energy, sexual drive in older men depends on the *muscle* inside his manhood. Did you ever think of the penis as having a muscle?

In fact, the key to the pop-up erection is the ability of the manhood muscle to relax totally. "When the muscle is relaxed, the blood can pump into the penis like air filling a balloon," says Dr. Lue. "But if the muscle is weak, it will not allow enough blood to come in, or it will allow too much to leak out to fill up a decent erection."

DHEA: A MAN'S MASTER HORMONE

A master hormone known as DHEA has earned scientific respect as possibly the most broadly useful natural body substance to build resistance to bodily aging and sexual slowdown. DHEA is naturally secreted by the adrenal glands, and in periods of rapid growth—infancy and puberty— it floods the body in great quantities. But it also declines in parallel with a man's advancing years.

Dr. Samuel Yen, a world-renowned endocrinologist at the University of California at San Diego, in his respected studies of DHEA, has reported that the hormone, used in replacement doses, activates the immune system. It steadily increases muscle strength and physical mobility in most men, while making their bodies leaner. Yen is careful to emphasize that the greatest benefits are usually psychological and very subtle. Most users experience an increase in their general feeling of well-being. Dr. Yen, a robust 68, uses it himself to maintain his sense of command—and his tennis game.

Some physicians who have used DHEA report privately that it had a bracing effect on their libido, but none will go on the record saying it enhances libido because so little is known about how it works. No one knows what the proper maintenance dose of DHEA is, but even small amounts can have startling effects. It is less risky than testosterone replacement, but it supplies the major growth hormone that declines along with testosterone.

CHEMICAL MACHISMO

Major breakthroughs in treatment for male menopause and/or erectile dysfunction are under way as this book is being written. Meanwhile, some of the older methods may prove to be more effective, although also more daunting and inconvenient. (See Appendix C, page 264, for sexual therapy resources.)

TESTOSTERONE

Testosterone patches have improved in comfort and efficacy since their introduction in the mid-1990s. Short-term testosterone therapy will give a boost to a man's energy and libido, and that may motivate him to make lifestyle changes to improve his health and potency. It may also help to bring his problem out of the closet so he can talk about it. But long-term testosterone therapy is pure quackery unless a man has a measurable deficiency of the hormone. "No physician can tell if a lack of desire is due to psychological inhibition or a hormone deficit" were the definitive words of Helen Singer Kaplan, the late psychiatrist and sex researcher who first identified the syndrome of low sexual desire in 1979.

There is also a significant element of danger in the testosterone patch. Studies have shown that about one third of men over 50, if studied carefully, would have microscopic evidence of prostate cancer. Prostate cancer's growth can be very much enhanced by testosterone. Hormone replacement therapy in men, then, risks causing otherwise indolent cancer cells to become malignant.

Any man who is on hormone replacement should have a frequent and regular digital rectal exam as well as a prostate-specific androgen (PSA) blood test every six months to a year. This is a major benefit in itself, since any abnormalities in his prostate or any rise in his PSA count will alert his doctor to do a sonogram and/or biopsy to rule out, or catch early, any prostate tumor. Since prostate cancer is very slow-growing, early detection is the best defense and almost ensures a cure.

INJECTION

"Give me a shot, Doc" is the usual quick fix sought by a man who answers an ad for male impotence. He doesn't want to talk about it. Then he gets into the doctor's office and shrieks, "You're going to give me a needle *where?*"

Dr. J. Francois Eid, the affable urologist who directs the heavy male traffic at New York Hospital's Sexual Function Center, has performed injections in the base of the penis on more than eight thousand patients. "Personally, I have not seen one of them—even if he is totally impotent—enjoy it." Even though the needle is tiny, the average man has a psychological needle phobia that makes it unlikely he will be able to administer the injections to himself at home. "You really have to be motivated to do this—because of the embarrassment at being impotent and the agony of not being able to satisfy your partner. Even then," says Dr. Eid, "over fifty percent of the impotent men who respond very well to a penile injection, and have a normal erection from it, will not follow through."

The most effective therapy to date is an injection of alprostadil, a substance that occurs naturally in the penile tissue. It dilates the blood vessels and provides a high-quality and very natural erection. The trade name is Caverject. It can be administered at home and is FDA-approved for penile injection. Both Dr. Goldberg and Dr. Lue say this method works for 80 percent of their patients—technically—but the psychological resistance is very high.

One problem is that injection therapy brings on a temporarily steely penis whether a man is turned on or not. Other objections are lack of spontaneity—a man has to inject himself twenty minutes before intercourse—and the cost, which is more than it costs to see a good movie: $10 to $24 a shot. A newer, cheaper injection therapy is called Edex.

SUPPOSITORY (MUSE)

A brand-new concept in treatment was introduced in 1996. A small pellet prefilled with alprostadil is applied not with a needle but as a suppository inserted into the tip of the penis ten minutes before intercourse. Alprostadil works by expanding blood vessels within the penis to increase blood flow and is the same safe substance as is used in injections.

About 98 percent of Dr. Goldberg's patients accept this treatment, trade-named MUSE (Medicated Urethral System for Erection). It's easy, painless, and concealable. "But it's not the magic potion that everybody thought it would be," he says. It works for no more than 30 to 40 percent of men with erectile dysfunction and usually produces a less than spectacular erection. MUSE is rendered more effective if a man does a "cock walk"—standing or walking around for ten minutes after insertion to increase the absorption of the drug and improve the quality of the erection. This treatment costs $25 per application. It can be used twice a day.

VACUUM PUMP

The least invasive method of all, involving no needles or surgery, this is a treatment best accepted by older men. It is a tube and rubber ring contraption that in effect "blows up" the penis. But only one third of men who buy this cumbersome device end up using it. Cost: $400 to $500.

Chemical machismo is not a lasting solution. To be Mr. Sure Thing instead of Mr. Excuse-Me-While-I-Inject-Myself takes effort—to inform oneself and to change lifestyle habits that over time can fry one's manhood. Even if a man can't be Forever Schwarzenegger, he can improve his sexual potency with a little information, a lot of attention to prevention, possibly a chemical assist, and a supportive partner.

COUPLES WORK

The other crucial element ignored by the "potency pill" approach is a man's relationship with his partner. The wife of an impotent man has a very special agony. She doesn't know how to discuss it with her husband without further deflating his ego. She doesn't want to talk about it to friends who know him because that would shame him. She may feel unfeminine, unwanted, rejected. She thinks: *It must be my fault. I am no longer attractive. I guess I'm getting old.* And of course she suspects: *He must have somebody else.*

Wives talk to me about these fears and frustrations. They don't know how to help their partners. They say things like *I can't stand losing it. I can't buy the idea that fifty is old. I just long to be touched.* At the 1996 Renaissance Weekend in Hilton Head, South Carolina, an attractive woman who was dating a divorced man of 50 asked me at a panel session:

> How do you chase the eight-hundred-pound gorilla out of
> the bedroom?

No one can shake libido like pennies out of a piggy bank. Many men,
if they have a decrease in libido—lack of sexual desire—will not complain about it. A man's partner has to recognize that there has been a
change in his sexual desire and not assume it is her fault. Experienced sex
therapists emphasize this point:

> The most effective sex therapy is practiced at home.

Dr. Lenore Tiefer, a senior clinical psychologist and sex therapist,
hotly disputes the medicalization of male sexuality. Male urologists, she
says, know that men don't want to go into therapy or talk about their relationships. So they tell the man suffering from male menopausal impotence, "You don't have a relationship problem. You have a medical
problem in your penis. And we can fix that." It's not so simple, Dr. Tiefer
has learned; it leaves out the wife.

Of the hundreds of cops, firemen, sanitation workers, and other blue-
collar men she has interviewed at Montefiore Medical Center in the
Bronx, most still expect, in their fifties, to get an erection merely by pag-
ing through *Playboy.* When the sexologist suggests that at this age a man
often needs physical stimulation, they balk: "C'mon, Doc, it's not *masculine* to have a woman get it up for me." Their wives often echo that rigid
code: "*He* should get it up." If their husbands haven't taken any sexual
initiative for some time, working-class wives often withdraw. And once
they have resigned themselves to a life stripped of intimacy, should the
husband start asking for sex again, they suspect he has a girlfriend. But in
the experience of Dr. Tiefer and other experts, "They lose it at the same
time with the wife *and* the girlfriend. Then they're totally devastated."

A random episode of impotence, whether in a longtime partner or a
first-time lover, usually has little to do with how a man feels about the
person lying next to him in bed. "He may be worrying about something
he forgot to do at the office or be distracted by something else," says Dr.
Renshaw. "Let it go," she advises. "An erection is a reflex event. A man

can't will it to happen, and the more anxious he gets, the less likely it be-comes."

If a man seems willing to continue making love after his erection fades, Dr. Renshaw recommends trying some relaxed, *nongenital* foreplay, such as taking a shower together or giving him a massage. But don't be surprised or hurt if his ardor chills along with his erection. He may be so ashamed, he won't cooperate. Leave it at that. If the chill turns into a repetitive freeze, it is usually up to the woman to raise the issue. She might start by saying "It seems as though we're having some problems with intimacy and sex. What do you think it's all about?" It helps if a woman volunteers what she is feeling, suggests Sandra A. Davis, Ph.D., a certified sex therapist and consultant for the Diagnostic Center for Men in Pittsburgh. "A woman might say, 'I guess I feel rejected, like I can't sat-isfy you,'" Dr. Davis adds. "Her partner will probably say 'No, it's not your fault,' and the discussion will go on from there."

A "potency pill" may be a temporary confidence builder for the man, but couples who have grown apart will almost inevitably need counseling to overcome anxiety and rebuild trust. The most telling and poignant revelation that came out of the Loyola study of 151 impotent men was the husbands' pattern of ignoring their wives' sexual needs. *None* of the men offered kissing, caressing, or manual or oral genital stimulation. One of the turn-ons for most men is watching their partner arouse her-self. But these men had apparently let their problem go so far, and were so wrapped up in their own pain, shame, or self-blame, that each seemed unable to enjoy even vicarious sexual pleasure by cooperating in his part-ner's arousal and climax.

Whose menopause is it, anyway?

Often, one partner blames the other's menopause for their lack of communication and intimacy:

> My wife is the problem—she's in menopause so bad, her glasses steam up at the dinner table.

> My husband is the problem—ever since his grant didn't come through, he's been impotent.

About one third of women experience a loss of sexual desire during menopause or perimenopause. Testosterone, the hormone of sexual desire in both men and women, declines with age in women as well as men. And in women, estrogen is also necessary to activate the receptors that allow them to use the testosterone that turns them on. Whoever thought sex was simple? Women who use hormone replacement therapy supply themselves with the estrogen that can revive their sexual desire and keep their sexual organs from atrophying. Some women, particularly if they have had hysterectomies and are suddenly estrogen-deficient, add a small topper of testosterone to their hormone replacement regimen. A decade of studies by Dr. Barbara Sherwin and the University of Toronto have shown testosterone replacement for menopausal women to be very effective in restoring their sex drive, which makes life much easier on a partner in MANopause.

Another cause of problems when both partners are in the menopausal years is a man feeling he is losing control in the power struggle with his partner. He is filled with anger or hostile dependence (possibly because he's no longer a big shot or she is now the major breadwinner), and the couple no longer knows how to resolve conflicts. So he takes a happy pill, and his already idling sex drive is turned off altogether. Prozac is a known depressor of libido, as are most other antidepressants. Anger is also a natural enemy of potency. And there are many reasons men may feel rage at this stage:

> All those years she was so worried about birth control and I was careful. Now she's menopausal and we don't need to worry, and now I can't function!

Or—he didn't expect to have a heart attack. Ever since he has been taking antihypertension medication, his sex drive has gone into neutral. He is kicking himself for all the opportunities for hot sex that he thinks are now gone forever. (Not true; see the section on treatments on page 210.)

Experts know, as mentioned earlier, that as a man gets older he needs more stimulation, directly to the penis, to produce a full erection. "It's difficult for some men to accept that," says Robert Perotti, a psychiatric social worker with a sex therapy practice in Chicago. "They're trained to initiate and take control." So he helps them reframe the issue. He assures them that there is a natural change in sexual behavior in middle life and that they can master it, choreograph it, and use it to their advantage. But first they have to learn how to receive as well as initiate. The man's fear is:

> If I give up control here, will she walk all over me elsewhere?

Perotti believes that modulating the man's need to be in control is one of the keys to overcoming middle-life potency problems He gives couples homework: Take turns being the initiator of sex play. It may be the first chance a man has had to be the passive partner. When he gives up that control and allows himself to receive from the woman, says Perotti, it is often a revelation. But it is an uphill battle, because men may refuse to relinquish control even to gain pleasure or regain potency.

As a middle-aged man himself, Perotti recognizes the resistance and denial he sees in most men: "They're going through a change of life with their bodies, just like women, and they're thrown by it." The therapist tries to verbalize the fears his male patients are hiding by talking about his own: "Sometimes I get scared. I'm ashamed because of the changes in my body. But changes in our bodies go on throughout the life cycle, and there's nothing wrong with it. Life is a *process*."

THE TESTIMONIAL WOMAN

Our level of self-esteem changes constantly over our lifetime. We are all familiar with destructive ways people try to restore their shaky self-regard: blaming others or putting down one's partner, for example. Men at this stage often try to prove their potency to themselves by seeking out an affair with a *testimonial woman*—usually younger and obviously sensual—who offers a testimony to his manhood.

> Will a novelty woman restore his potency?

A handsome entrepreneur who sold his business and felt at loose ends in his fifties told me he had exhausted porn videos, and he wasn't turned on anymore by the mother of his children, although she was still beautiful and dear to him. He followed the pattern of his married friends in high finance, law, and the arts. The only way to put the kick back into the champagne, they told him, was to find a woman who was different, exotic. And the first time, yes! he did feel the old athletic performance level—certain as tossing horseshoes! In subsequent performances it was more like spring training: hard work and not a lot of hits. "After a while," the entrepreneur reported, "most of my friends and I decided we'd rather play golf."

Besides threatening a marriage, these flings are not always curative and may drive a man further into sexual abstinence out of shame. In a study of 151 married men who sought treatment for impotence at the Sexual Dysfunction Clinic at Loyola University, the amount of time they had endured this self-abnegation, silently, was telling: *from two to ten years!* Had they tried "having a little piece on the side"? One third of them had attempted an affair, often trying more than one other woman, including prostitutes, but most had failed ignominiously in these adventures as well. The remaining two thirds of the husbands confessed they were too filled with anxiety about their performance even to attempt a sexual liaison with anyone else.

TEAMING UP TO FIND THE RIGHT TREATMENT

A man's withdrawal from sex may exaggerate a power struggle between members of a couple. She implies, "If we don't improve in the bedroom, I am going to leave you." An ultimatum is a further challenge and will likely make things worse. If a woman can be made to understand that this sexual freeze is not a reaction to her and is probably reversible, she and her partner can usually find relief by working with a specialist or clinic for sexual dysfunction.

> Most males go to sexual dysfunction clinics because of their spouses.

The wife is usually the one who has to audition the right sex therapist or scope out the availability and results of doctors or clinics that specialize in male sexual health. If she and her husband *go together* to a good sex therapist or a sensitive doctor who raises the issue with the two of them together, the very fact that the eight-hundred-pound gorilla has been identified usually makes a 50 percent improvement right away. If both partners are committed to treatment, they have a very good chance of correcting the problem and saving the marriage. The appendix to this chapter (see page 264) offers suggested screening questions to ask when auditioning for the right health professionals to be your partners.

For many men, the wall that goes up against "treatment" is tantamount to the resistance of an alcoholic who insists, "I do *not* have a drinking problem." The lack of information and understanding of this complex phenomenon may deprive such men of a fuller life that includes sexual intimacy, love, trust, and the ability to keep their mate happy.

The process is circular: The care or carelessness a man shows toward his physical condition is influenced by his mind-set. And the greater care he shows for himself, the stronger will be his resilience in the face of changes that temporarily slow him down. No matter what bullets the drug companies try to sell men, the real magic comes from finding a new level of intimacy with one's mate. If men push their doctors to treat this time of life more holistically, a great weight may be removed from both mind and body.

> In the near future most men should be able to manage the middle-life male potency crisis as successfully as women have learned to manage their menopause.

PART V

INFLUENTIAL SIXTIES

How dull it is to pause, to make an end,
To rust unburnished, not to shine in use.

As tho' to breathe were life!

'Tis not too late to seek a newer world.

To strive, to seek, to find, and not to yield.
—FROM "ULYSSES," BY ALFRED,
LORD TENNYSON

Chapter Eleven

PASSAGE TO THE AGE
OF INTEGRITY

The sixties used to mark the beginning of a slow fade to retirement and hobbies and a creeping sense of uselessness. But the new story for an American man who reaches age 65 today, having passed through the main danger zone for heart attacks, is an average life expectancy that has advanced to 81. Thus a new stage is being inserted between middle life and old age, one lasting roughly fifteen years. What can give this stage its own meaning? Fifteen years is too long to spend on shaving a few strokes off your golf handicap. For some, the meaning is derived from learning how to love and play again after a period in which one has "rusted unburnished."

The surgeon had begun to feel ancient as his fifties ran out. The death of his wife had left him feeling emptied of passion. He had taken up golf because, as he said, "That's what old guys do." But he was only playing to the old age expectations.

For his sixtieth birthday, somebody gave him a bicycle. How strange and incongruous this artifact of childhood looked in the garage next to his serious black doctor's car. He thought, "Will I ever learn to play again?"

For lack of anything better to do, he began riding the bicycle on weekends. He enjoyed it. The heaviness of aging that had heaped upon his shoulders began to lift off. One spring day, on the golf course, he met a woman who was enthusiastic about both biking and golf. They began discovering the back roads of their community together. Come fall, she signed them up for a biking tour of Italy.

"I just came back from the three greatest weeks of my life!" the surgeon blurted out moments after we first met. His eyes danced as he elaborated. "I kept thinking to myself as we biked around Tuscany, purring along between olive groves at our own pace, *Goddamn! This is as close to total control over my life as I'll ever get. I'm my own transportation, my muscles are making the wheels go 'round, and the sun is warming my back and the vineyards are pleasing my senses, time is suspended, but I know at some point I'll stop to have a delicious lunch with my new lady and fall into lovemaking. Does life get any better?*"

He snapped out of his reverie and offered a testimonial: "This passage into my sixties is the best—and I *never* would have believed it."

SECRETS OF WELL-BEING IN THE SIXTIES

"I want to count," said a former corporate executive as he crept up on his sixties. The handwriting was on the wall: he could not base his life's worth much longer on the position of power he held in his company or even at home (his children merely tolerated his advice). If he wanted to count in his sixties, he would have to exercise his voice more subtly—through influence.

It would be nice if men could shift seamlessly from positions of power to positions of influence. But men who have been living out a heroic quest, building a record of achievement for which they have been recognized, often become legends in their own minds. As they grow older, something usually punctures that myth. They lose an election, lose a company, lose a wife, or lose out to a younger rival for their position—they face some devastating setback they were unable to predict or prevent. This is where the men are separated from the Protean Men: the latter have built up a critical stockpile of resilience for meeting the tests of the last third of life.

Resilience is the ability to roll with the punches; it is faith, even in the bleakest and loneliest of times, that you can be stronger than life's perversities. Who has it? People who have met and mastered most of the passages and predictable crises of life up to now are, by definition, resilient. By late middle age, such men should have banked the inner resources to survive setbacks again and again; they are stronger than they probably think they are.

An impressive study of the sources of well-being in Harvard men at age 65 found that, by that age, their emotional health was not grounded in a happy childhood or awards or other testimonies to a successful career. It was the men who had developed the resilience to absorb life's shocks and conflicts—without passivity, blaming, bitterness, or self-destructive behaviors—who were best able to enjoy their third act. According to the Grant Study of these 173 Harvard men, followed up at five-year intervals by psychiatrist George E. Vaillant, the most valuable asset they had gained during the Age of Mastery was the self-awareness to control their first impulses. Instead of lashing out in anger or looking for others to blame or retreating into depression when faced with emotional crisis, they have learned to sleep on major decisions and to wait until they can respond in a calm, measured way. Resilience, though, is not a solo act. A man's ability to roll with the punches is vastly improved by developing, and constantly refreshing, a pool of people who can offer him stimulation and emotional support.

But it is natural in your later years to feel nervous that you have not accomplished all that you wished. Is there still time to create a legacy? To make a difference?

One of America's greatest living literary legends, John Updike, recently ruminated on the legacy he has already created: forty books, all jacketed in polychrome covers and sitting like a row of soldiers opposite his writing desk. "Somewhere in their several million pondered, proofread, printed words I must have done my best, sung my song, had my say," wrote Updike in *The New Yorker.* "But my panicked awareness, as the cutoff age of sixty-five approaches, is of all that *isn't* in them—almost everything, it suddenly seems. *Worlds* are not in them. In the face of this vacuity arises the terrible itch to—what else?"

Perhaps our greatest fear as we grow older is of our own irrelevance. Thus, paramount concerns of the sixties are:

> What will my life add up to?
> Is it too late to put more meaning into my life?
> Do I want to be remembered as the man I have been up to now?

These kinds of questions color many of the attitudes and choices that come up in the sixties. Although you may well have another quarter century of living to do, the shadow of age begins to fall across your path. It is important not to allow that awareness to overshadow the new and deeply meaningful passage ahead—one leading to the illumination (or despair) of the Age of Integrity.

We can all recognize despair. But what does "integrity" really mean? It was Erik Erikson who conceived of the eighth and final stage of the adult developmental life cycle as a struggle between integrity and despair. Even he admitted that integrity is hard to define, suggesting that it involves the capacity for postnarcissistic love and the serenity to bless one's own life history as something that had to be.

Men I have interviewed in late middle age often speak of their yearning for *balance* and for being *authentic.* It sounds very much like the concept of integrity. To me, integrity means the work of integrating all the serial identities that have served you through adolescence and middlescence, shedding outlived roles, letting go of the "big-shot" ego, retiring the victim and the killer, honoring your better nature, forgiving your parents and yourself for what had to be, and arriving at *coalescence.* You are who you are. The Protean Man must now commit himself to finding his most natural form and holding to it with some consistency. Traits found by the Grant Study to be important as men grow older are dependability, good self-organization, and pragmatism.

An architect gave a simple description of this change. He recalled himself as a hotheaded artist in his forties, shouting all day at people who worked for him in his studio, then going home and behaving like the benevolent father and honest husband, while fooling around with women on the side and lying about it—even to himself. "It becomes more difficult to lie to yourself as you get older," he acknowledged when I interviewed him in his sixties. "By now I don't feel that I am playing one role in my work life and another role in my love life and another in my family life and friendships." Groping for how to describe this change in perspective that came over him as he moved into his sixties, he said, "You don't want to feel that any part of your life is *unauthentic.*"

IMAGINING THE PAUL McCARTNEY RETIREMENT HOME

When thinking about baby boomers moving into retirement age, instead of thinking about Grandpa we should imagine Paul McCartney, Mick Jagger, or Keith Richards in their golden years. A witty boomer who chairs the California Association of Homes and Services for the Aging, Mel Matsumoto, sketched out his whimsy of a Purple Haze Retirement Commune that might accommodate such aging hipsters. Wings of the home could have cool names like Penny Lane and Strawberry Fields. Forget Jell-O and bingo. Residents, naturally suspicious of any prescribed medications, would demand alternatives: medicinal marijuana and a broad menu of recreational drugs and hormone cocktails. They would not hesitate to stage protests. When pressed to take urine tests, they could be expected to sit down in administration offices and shout, "Hell, no, we won't go!" Predictably, they would be unmanageable because there would always be more of them than the staff. And by this age, they will have nothing left to lose.

Maybe their retirement communities won't be made of brick and mortar at all but will be virtual communities, networked by technologies we can't even imagine as yet. Most men, however, still base their fantasies about retirement on age cues from fathers who were not expected to live beyond 70, and who were conditioned to think of this stage as nothing more than the end of work.

The "do nothing" fantasy was expressed by a charismatic African-American man, Gerald Brooks, who had grown up in the inner city of Saint Louis. Gerald started in the mail room of a big defense contractor, worked his way into public relations, and earned a college degree after ten years of night school. In middle life he runs the marketing department of the Saint Louis Public Library, a model nonprofit organization.

As Brooks tooled me around town in his huge van, it was plain that he thrives on his influential role as a cultural bridge-builder between the racial and social divides of his community. Everywhere, people greeted him like a personal friend. He also serves on many boards as a city father.

If and when he retires from paid community service, I asked Brooks, what would he look forward to about retirement?

"Retiring means waking up and doing whatever I want to do," he said cheerily. "And if it means waking up at ten o'clock every morning and staying in bed, reading the newspaper and watching TV until eleven, and then getting up and starting my day, that's fine."

DON'T RETIRE! REDIRECT!

But it doesn't work that way today. Men live too long to be stimulated by the big sleep. Some men who choose to take early retirement or sell their company have the magical illusion that it will be all fun and games or a magical rebirth. These are the kinds of fantasies they spin:

> I'm going to have a ball. I'm going to travel, I'm just going to enjoy my family and play golf every day. I don't want somebody telling me I have to be somewhere at a certain time.

It soon becomes embarrassing to be the only man under 70 who is out on the golf course in midweek. A healthy man in his sixties is not ready to hang up his gloves entirely. But now he doesn't know what to do with himself. The very word "retire" is synonymous with *discard, dismiss, resign, retreat, seclude oneself, be unsociable, go to bed*—everything that is physically and mentally detrimental to a person in the Age of Integrity. We should retire the very word "retire." Let's replace it with the active word "redirect."

> Are you retiring?
> No, I'm redirecting.

"'Tis not too late to seek a newer world," wrote Alfred, Lord Tennyson in his poetic ode to aging men, "Ulysses." If that was true for warriors and kings in 1842, it is emphatically true for both ordinary and extraordinary men today. Baby-boom men who live for fifteen or twenty years beyond the traditional retirement age will be the powerhouse age group over the next twenty years. The projections are mind-boggling. During the twentieth century, the number of Americans aged 65 or over has jumped off the charts—doubling more than three times! Between 2010 and 2030, when the baby-boom population enters the Age of Integrity, the Census Bureau expects the 65-and-over crowd to swell to 69 million people. Roughly *one in five* Americans could be 65 or over by 2030. By the middle of the next century, it might be completely inaccurate to think of ourselves as a nation of the young: there could be more persons who are considered "elderly" (65 or older) than those considered "young" (14 or younger).

So it shouldn't be surprising that retirement is one of today's most troubling passages for Americans, as confirmed by national surveys. Having defined themselves largely by their work, many members of the baby-boom generation are bothered by the question: *What do you do when it stops?* And the higher the status conferred by one's work, the steeper the slide to anonymity.

A professional man who had not retired but whose career had, typically, faded away in his sixties, approached me after I gave a lecture at the Saint Louis Public Library. He wanted to know, "Do many men who reach their eighties, after retiring around sixty and mostly just loafing or doing hobbies, do they often regret that they haven't accomplished more?"

Most men want to feel before they die that they have made a difference, I said. And the years after retirement from one's primary career offer a great opportunity to leave things a little better than you found them.

This was not the answer he wanted to hear. "I don't want to keep going for success and a higher dollar income," he insisted.

"It's not about success and money," interjected a lawyer who had consciously changed careers, or the major focus within his career, roughly every seven years and was excitedly anticipating his next passage. "It's about trying to find another way to put what you know to work."

"But that's being goal-oriented all over again," protested the man.

"No," the lawyer corrected him, "it's being *process*-oriented."

The process of redirecting also has its very practical aspects.

LOOKING FOR YOUR POSTCAREER CAREER

People used to count on a three-legged stool to support their retirement years: a pension, Social Security, and personal savings. All three legs of that stool are now increasingly wobbly. Since older Americans now desire—and need—a fatter financial cushion to support them for longer lives, they will increasingly need a fourth leg on the stool. It's called work. A working retirement.

The percentage of Americans 65 and over who work full-time declined after World War II, when pensions became commonplace, and by 1985 had plunged to a record low as the last members of the World War II generation entered their sixties. But over the next ten years, 1985 to 1995, their ranks almost tripled among full-time working people. Indeed, the fastest-growing stream of full-time employees entering the workforce has been people over 65—almost 4 million of them.

Some remake themselves, repackaging all the skills they have gained and offering their expertise as consultants. Some start small, low-overhead businesses. Or they find time to contribute to their communities—or the country.

Smaller companies and nonprofit organizations, given their limited resources, are more willing to hire older people.

> One out of ten Americans today works for a nonprofit organization.

Most people working for nonprofits are in their middle or later years, and increasingly they are men who were once shining successes in commercial business. Retirees who have pensions and Medicare or portable health insurance policies can often afford to work for less than market rates. And, given the robust job market in America of the late 1990s, pockets of labor shortage are being revealed along with the executive brain drain resulting from overzealous downsizing, The agile senior thus has good prospects for a postcareer career.

But this is not yet the norm—far from it. Men are continuing to take earlier and earlier retirement, even as they live longer and longer. The average age for men to collect the gold watch was 67 in 1950. Now it is down to 63. It doesn't take a Ph.D. in statistics to figure out that if men can expect twenty-eight years of additional life (since 1900), they should plan to spend a good part of those bonus years doing something useful. But society's institutions are appallingly behind the times in preparing for this new reality. American government policy penalizes people for mixing work with retirement. As a result, a huge pool of restless, still-vigorous men is floating around the country, into and out of part-time jobs or entrepreneurial efforts, searching for the right fit.

> What a man needs for a satisfying third act is something he *has* to live for—an internal mission.

No matter what your record of external achievement, you will need an internal mission to fortify your resilience in meeting the obstacles and exit events ahead. The optimum goal is to find a pleasurable commitment that allows you to exercise parts of yourself that had to be ignored earlier. A mission can give this stage of life its own meaning and might even guarantee you a sliver of immortality.

Reaching young people is one of the most effective ways to extend your influence. Henry Fenwick, the sophisticated sixtysomething editor of *Modern Maturity*, the official magazine of the American Association of Retired Persons (AARP), has seen and read the stories of thousands of men who have passed 60. "The men that I'm most impressed by in their sixties, seventies, and eighties are those who have formed the most effective bridges to the younger generations—either through family or through mentoring," he says. "The fame or credit no longer necessarily redounds to you—it may go to a younger man or woman."

When should you start planning to redirect?

Yesterday.

Career counselors generally advise people to start experimenting and planning for a postretirement career by age 45. Should you need to change fields entirely, it will naturally feel awkward to be an amateur again. But it is absolutely essential to take on the humble role of "learner" if you are going to retrofit yourself for a working retirement. The best plan is not to cut loose suddenly but rather to open a parallel track—gain some new experience, make some mistakes, find out what you *don't* want to do—before going off on your own. You might also invest in a promising business well before traditional retirement age, with an option to buy at a later point.

Our major corporations should be offering *flexible* retirement plans, so that valued senior employees can taper off gradually as they build up skills and contacts for the next serial career. The challenge for our social institutions is to prepare attractive positions for people who are at the top of their game, to utilize retiring executives, skilled workers, and artisans. We need to match the resources of older, experienced men with our most glaring problems as a society and develop roles that grant them respect and allow them to contribute.

HIS AND HER RETIREMENT FANTASIES

Decisions about retirement obviously have a major impact on one's partner. How many men and women truly know the fantasies or fears of retirement inside their partner's heads? Not many, judging from focus groups. When Peggy,* a Los Angeles dance instructor married to a general contractor, was asked to guess at her husband's retirement dreams, she said honestly, "That's one thing we've never talked about. I'd say a home in the mountains and one at the ocean, relaxation, and being near the kids."

In a separate focus group, her husband had mentioned none of those things: "Those are Peggy's dreams. I want to study and travel and maybe open a new business."

In conducting focus groups with preretirees, a Prudential executive was struck by the dissonance between men's and women's fantasy requirements. "Guys say, 'It's going to be great. We're going to travel a lot, and I'm going to be with my wife a lot.' They start to giggle, like there's going to be a lot of sex. Their idea about retirement is a really hot vacation. When you ask them, 'What's it *really* going to be like?' they'll say, 'I don't know.' "

Men almost universally mention travel as a requirement for enjoying retirement and often dream of buying a ranch or becoming gentleman

---

*A pseudonym.

farmers. The women are predictably concerned about uprooting, leaving old friends and children, and especially being out of range of grandchildren. They also worry that their husbands, once deprived of the stimulation of work, will grow stale and bored.

Frank Lalli, one of the most successful magazine editors in America, spends 150 percent of his time working at *Money* magazine, doing magazine industry pro bono speeches, or reading his reader mail over the weekend. He has begun to dream about early retirement—not from life, but unburdening himself of the rigid responsibilities of being a corporate executive who must put out a magazine every month that will excite his 3 million readers. When he starts to daydream about retiring, his wife, Carole, a freelance book editor and food and wine critic, gets a panicky look: Not yet!

What projects and activities could replace the challenges and satisfaction of work? she wonders. Since she has left a nine-to-five-plus job, she has indulged in her city's cultural life and committed herself to more and more community work. Her dream is to find a demanding project she and her husband could work on together.

Her husband agrees. But Lalli doesn't want to put off retirement so long that they won't have the energy for the kind of travel that occupies his fantasies. "We dream about spending three or four months a year in Italy," he says. "If we wait another ten years, maybe I won't feel as energetic or healthy." He adds with a smile, "Now I jog every day. In ten years I may be down to a crawl. Look, we've worked very hard, and I want to be sure we get the rewards."

It is predictable that couples will be out of sync when it comes to the point of actually planning for the last third of life. Men are generally in a greater hurry to retire for a very realistic reason: the mortality clock starts ticking for them earlier than for women.

> Couples must share the pictures in their heads of what retirement will be like.

When they fail to share these pictures, they may run into abrupt changes or role reversals that were never anticipated.

In 1992, the year George Bush left the White House, he retired to a blur of round-the-world golf games. He had no Plan B. It was his wife,

Barbara, who had to try to find time to call home and say "Hi." She was traveling the country to promote her best-selling autobiography, prepping for TV interviews, and autographing books for the adoring crowds who now turned out to see *her.*

Whichever member of a married couple retires first generally expects the other one to slow down, too. This can become a source of constant tension. One of the questions I hear frequently from older wives is this: "I'm very involved in civic activities, I have a position in the community that's important to me, and my husband has recently retired. He's led a satisfying career, now he's ready to put his feet up—and he wants me home at his beck and call. Is that fair?" No one has the right to kill off another's passion. As previously stated, the secret in providing meaning for your Second Adulthood is to find your passion and pursue it. If a wife finds joy in teaching literacy to underprivileged children or in starting her own business or in taking a leadership role in her community, it is certainly not appropriate for a husband who has now elected the leisure life to expect her to do another round of day care. Her mothering duties are done.

Couples need to try to forge their new retirement identity together. (See Appendix D, page 267, for preretirement couples exercises.) This may very well necessitate a move, letting go of the clutter of the years and outmoded habits along with it. Holding on to the structures and possessions of the past may seem comforting but actually imprisons the spirit. The more you let go of the restrictions of your old environment and let your imagination roam, the easier you will find it to change inside. A new and vibrant energy can be released, whether as the result of planting a new garden, making new friends, indulging a new grandchild, or committing to improving your health for the long haul.

Chapter Twelve

PROGRESS VERSUS DESPAIR

Somebody should pass out a higher handicap to men as they step onto the sixth green of life. Sand traps and pitfalls, exit events and life accidents do increase in the sixties, making it imperative that those who want to keep up their game know how to spot signs of trouble and combat any creeping despair.

We talked in Part III about the dangers of "disguised depression" in men like Joe O'Dell, who lost his job as a food technologist in his late forties and was out of work for eighteen months. He had no previous history of depression. His midlife slump was directly linked to one of the losses common in middle life.

An even deeper level of despair sometimes overwhelms men anytime from their late fifties on. It is *not* always related to any situation or event. Rather, these men can appear to the world to be at the top of their game. But a depressive tendency that may have broken through only briefly in earlier stages can abruptly surface, unrelated to any specific event, and lead treacherously in a downward spiral to a suicidal depression.

Do you find yourself thinking there is no way your life could get better, it never has, and it never will? You're worthless. You've worked your whole life and have nothing to show for it. You're emotionally bankrupt. Alone inside.

If this description fits the way you feel about yourself, you are very likely in depression. It is the disease talking. One of the hallmarks of depressive illness is that it envelops your entire history and future like a dense fog, making you believe that you have always felt this way and always will.

"My indolence has sunk into grosser sluggishness. A kind of strange oblivion has overspread me, so that I know not what has become of the last year. . . . My time has been unprofitably spent, and seems as a dream that has left nothing behind. My memory grows confused, and I know not how the days pass over me." These words were written 150 years ago (in 1764–75) by the great lexicographer Samuel Johnson. It reminds us that depressive illness among men in middle and later life is not some trendy phenomenon born of the pressures of modern life. And it may be unrelated to a man's actual status and accomplishments in the external world. Winston Churchill, a sufferer, called it "the black dog."

When men move into their sixties, their suicide rate soars above that of women. Men committed 81 percent of the suicides among older Americans in 1996, a rate that is rising after decades of declining. Of the four leading risk factors for suicide, according to a 1996 federal study, depression is number one, followed by alcohol abuse, social isolation, and physical illness.

This level of depression is more likely to be reached after 60 and in later stages of life. Just as with women, men's hormone levels are declining more rapidly at this point, but as pointed out in the previous chapter, few men are availing themselves of hormone replacement the way women routinely do. Also, men who have a propensity for serious clinical depression are sometimes able to deny or disguise it with various behaviors until their sixties, when the body's defenses and the mind's control become more vulnerable and when they may not have the same life structure to offset their feelings of despair. Certain defenses and adjustments that were healthy and that worked satisfactorily at earlier stages— immersion in work or physically demanding sports—may no longer be relevant. And palliatives that may have been tolerated by the body, such as chronic drinking or overeating, may suddenly backfire.

THE BLACK TEMPEST

A contemporary example is Robert Hughes, *Time* magazine's well-known arbiter of modern art and culture. He appeared to be on top of the world as he sped along toward his sixties creating—under horrendous deadline pressure—both a 600-page book, *American Visions: The Epic History of Art in America,* and a tie-in public television series. His personal life also seemed enviable: married to a beautiful, spunky redhead who created the gardens and nourished the ambiance of their Long Island retreat. But even his feverish pace of work failed to keep him from despair. While finishing the TV series, he fell into a deep depression.

"If you have one of these 'collapse-os,' the reasons for it . . . go back a long way. It's not just something that happened because you were tired from working . . . these things serve as a trigger . . . I woke up . . . but there were all sorts of gunpowder trails," Hughes told Charlie Rose in an extraordinary public television interview in May 1997. He recalled the artist Robert Motherwell once asking him, years ago, "Have you ever been to a shrink?" Hughes said, "No." Motherwell said, "Well, yeah, it shows."

What was it that showed? Charlie Rose inquired.

"A certain lack of reflection, a certain impulsiveness, which I've always had."

Hughes tried to pull out of it by working even harder, but that only increased his isolation. He cut himself off from his friends, refusing even to return their phone calls. "You feel like a beast in a cave," he told Rose, conjuring up the Homeric legend of the cave of Polyphemus, "strewn with bits of carcasses that he'd half eaten—that's what I felt like."

At the blackest point, he pulled out his shotgun, marched to the end of a pier, and threw it out into the water. "I didn't want it in my hand," he said. "You want to deprive yourself of opportunities to do what you might afterwards not live to regret."

Charlie Rose asked if Hughes might write about this.

"No. Bill Styron's written about it."

Robert Hughes was referring to a classic book about depression, *Darkness Visible,* by one of America's most celebrated novelists, William Styron. Having suffered from a nearly fatal suicidal depression himself,

Styron knows the nature of the mental storm that Hughes was battling. He calls this level of despair "depression's black tempest."

Even though Styron says his depression struck him quite suddenly, almost overnight, he acknowledges, "Doubtless depression had hovered near me for years, waiting to swoop down." He raised the possibility that his age had something to do with it: "the dour fact, for instance, that at about the same time I was smitten I turned sixty, that hulking milestone of mortality."

All through his brilliant writing career, forty years of it, he had used alcohol to shield himself from anxiety and to keep his demons at bay. Suddenly, his palliative turned toxic: "I could no longer drink. It was as if my body had risen up in protest, along with my mind, and had conspired to reject this daily mood bath." As with many drinkers when they grow older, his liver simply rebelled. "The comforting friend had abandoned me not gradually and reluctantly, as a true friend might do, but like a shot—and I was left high and dry."

It is fair to say, as Styron did himself, that he was already clinically depressed and probably had been on the verge of clinical depression for many years. In Styron's case, not only was there a genetic risk, but he had never resolved the trauma of losing his mother to death when he was 13. The emotional havoc wrought by the death or disappearance of a parent, especially a mother, before or during puberty, is repeatedly cited in the literature on depression.

> Incomplete mourning for any great loss in life is one of the gunpowder trails that may blow up in later life into clinical depression.

Styron's response to anxiety and sadness was the most common one used by men: he medicated the stresses with alcohol. When he had to stop drinking cold turkey, he was flooded with a clinical depression for which he had no psychological defenses.

Men are five times more likely than women to use alcohol and drugs to reduce the sad feelings of depression. (Women usually use food.) Men are also more likely to do violence and to have accidents (with cars or hunting), and much more likely than women to end their own lives. Think of the Clintons' former lawyer and friend Vince Foster: a middle-aged man separated from his wife and family, working long hours under severe deadline pressures and performance criticisms, goes to a park alone and puts a gun into his mouth to punish himself. How did things go so far?

"Under an increasing burden of intense external stress" and the "rigid hold of perfectionistic self-demands," he suffered a "breakdown in his usual ability to handle that stress, primarily due to the impact of a mental disorder which was undertreated." That was the conclusion of an exhaustive report by the Whitewater independent counsel that verified that Foster was "clinically depressed in early 1993, and perhaps, subclinically even before this." But apparently Foster was so good at covering up his emotions that even people who described themselves as among his "best friends" were not aware that he was experiencing any type of stress. Four days before his death, he broke down and cried while having dinner with his wife. But it was only the day before that he contacted a doctor and admitted that he was under stress. He received a prescription for an antidepressant and had time to take only one tablet—the night before he put an end to his depression with suicide.

Depression in men is a swallowed grief, according to therapist Terrence Real, who writes about male depression in his book *I Don't Want to Talk About It.* It may be grief over a loss from childhood, such as the death of a man's mother, so searing a sadness that he denies the feelings for many years, more or less successfully, until middle life. The depressed psyche then attacks itself in the manner of autoimmune disease.

DON'T BACK UP, SEVERE TIRE DAMAGE!

The wunderkind, who achieves more and earlier than the norm, is particularly susceptible to a middle-aged crisis—especially since he will probably deny that any steps may have been skipped in his rush to success. "Infant gods" rarely make much effort to build up inner resources or spiritual strength. The wives of superachievers often create the psychological sanctuary that frees their husbands to be "on" all the time.

But these men, so seldom introspective, may be secretly scared to death that if they let down their guard, they will be reduced again to the powerlessness of a little boy. Somewhere in the hidden recesses of their background, each wunderkind I have interviewed recalls a figure who made him feel helpless, worthless, or insecure. It might be a controlling mother or a father who withheld his blessing or an absent or alcoholic parent. The great crisis for such a man is triggered by the *achievement* of his success. All along he has assumed, unconsciously, that once he reaches the top of his game, the inner dictator who once made him feel helpless will be disempowered once and for all. It is not so simple.

Wives or partners of superachievers may have to be particularly vigilant as their husbands hit their sixties, because these men will usually go to any lengths to avoid looking inside. When their usual defenses fall apart, watch out: they may slip into depression but mask it with hyperactivity or regress to acting like big bad boys. This pattern is graphically demonstrated by a Washington politico whom I will call Phil.

The woman talking was the wife of a political pollster who had hit 60 and the peak of his professional esteem—and spiraled into a suicidal depression. She was as startled as he. Phil and Janice* had lived together for two decades, and using 20/20 hindsight she could see that he had been mildly depressed for some time. It had started with a lagging libido. Then his analyses of the American political system had become more and more pessimistic; he saw only the decadence all around him. But the weevil was in his soul. A total performer, he had no idea what dream he was living for anymore. It wasn't success, he had that; nor recognition or critical respect, he had those. What about giving back? Maybe try teaching? She had suggested they get out of the box, move outside the Washington Beltway.

He was immovable. He wanted nothing changed. Even his walk stiffened. He was determined to stay at the center of action. During the last national campaign, Phil had followed the same regimen as always: up in the predawn hours to start making international calls, working for a five- to eight-hour stretch, then a long, boozy lunch followed by a long siesta, then back to making calls to California, being available to evening news shows, and writing memos for his clients. But this time his dark moods drove him to seek more frequent comfort in the bottle. He drank, got darker, drove himself harder. When he suffered night panics, he drank

---

* Pseudonyms.

some more to blot up the panic, and when that stopped working, he found some wild friends to go out with to rowdy bars, where he picked up girls and buried himself in the oblivion of strange women's bodies.

"Talk to me," his wife coaxed. "I'm your pal. You can trust me. We'll do whatever we have to do—go to doctors, see a therapist, live apart, get a divorce—whatever you need to pull out of this free fall."

Silent, he retreated into his fort and reinforced its walls. No one could talk to him. He worked harder.

Not until he found himself walking on the edge and looking over, longing to jump, did he tell his wife he needed some help. Janice dialed the several psychiatrists she knew and, by chance, found one at home. "He saved him from killing himself, in the short run," she told me. "Then he began seeing another therapist to do more serious long-term work. But once he was given antidepressants and felt well enough to function again, bye-bye shrink."

By the time Phil won the campaign, his marriage had deteriorated. His depression was being masked by hyperactivity and drugs along with the alcohol. And he was out in the limelight again, being applauded for his power behind the scenes. He told every interviewer who would listen his lion-in-winter story: how he had worked twelve to eighteen hours a day taking the pulse of the American people and translating it for his clients into wins, even while having a nervous breakdown. He bragged about it.

"He's totally regressed to the wild young man he was when I first met him," lamented his wife. "He's on massive doses of antidepressants, which is what's keeping him up. But he's not looking ahead. And he doesn't want to look inside. He'd rather go back to smoking pot and picking up girls and trying to prove he's still the young hellion he used to be twenty years ago."

How can one predict or prevent such a disaster disrupting the usually serene sixties?

HELP IS NOT HARD TO GET

Most depressive illness can be prevented. Or at least a vulnerable person can learn preventive measures to take before despair develops into full-blown depressive illness. This is especially true of the depressions that are triggered by life events, such as sudden job loss, death of a spouse, or retirement, all of which occur more often after 60.

Depression was cited by more than two thirds of the physicians in a recent Gallup Poll as the most common emotional health problem of middle-aged men. Yet fewer than one quarter of the men queried said they would be very likely to see a doctor if they were feeling depressed. A person who has suffered a depressive episode earlier in life is more susceptible to the recurrence of depression as a reaction to a negative life event. When the early signs appear, it is imperative that the disease not be denied or disguised. Depression is a progressive illness: if left untreated, it will in most cases recur with more frequency and intensity, not unlike alcoholism. It is a mood cancer. It can rob a man of his life's worth and make him sicker than most physical illnesses other than heart disease and cancer.

The pollster described earlier was a sitting candidate for major depressive illness. Backing up to play the "bad boy" of one's impulsive youth may lift the fog of depression temporarily, but it is a short-term solution. The most important steps toward solution are to recognize the warning signs of depression, acknowledge that an illness is coming on (like flu), and reach out for help. Many men still believe that seeking help is a sign of weakness. But it is not weak to try to prevent a treatable illness before becoming seriously incapacitated. It is both sensible and considerate of those around you.

> Depression is the most treatable of all mental illnesses among men.

About 80 to 90 percent of depressed people can be treated successfully outside a hospital with psychotherapy alone or in combination with drugs. The symptoms of depression can be significantly reduced within twelve to fourteen weeks, according to the American Psychological Association's National Task Force on Depression. The big stumbling block today is not a lack of effective treatments, it is a lack of candor and education—on the part of men *and* their doctors.

Dr. Harry Wexler, the psychologist and substance abuse expert, raises an interesting question: "Could there be a need to rebalance the brain chemistry in men in middle and late age?" He is impressed by drugs like

Prozac, not only for their impact on depression but even more for providing impulse control. In many men Prozac slows down the intense fight-or-flight reaction and the dangerous "flooding" condition described earlier, when men faced with emotional confrontations pump out stress chemicals and push their blood pressure dangerously high. There is no scarcity of couples who have spent twenty or thirty years locked into the same pattern of fights, retreats, and recriminations without ever really changing.

"And it *must* change if the men are going to get through their fifties and sixties alive and well," says Dr. Wexler.

But Prozac is not a panacea, though the number of prescriptions for the drug and its siblings, Zoloft and Paxil, has jumped by 20 percent in only the last two years. Prozac boosts serotonin levels and makes some people feel better, but this does not mean their depressions were caused by a deficiency in serotonin (any more than headaches are caused by an aspirin deficiency). Two important facts:

- Prozac and other serotonin-uptake drugs help only about two thirds of depressed patients.
- Up to one half of patients on these drugs will experience impotence, decreased libido, or inability to reach orgasm.

According to a leading expert on depression, Dr. Ellen McGrath, who led the American Psychological Association National Task Force on Women and Depression, there are usually multiple causes for a clinical depression. She adds one possibility that you may be surprised to hear: "In some men, chronic depression may trigger a heart attack."

> Depression may be as strong a predictor of a looming heart attack as high blood pressure or a soaring cholesterol count.

A study that traced people thirteen years after they had been screened for depression found that those who were depressed were *four times* as likely to have a heart attack as those with a more cheerful state of mind. Adults with several symptoms of depression also face a 50 percent increased risk of dying from a stroke, as demonstrated by a twenty-nine-year study conducted by Dr. Susan Everson at the Public Health Institute in Berkeley, California. The new findings add to mounting evidence that depression is a red alert that one's cardiovascular health may be in peril.

Yet most cardiologists do not screen for depression, and most internists don't look for it. Doctors may tell patients to change their diets and get exercise, but if a man is depressed, he doesn't have the energy or motivation to take these preventive measures. Yet it is not difficult to identify depressed people. Wives may have to be the first line of defense. (See Appendix E, page 268 for a checklist of warning signs of depression.)

I AM **NOT** HAVING A HEART ATTACK!

The lengths to which men will go to deny any signs of weakness in their bodies never ceases to amaze me, but one story I heard in a Miami men's discussion group stuck in my mind.

Enrique,* a 61-year-old Cuban American, was proud of owning his own plumbing business. His hands were as big and powerful as paddles—or had been—and those hands had built his business from nothing into a supply and repair service that served both his neighborhood and some of the carriage trade. A charmer he was, always joking, backslapping, making everybody feel like part of his family. But that began to change when his eldest son came home from college. Enrique Jr.—Rick, he insisted upon being called—was a computer whiz, and gradually he took over the family business. The father, ashamed to say that computers and databases were utterly foreign to him, backed off. Then arthritis began creeping into his fingers and his son said he shouldn't try to be a plumber anymore.

After five years of being overshadowed by his son, Enrique's heart felt empty. He would go into the office now and then, but Rick wouldn't even let him sign contracts. Enrique's anger began boiling up in his chest. He ignored the pain. He didn't tell his wife about his shortness of breath. Or the lacing that tightened across the inside of his chest when they took aerobic walks together. She began to be impatient with him.

---

* A pseudonym.

"Rique, why can't you keep up?" She would be in her new purple spandex shorts and jogging top, a woman in her Flaming Fifties determined to reclaim her figure.

He walked faster.

Why didn't he talk about his symptoms to his wife?

"I guess I didn't want her to think she's living with an old man," Enrique told me. "I don't *feel* old when I walk faster. I just punch through the pain." Until they took their first full week's vacation in several years, crossing half a dozen states. One night as they were camping in a state park, Enrique leapt up and went running off into the swallowing dark of woods. "Where are you?" his wife shouted. "What's happening?"

Pain. Like a truck tire rolling over his chest. He didn't answer his wife. Instead he threw himself across the hood of his car. Spread-eagle, pressing the throb in his chest into the hard metal, he thought he felt better.

"What are you doing?" his wife shrieked. "Is it your back?"

"My chest," he said finally.

She tried to talk him into lying on his back on the ground. "I'll run and call 911 right away!"

"No!" His command cut through the night quiet. "I'm gonna be fine."

"Rique, you're having a heart attack!" She ran for their trailer.

Enrique outran her and tried to bar her from the door. "I don't need any ambulance, you hear me?"

She ran toward the park ranger's cabin. No sooner had she picked up the phone and dialed the emergency number than Enrique came to the door shouting, "Put down the phone! I am *not* having a heart attack!" To him it was as if his own wife was sending out the news of his inadequacy on the World Wide Web. He needed help. But at that moment he felt so overwhelmed by shame, he would have preferred to die than to admit it.

———

The shame a man may feel about aging and encroaching weaknesses is a risk factor seldom mentioned in discussions of heart disease. The Action Man just pushes harder, determined to "punch through the pain," until he drops.

The wife of such a man has her own conundrum: *Did I push him too hard? Why didn't I see or sense the symptoms before this?*

"Why didn't you tell me?" whispered Enrique's wife as he awaited an emergency angioplasty.

"I was afraid to. You'd start taking over things for me. I don't want that kind of help."

There is terror for a man of losing his own strength and control. For some, it is greater than the fear of dying. Rationally, a man who is sick knows he must submit to being helped. But contemplating helplessness and dependency, even temporarily, may resurrect the fears of being a mama's boy. Every cultural message has told him that men provide and protect. What happens when *he* is the one who needs to be protected and provided for? He may resist mightily or, alternatively, revert to acting like a little boy and expecting everything to be done for him.

Action Men must learn to let go. No one fights disease and emerges victorious all alone. It is essential to admit to oneself: *For now, in order to live, I am going to need help.* Men who learn this, and experience their vulnerability as another dimension of their enlarged humanity, often come to a deeper appreciation of things such as family, friends, nature, music—the enduring elements of life.

Doctors were able to open up the most important highways carrying blood through Enrique's heart. The experience gave him a greater respect for his body and his wife. With her help, he changed his behavior: he stopped being passive around his son, but he also stopped trying to pretend that he was as physically energetic as his younger wife. In family counseling, father and son learned to respect their very different but equally valuable strengths. Enrique was recognized by his family as the heart and soul of the business. His unrecognized depression lifted.

The most important messages Enrique's story carries for all older men are:

- *Don't tune out of your body.* Listen to what it's telling you.
- *Don't hide signs and symptoms of health problems* from your family or your physician. You need to build a team to ensure your continued health and well-being.
- *Don't press the pedal to the metal until you drop,* figuring you will change your lifestyle *after* the first heart attack. Men have only a fifty-fifty chance of surviving the first attack.

- *Exercise, exercise, exercise.* It remains the single most potent antiaging medication known to humankind.

ABSORBING THE BLOWS OF FATE

A man may have been resilient in the face of earlier challenges, but the blows to body and ego that may spring forth suddenly in one's sixties demand greater honesty and humility. Events may change a man's life drastically and prevent him from doing what he loves most. The vignette that follows concerns a man who properly felt betrayed but who took what life handed him and made something valuable and satisfying out of it.

It shouldn't have happened to Aaron Bloomberg.* So everyone said. Such a generous man. So dedicated. Well respected. A full teaching professor who always maintained a full private practice. He was known in his city as the "godfather of urology." Until he was stabbed in the back by his own men in a story as old as Julius Caesar's.

When Dr. Bloomberg joined fifteen other men for a discussion group, he did not share the story of his professional betrayal. He spoke of only one traumatic passage in his life, the loss of his first wife, who had died of lupus erythematosus. "I was brokenhearted," he said, choking back a sob in his throat, "and that was twenty years ago." But before she died, his wife had given him the kindest of gifts: "After I'm gone," she told him, "wait a year, and then marry someone sweet, like Diane."

He had followed her instructions to the letter. Marrying his wife's close friend Diane, twenty years his junior, reignited his sexual vigor exactly a year after he was widowed. They then adopted two newborns, mostly for Diane's sake. (Dr. Bloomberg's own children were almost out of college.) He was by then 59 and pleasantly surprised to find a whole new nurturing side of himself released by late fatherhood. Life seemed full and secure. He followed the same disciplined work ethic as always: up at five A.M. and in the hospital or the office by six for a full day of seeing patients and teaching part-time at the medical school on a voluntary

---

* A pseudonym.

basis. He kept up that commitment for forty years. By the time I met him, he was 77 years old but didn't look as though he had passed 60. He never wanted to retire.

In a private interview I pressed Dr. Bloomberg on what his toughest passage had been. He evaded the question, not accustomed to giving in to self-pity. A fit, formally dressed, distinguished-looking man with a strong face, the doctor told me he had come from the "other side of the tracks." Self-sufficient since he was eight years old, he had been through combat in World War II. "So I can take heartaches and disappointments better than most." He finally acknowledged that the most important passage in his life had come when he was 76.

"The fellas I had brought in and fathered—the interns and residents at the hospital—pushed me out. They wanted me to retire." His "surrogate sons" kept him from doing surgery for a full year. "They wouldn't even let me do a vasectomy." His eyelids drooped like dead weights. "It was cruel."

But instead of crawling away to nurse his wounded pride, Dr. Bloomberg tried to find another way he could be useful—without worrying about the step-down in prestige. A colleague told him that a younger, visionary physician might need some help in establishing his struggling male health clinic. He wanted to teach men to take care of their health preventively, not a practice that was easily reimbursable under the new rules of health maintenance organizations, and he was having trouble hiring good people. Dr. Bloomberg was enthusiastically welcomed into the clinic, where his wisdom and expertise are properly appreciated.

But would his energy hold up?

He began working out at a spa four days a week. By now, he goes through a full two-hour workout on each visit. "I walk in limping," he says, "and I come out jumping."

Not one to let personal disappointment deprive himself of purpose, Dr. Bloomberg continues to help teach young residents in urology. His story is a testimony to Tennyson's poetic truth: it is never too late to "shine in use."

PART VI

WHAT KEEPS A MAN YOUNG?

Every man desires to live long; but no man would be old.

—Jonathan Swift

So teach us to number our days
That we may apply our hearts to wisdom.

—The Bible, Psalm 90:12

Chapter Thirteen

UNCONVENTIONAL WISDOM

The first American to orbit the earth, John Glenn, defied conventional wisdom about aging when he asked to be rocketed back into space at the age of 77. Having passed the astronauts' rigorous physical every year since his pioneering mission thirty-six years earlier, he was able to shake up stereotypes and win a place aboard the shuttle *Discovery* for a flight in the fall of 1998. Once again, Glenn becomes a pioneer, but now his mission is to explore the new human frontier: stretching our notions of the adult life cycle and establishing a new aristocracy of aging.

George Burns, who began a solo career near the age of 80 after the death of his wife, Gracie Allen, liked to tell the story of how NBC-TV came to him when he was 90 years old and asked him to sign up with them for a five-year contract. The comedian said, "Five years!? How do I know *you'll* be around for five years?" Two years later, NBC's parent, RCA, was bought up by General Electric. George Burns stayed around until his one hundredth year.

A 94-year-old man went to see an orthopedist about his knee. The physician asked, "What's the problem?"

"Every time I turn my right knee, I get this sharp pain," the man said.

The physician, all of 48, dismissed the nonagenarian: "Well, what do you expect at age 94?"

The man came right back: "My left knee is 94 years old, too, and *it* doesn't have any problem."

All three vignettes express the kind of personal feistiness and refusal to accept conventional wisdom—including outmoded views of when a man is old—that is a key ingredient in the survival of centenarians. A long-term study on a large group of one-hundred-year-old men conducted by Emory University found that what has kept them going is not diet. They drink in moderation, and some were smokers in the past. What stands out most strikingly in this enviably robust population is their personal resilience and self-reliance. They do not easily accept others' authority. They prize autonomy. They tend to be their own bosses and do not retire early. All have suffered losses and major setbacks. But whatever is taken from them, they find ways to adapt and to maintain their independent spirit.

> "I don't *feel* old!"

That is the most common refrain when one talks to people over 65 or 70 today. Not only are Americans over 65 living longer, but more of them are remaining healthy, frisky, and optimistic enough to enjoy this unexpected extension to their lease on life. Dramatic reductions in deaths and illnesses from heart disease and stroke, together with lens implants for the eyes, plastic hip replacements, and many other prosthetic devices, make it possible for people to continue to engage in life in a profound way that simply wasn't possible even twenty years ago.

The percentage of people over age 65 who are disabled—which used to be one quarter—has dropped significantly in the past fifteen years, according to national medical surveys. Now it is slightly more than one in five. Mass public health education constantly teaches people how to take better care of themselves, and there are better and better diagnoses and treatment of the specialized problems encountered by an aging population. So instead of feeling like a burden on their children or society, many seniors are participating creatively in a variety of activities, including writing novels and memoirs. The oldest old—those aged 85 and over—are the most rapidly growing elderly age group. Between 1960 and 1994, their numbers rose by 274 percent. In contrast, the elderly population in general rose by 100 percent and the entire U.S. population grew by only 45 percent.

But there is a striking difference in longevity between the two sexes. Comedian Jay Leno on *The Tonight Show* referred to a recent study reporting that overly competitive people—people who constantly disrupt conversations and always have to prove that they are right—tend to die younger. Quipped Leno, "Scientists call these people men."

DO MEN HAVE TO DIE EARLIER THAN WOMEN?

The good news first: The increasing average life span has selectively favored women of American society over the past 150 years. But the gender gap in longevity began to level off in the 1970s and 1980s and appears to be progressively declining.

> The longer men live, the longer they can expect to live—and the narrower will be their life expectancy gap with women.

The most dramatic difference in life expectancy between males and females exists at birth, with girl babies projected to live an average of seven years longer than boy babies. Genetically speaking, femaleness is the stable, default position. Women are born with a pair of X chromosomes, which are the most reliable and conservative of all ingredients in the primal soup. The Y chromosome, which carries the gene for maleness, has recently been found to be "unstable and flighty" by comparison: it jumps around among the other chromosomes. These startling discoveries from the Human Genome Project may help to explain why many conditions caused by defective genes on the X chromosome—such as hemophilia and color blindness—turn up only in men. The explanation is that, in women, a defect on one X chromosome can be compensated for by the other, normal one. In a man, a defect in a gene on his X chromosome cannot be compensated for and thus leads to the X-linked disorder.

At all stages of life—infancy, childhood, young adulthood, and up through middle age—men continue to have greater vulnerabilities to premature death than women, from malignancies through pneumonia. "Men are doubly disadvantaged," notes Dr. William Hazzard of the Wake Forest University School of Medicine, who has been tracking the biological differences in the sexes in terms of longevity. "Men don't have the cardiovascular protection of estrogen—the female hormone—while they do have the male hormone testosterone, which drives the behavioral differences between the sexes." Dr. Hazzard is referring to the more typically male behavior in taking high risks and acting out frustration and anger in violent ways, which lead to higher rates of homicide, suicide, and accidents.

But the gap starts closing in Second Adulthood:*

- A man who reaches age 50 is only five years behind the average woman in his projected life span—his 77 years to her 82.
- By age 65, the sexes are only four years apart in expected life span—his 80 years to her 84.
- Men who reach age 70 can expect on average to see their eighty-second birthday, while their female counterparts can expect to last to 85—a difference of only three years.

> The key for men is to make it through middle age.

All the noncardiac male vulnerabilities taken together are outweighed by the risk of heart disease. Men die earlier than women primarily because of the impact of atherosclerosis (narrowing of arteries with age

---

* Statistics from U.S. National Center of Health Statistics are based on white men and women in 1993.

from high cholesterol deposits in arteries). The danger zone is between ages 45 and 65. But the risk in men could be greatly reduced if they elected to change the lifestyle behaviors that contribute to heart disease. Dr. Hazzard estimates that if men would "get it" and make the alterations in their behavior recommended to preserve their hearts, they could extend their life span by *at least five or six years.*

After age 70, it is psychological attitude and behavior that mostly determine the quality and duration of the third age, much more so than a man's genes. Therefore, successful aging in the later years becomes a career choice.

We are never too old to benefit from exercise, for instance. Long daily walks at a reasonable clip are part of the daily discipline of anyone who wants to remain youthful. Men who walk at least half an hour every day, six days a week, can cut their mortality rate *in half* compared to their sedentary counterparts of the same age. (That was the striking conclusion of a massive study on 13,000 men and women at the Cooper Institute for Aerobics Research in Dallas, Texas.) In another groundbreaking study, Tufts University researchers found that even men in their eighties or nineties who had been typically inert nursing home residents, given a vigorous workout for their legs on exercise machines three times a week, strengthened their aging muscles and found they could move more quickly, climb stairs, even in some cases throw away their walkers. Perhaps even more important, those octogenarians who started exercising were also less depressed and more likely to take part in spirit-boosting social activities.

Certainly, the information is out there for men who want to maximize their vitality and virility for a long life. The awareness of preventive medicine, the hot new science of psychoimmunology, the potency of Eastern herbal medicine and spiritual health practices when used in connection with Western medical technology, all are adding to the armamentarium we have to battle disease and encourage a consistent life force into the advanced years.

We have to rewrite the script completely. Traditionally, people have spent their whole young and middle adulthood working hard so that they could be "comfortable" in old age. But that's the last thing we want to be: too comfortable. We want to be active, engaged, useful, and sometimes tossing in our sleep at night—thinking about how to pursue our passion tomorrow.

UNRETIRED CHAMPIONS

The bandleader's knees begin bouncing gently as his players strike up the old song "Night and Day." A grande dame wrapped in an ostrich-feather boa sweeps across the ballroom to give him a hug. He instantly turns into a young debonair, gracefully bowing in his finely tailored tuxedo. Guests drift into the elegant ballroom of Manhattan's Essex House, smiling as they step into the warm bath of familiar old dance-band music they associate with their senior proms, weddings, society balls, anniversaries. Best of all, one of the rare holdouts against rock 'n' roll is still here to entertain them: Lester Lanin, an unretired champion at ninety plus.

Lanin is sensitive about precise references to his age, and he should be. Hopping from one foot to the other as his band moves up tempo—*I get no kick from champagne*—he is a trim, agile, handsome man. His players use no music. They may have played "Cheek to Cheek" a zillion times, but it is understood that they will watch Lester. The bandleader is in control of every instrument in his orchestra—and that is probably the key to his long life.

The long and prodigious careers of many legendary figures in the music world—Arturo Toscanini, Leopold Stokowski, Arthur Fiedler, Georg Solti—suggest that orchestra conductors are a remarkably long-lived group. Statistically, they do enjoy superior longevity, a conclusion based on a twenty-year follow-up study of 437 active and former male conductors in the United States by the insurance giant Metropolitan Life. But the reason was not merely the commonly observed fact that conductors wave their arms around and thus enjoy a consistent aerobic workout.

Conductors, like top corporate executives who enjoy greater longevity than ordinary business executives (according to a previous Met Life study), are in total command. During a musical performance, all eyes are upon them. They found and organize orchestras. Active teachers and mentors, they train apprentice conductors and help launch the careers of composers. They become pillars of the cultural life of their communities. And just as top corporate executives seem to thrive on stress, conductors seem able to turn the high stresses in their profession to productive use. The study concludes, "The exceptional longevity enjoyed by symphony conductors lends further support to the theory that work fulfillment and worldwide recognition of professional accomplishments are important determinants of health and longevity."

Others are inspired by Lester Lanin. One of his players, for example, had set aside his instrument for four decades while he pursued a career as a university professor. Several years before he was about to be forcibly retired at 65, his lady friend prodded him to make plans. "What do you want me to do," he replied crankily, "open a newsstand?" But he watched too many of his contemporaries leave work they loved, move to Florida, and die. So one day he dusted off his instrument, rented a studio, and began a disciplined daily regimen of taking the subway before nine A.M. and practicing in his studio for two hours. Just before he turned 70, he felt he was ready to play with Lester Lanin's band again. It was music to his ears when he called up the bandleader and landed the job. He recently passed 80 and was still playing vigorously.

I told the musician about the Met Life study. He said, "Lester's that way. We know 'Night and Day' and the rest of the repertoire inside out, but we always have to watch Lester for the phrasing. That's what makes his band distinctive: he *conducts.*"

Many men who work past 65 do so even though they don't need the income, because they firmly believe it keeps them healthy, physically charged, and mentally stimulated. And they're right. Intense involvement in work that one loves has paid off for giants such as Philip Johnson, the architect who was still actively working when he passed the 90-year mark. Albert H. Gordon, the investment banker who founded Kidder Peabody, which became PaineWebber, remained until recently, at age 96, one of the company's largest rainmakers. Strom Thurmond was reelected to his ninth term in Congress at the age of 93, having first entered the Senate in 1954.

These are extraordinary men, of course. We consult the exceptional among us to inspire our more ordinary lives by displaying their own potentialities—and weaknesses. They guide us, warn us, fire our imaginations, and remind us to listen for the call of our guardian spirit.

Many of the most revered writers extend their creativity, and their lifeline, well beyond 65. Norman Mailer was on his thirtieth book at age 74; Saul Bellow published *The Actual* at 81; James Michener was prodigious right up until his death at 90. Psychiatrist and Pulitzer Prize–winning author Robert Coles, by comparison still a pup at 67, continues to see himself as an "explorer," a "work in progress," not a finished product needing to be collected, honored, boxed up, and put on the shelf.

Great artists seem to endure even longer than writers: consider Pablo
Picasso, who lived and worked until 91, Henri Matisse until 85. Claude
Monet prepared the canvas of his Second Adulthood when, at 55, he
found a piece of marshy meadowland across a railroad track and saw the
possibilities for the garden at Giverny. For the next thirty years that garden served Monet's passion for sensation, allowing him to paint despite
his cataracts—indeed, to transcend the boundaries of immediate experience *because* of his physical limitations—and to produce the prized water
lily series. Michelangelo is the ultimate model of the creative spirit nour-
ishing the corporeal self. Although he lived in a century of plagues, when
most people had short, brutish lives, the master painter was still working
on the plans for completion of Saint Peter's in Rome when he was only
years away from ninety.

Another fast-growing tribe of young oldies is college students who
can get into movies on a senior discount—many of them today in their
seventies, eighties, even nineties. It is no longer unique to see a 70-year-
old enroll in an undergraduate or graduate program and pursue it for as
many years as it takes to get the degree. Unlike the Generation Xers who
share their classes, according to college officials, these older, wiser students bring more enthusiasm and focus to their studies. They don't *have*
to be there; they *want* to be there. The motive may be practical—the re-
tiree who needs computer training—but just as often these are men with
the means, and perspicacity, to make use of earlier retirements and longer
lives to study history, art, or another region of the globe. Filling in gaps
in their knowledge will help integrate their experience of the world. And
they may be stimulated to turn around and teach. There is a strong trend
in the United States toward men switching into teaching in their fifties,
sixties, and seventies.

But there is obviously more reluctance on the part of men than
women to return to the status of student. This is unfortunate, but here
is the definitive fact:

> Two out of three older returning students in the United
> States are women.

Europe is far ahead of the United States in encouraging seniors to invigorate their minds indefinitely. Free university courses are widely of-

fered for those in the Third Age. But then, Europeans have centuries of history to consult. Diogenes, the ancient Greek philosopher, kept up his simple, healthy, highly active life well beyond the age when most of his contemporaries had passed on. When one of his disciples urged him to slow down, Diogenes replied, "I know that many people feel that old age is a time to take it easy, but I compare my life now to being the last runner in a relay race. Would you have me slow down as I near the finish line?" Consequently, the philosopher lived well into his nineties.

Another prod to investing in a long and healthy life is consideration of your offspring.

> What is the greatest gift you can give your adult children?

Money, stock, a piece of the business, the promise of a legacy, all these are nice things to pass on to children, but not necessary. The best act of love you can give your children is to take the trouble to stay healthy and alive as long as you possibly can.

Okay, you may say, what are the incentives?

GROWING AND REGENERATING BRAIN

Here is the really good news: Our most basic fears about mental decline with aging are challenged by recent research. Brain cells do not automatically die off as we age in 100,000-cell lots, as was erroneously reported. There is some cell death, but mostly brain cells shrink or grow dormant in old age, particularly when there is a lack of stimulation or challenge.

But if we introduce vigorous mental stimulation on a daily basis—doing computations or crossword puzzles, learning a new computer program—even an older, developed brain can grow, sprouting new neural foliage and making new connections. Students at the University of California at Los Angeles keep asking Professor Arnold Scheibel when he is planning to retire. The eminent professor, formerly director of the Brain Research Institute at UCLA, is still teaching in the Department of Psy-

chiatry and in Neurobiology. In 1977, he was 75. He had no plans to retire. His wife, Dr. Marion Diamond, an equally eminent neuroscientist,
is former director of the Lawrence Hall of Science at the University of
California at Berkeley and is still actively teaching, researching, and mentoring. In 1977, she was 70. She had no plans to retire. Why?

"Because of what we have learned from our rats," says Dr. Diamond,
an attractive, statuesque blonde with a mind like a whiplash. "Just because we have wrinkled faces doesn't mean that the brain doesn't have potential. The brain is able to maintain its plasticity throughout life."

She explains the science behind her faith in the regenerative possibilities of even aged brains. "We started with young animals and put them
in enriched environments, where they had a lot of objects and friends to
play with. They grew brain cells. The animals in impoverished environments [without toys or friends] showed the opposite reaction. Then we
experimented with middle-aged animals, keeping them in enriched environments for up to ninety days. Their brain cells showed even greater en-
hancement." After forty years of experimentation and analysis, Dr.
Diamond can give this assurance:

> There is no significant loss of brain cells in the healthy brains
> of people who are living normal, healthy lives—all the way
> up through old age.

By dissecting older *healthy human* brains, Dr. Paul Coleman, a neu-
roanatomist at the University of Rochester, replicated Dr. Diamond's
work on rats and supported her findings. Again, in people who had been
reasonably healthy and mentally active up through advanced age until
shortly before their deaths, there was no significant loss of brain cells.

More recently, astonishing new research at Rockefeller University has
found that certain nerve cells in the brain can actually *reproduce.* Prelimi-
nary evidence suggests that these newborn brain cells can migrate along
chains very speedily to repopulate several different areas of the brain,
says Professor Arturo Alvarez-Buylla. Now the challenge for scientists is
to understand what directs these migrations and to learn how to steer
new brain cells to repair damaged or depleted territories in the human
brain.

How long do you *want* to live?

It is one of the most profound questions to ask yourself. Most people I have interviewed reply, "I want to live as long as I'm healthy." The going bet of some affluent, well-educated boomers as they back across the fifty age line is that they will double their life span. "I expect to live to one hundred," they tell me. Just another pipe dream of agephobic Americans?

An endocrinologist who has pioneered in studying human sex hormones, Dr. Estelle Ramey, doesn't think it's fantasy at all. "The point to remember is that if one member of a species can live to a particular age, that means all members of the same species have that potential," Dr. Ramey said. "And 120 is about as long as any human can live."

It pays to make the effort of maintenance, because every day it seems there are amazing new discoveries for how to fortify the human machine and nourish the brain. According to neurobiologist Caleb Finch, principal investigator at the Alzheimer Disease Research Center at the University of Southern California, "There is no part of an organism that can't be manipulated in some way these days, given the understanding of genetic information."

SPIRITUAL HUNGER

Man does not live by brains and body alone; he requires spiritual nourishment. And it is natural with advancing years to feel a greater hunger for the presence of God in one's life. Most of the people over age 60 I interviewed spoke of actively searching for spiritual commitment and companionship.

Often, the need is recognized when one of the mainstays to which a man has attached his love and essentiality—career, family, physical strength or health—collapses, and at some point, these things usually do go. The pain of loss, the joylessness, alienation, or disconnection he feels, may move a man to seek a higher power to elevate his sense of purpose in being.

I believe that each soul has a destiny, a personal calling, a reason that we are alive. James Hillman describes in his provocative book *The Soul's Code* Plato's concept of a soul companion: the *daimon*. Each human being is imbued with a soul that has a unique calling, and the daimon is the carrier of that personal destiny. Our task is to "grow down" into the realm of human affairs where we can most freely and fully express that calling. When you experience one of the "exit events" of life and feel your loss to be inconsolable, it is most important to reconnect with your daimon, then to reestablish duties and customs that will allow you to give back from your better nature.

God, or destiny, sends us storms but usually also provides a breathing space—a time when it is possible to see ourselves clearly, perhaps for the first time, and to glimpse the love of the divine. There are many ways of searching for one's daimon. It need not be through formal or hierarchical religion. What is essential is to detach from your normal and necessarily narrow thinking patterns, to clear your head and relax into a receptive state, where you will be ready to find the passion that is yours alone.

One of the many doors to this inner room for creative stocktaking is meditation. One inhales deeply, taking in light and energy, holds the breath, then exhales tensions and one's knot of negative thoughts. Once you let down the defensive walls and allow fear, sadness, or remembered joy to be felt, the subconscious is able to send insights and creative solutions to the surface. If you can learn to induce this state of awareness, below the conscious thinking/planning/controlling level, you will have a much clearer awareness of what is really going on around you, and calm and courage will seep in from somewhere else.

LOVE IN THE TWILIGHT OF LIFE

Even this late it happens;
The coming of love, the coming of light . . .
Even this late the bones of the body shine
And tomorrow's dust flares into breath.

The poets always express it first. The above lines from poet Mark Strand's book *The Late Hour* are now confirmed by social science. Especially after 60, a man almost invariably needs a partner to keep him alive and shining.

> The strongest factor in male survival is being married.

The hard evidence came out in a large-scale study of survival factors in more than seven thousand American adults by the University of California at San Francisco. Men from the ages of 45 to 64 who live with wives are twice as likely to live ten years longer than are their unmarried counterparts. And that holds true despite differences in income and education and even among men with obvious risk factors such as smoking, drinking, obesity, and sloth. As shown by previous studies, there is something special about sharing daily life with a wife that protects men from depression.

Some men, however, are unlucky enough to outlive a good wife. The death of a longtime life partner inevitably plunges one into waves of intense loneliness. But the waves are dry. The soul is parched. Who is there to care or to be cared for? The whole web of family, friends, neighbors, shared customs, private jokes, accumulated habits—the result of years of working together to build a satisfying life—seems to unravel. Life loses color. It becomes black and white, and, for a while at least, the hollowness of mourning takes over.

But it is never too late to find love again.

One of the sweet repetitions I hear from both men and women interviewees over 70 is the story of rediscovering their first love. By design, or more often by accident, they bump into an old flame and—Shazaam!—the fire flares more brightly than ever. Each has preserved the youth and beauty of the other in the coils of memory and still sees the other through rose-colored glasses. Often widowed or divorced at this stage, no one can keep them apart, not even their scandalized middle-aged children!

A LUSTY WINTER

Even Shakespeare recognized four centuries ago that aging did not necessarily condemn a man to frailty and impotence. The servant Adam in

As You Like It says, "Though I look old, yet I am strong and lusty" (Act II, Scene 3). Having resisted the Falstaffian excesses of drinking and overeating, he is enjoying his age as a "lusty winter."

A contemporary story that proves the point most poignantly is told by writer Aaron Latham in his little gem of a book, *The Ballad of Gussie and Clyde.* It is the true story of his father, a retired west Texas football coach, about whom Latham writes, "Clyde might be in his eighties, but he was nonetheless . . . a Marlboro Man who had charm instead of sissy cigarettes."

A little over two years after Clyde's eightieth birthday, his wife of more than fifty years died. As he had become immersed in the details of his wife's illness during her last six months, the tall, strapping Texan had begun to limp. By the end, he could barely walk at all. He lived in Spur, Texas, a shrinking town of 1,300, and he had no other living relations nearby. His son was afraid he would fall apart. But a brief moment shared by father and son suggested that Clyde still sustained the capacity for joy. As Latham describes it:

> A few days after the funeral, my dad and I played a round of golf on Spur's hardscrabble golf course . . . he surveyed the landscape: scrawny mesquite trees, dying grass, rocks, sand, and a diseased, tick-ridden jackrabbit. "It's a pretty old world," my father said. My dad knew that he had a lot of trials ahead of him, loneliness, a dying body, but it was still a pretty old world. . . . I thought it was one of the bravest, most existential statements I had ever heard.

Clyde didn't pull into his shell. He walked to the drugstore every day and had coffee with people he had gone to grade school with; he played golf religiously, and that kept the conversation going. About a year and a half after his wife's death, he heard that one of the "Willis girls" had lost her husband. He remembered the spunky Gussie Lee Willis (Lancaster) vividly, although it had been fifty years since she had fled from Spur and settled in Sacramento, California. He called her up. To his delight, she answered. They talked. Compared notes about widowhood. He kept calling her. And after some weeks of long-distance "dating," Clyde suggested that Gussie come back to her old hometown to see the old buildings, the old people, him. She said maybe, someday.

Gussie's name began coming up regularly whenever Latham called his dad. And his dad's voice was always animated when he spoke of plans for Gussie's visit. They made one plan after another. But at the last moment Gussie always backed out. Latham was becoming more and more exasperated with this octogenarian tease who seemed to be tormenting his father. The final straw was on the second anniversary of his mother's death. Gussie was supposed to fly from Sacramento to be with Clyde. She called and said she might not be able to make it. That afternoon Gussie called Clyde again—she had made it halfway, to Dallas—and she was attempting to work up the nerve to fly halfway across Texas by herself.

"I'm leaving for the airport right now," Clyde said, pinning her down. "I'll be there when you step off the plane." He was there, but she wasn't. Again. Clyde studied every passenger coming off the plane and didn't see Gussie. The comic peril in meeting up with an old flame after fifty years is described by Latham:

> Gussie marched right up to him and demanded: "Are you Clyde Latham?" . . . smiling, he admitted: "Why, yes, I am. I'm sorry I didn't recognize you right off," he said. "I know why," Gussie said. "You weren't looking for a little old lady." "No, that's not it. I was looking for a little old lady. That was the problem. When no little old ladies got off the plane, I was stumped."
>
> "Liar."

By the end of Gussie's visit, they were holding hands. It felt so good. But no sooner had his old friend departed than Clyde missed holding hands with her. Unbearably. Not twenty-four hours had passed before he was on a plane to Sacramento to tell her he couldn't wait any longer. He wanted to marry her—right then! Neither of them had ever dreamed they could feel this way again, not at their ages, not with hearing aids. But that very night, when they thought they were having a private conversation, a granddaughter couldn't help overhearing their exuberance. They had taken out their hearing aids and were shouting: "I'M SO HAPPY. I LOVE YOU, CLYDE." "I LOVE YOU TOO, GUSSIE."

After they were married and *The Ballad of Gussie and Clyde* was published, the happy couple and their author-son Aaron drove all over Texas in a Winnebago selling the book. At every stop, Latham would give a reading. Audiences were particularly intrigued by his description of octogenarian lovemaking. His father had assured him that yes, they did have a love life.

But it was only at the final stop on the tour, before a public audience in San Antonio, that Gussie herself asked to speak up.

"Let me tell you what it's really like," she said. "Clyde rolls over in bed and touches my shoulder, and I say, 'Oh no, that's my arthritic shoulder!' We hug and he says, 'Oh, my arm's gone to sleep, move, Gussie!' I say, 'I'm trying, but my arm's gone to sleep too, I can't move.' Then he says 'Oh, my back.' And I say, 'Oh, my knee.' And finally," Gussie told the audience, "we're so exhausted we just fall asleep. But the next morning we wake up, and it's just like Christmas. We have these big Christmas-morning smiles on our faces, and we say to each other 'Weren't we great last night?' "

She stopped the show.

Appendix A

CHAPTER SIX: PASSAGE TO YOUR SECOND ADULTHOOD

COPING WITH JOB LOSS

Advice from five top career counselors (identified below):

First Stage

Borders on euphoria. *I'm better off not there. This will force me to rethink priorities. I'm probably worth more than this.* Flurry of activity. Formulation of a "plan." Necessary stage to make sense of this loss.

Second Stage

After four to five weeks, the rubber hits the road. Expect indifference from many former business associates. The best information often comes from total strangers or new acquaintances. It may take three or four calls to get one callback.

Third Stage

If there are cracks in the family or marriage picture, they usually become apparent after six weeks. There will be more pressure on a man to help out at home or respond to favors requested by friends and relatives "since you're not working." It becomes imperative to set up one's own structure. Sales/marketing types may charge right through. But more introverted people go into a shell. They won't make the ten or twenty phone calls they need to make each day for fear of being rejected.

Fourth Stage

The six-month mark is the wall. Band-Aid solutions begin to peel off. Self-confidence begins to crack. Holidays that were formerly a source of joy—birthdays and anniversaries—now mark only the passing of time. Even three-day holiday weekends can be an ordeal: they keep you out of action, but they also force you to think. It isn't as easy to keep your feelings compartmentalized. The sense that you are not living up to your responsibilities for other people may be more painful than your own personal survival.

Fifth Stage

Crisis of former stage either develops into a chronic state of despair and self-reproach or ushers in a vigorous stage of personal transformation. You may realize that your values and priorities have shifted. Realistic options take shape: some get coaching, others reinvent themselves and start consulting, new ventures, teaching. Major changes in lifestyle are likely at this time.

STRATEGIES FOR SURVIVING JOB LOSS IN MIDDLE LIFE

In Preparation

- *Get plenty of rest.*
- *Make sure you look good.* People take impressions from passing you in the hall (i.e., "This person looks energetic and healthy—he can probably take on a lot of responsibility"). You may need to get a new suit or a suntan.
- *Cultivate business relationships.* Triple the amount of time you spend cultivating business relationships. Consider resources such as a financial planner, lawyer, career counselor.
- *Get outside—see anybody.* Have lunch at least once a week with an executive outside your company. Do a lot of listening. Be as helpful as you can to others—they may return the consideration.
- *Expand your friendships.* Most men have only one friend in whom they can confide: a wife, a brother, an old college buddy. Now is the time to *make friends among your male peers.*

After the Job Ends

- *Impose a structure.* Decide a time and place to "go to work." Don't stay in your sweatpants past a certain hour. Make a schedule or an agenda for yourself, and stick to it.

- *Make exercise a must.* It becomes too easy to be sedentary, and doing nothing is exhausting. It's much better to release those endorphins and feel juiced again.
- *Ease up on drinking.* Alcohol is a depressant. Increasing your drinking to medicate your sadness usually backfires by increasing depression.
- *Catch up with who you've become.* Use this time to examine your values and how they may have changed. It will make your next job decision much wiser.
- *Use outplacement or counseling services or retain a personal career coach.* They can help you understand what reactions to anticipate from family and colleagues, as well as assist in the more obvious steps, such as making up a marketing plan, preparing a résumé, and interviewing.
- *Consider a parallel career.* What could you do outside the salaried workforce that has personal meaning and allows you to contribute? Offering your expertise to a nonprofit organization can be a source of enormous satisfaction and support your sense of self-worth.
- *Explore your creative side.* What activity do you do that makes time pass and you don't even know it? (Sleeping doesn't count.) Go back to childhood, where the essential "you" is. What did you love to do when you were 12 years old? Now is the time to unlock your dormant creativity.
- *Have a physical checkup.* If you're feeling depressed and becoming inactive, inquire about an antidepressant to get through the rough patch. Meditation can reduce the physical toll of stress and prepare your mind for important insights.

RESOURCES: CAREER COUNSELORS

Below are the top career counselors who contributed to this book:

Robert J. Graham. M.A.
Career Counselor
The Cambridge Group
1175 Post Road East
Westport, CT 06880

Robin Holt, M.A.
Career Counselor
Alumnae Resources
120 Montgomery Street, Suite 600
San Francisco, CA 94104

Dr. Marilyn Puder-York, Ph.D.
Executive Coach
(Private practice:)
200 Rector Place, Suite 18D
New York, NY 10280

Dr. Dee Soder, Ph.D.
Executive Coach
The CEO Perspective Group
50 Rockefeller Plaza
New York, NY 10020

Anne Weinstock, M.A.
Career Counselor
Manchester Partners International
383 Main Avenue, 4th Floor
Norwalk, CT 06851

Appendix B

CHAPTER EIGHT: LOVE AND WAR

WITH WIVES, FATHERS, CHILDREN

RESOURCES: COUPLES THERAPY

Below are some outstanding psychologists and psychiatrists specializing in couples therapy who have contributed to this book:

Melanie Horn, Ph.D.
2477 Washington Street
San Francisco, CA 94115

Arthur L. Kovacs, Ph.D.
Founding board member, Society
for the Psychological Study of Men
and Masculinity
1821 Wilshire Boulevard, Suite 411
Santa Monica, CA 90403

Ellen McGrath, Ph.D.
Director, Psychology Centers
9 Garden Place
Brooklyn Heights, NY 11201
or
380 Glenneyre Street, Suite D
Laguna Beach, CA 92651

Michael A. Perelman, Ph.D.
Clinical Assistant Professor of
Psychiatry
New York Hospital–Cornell
Medical Center
133 E. 35th Street
New York, NY 10016

Eliot Sorel, M.D., F.A.P.A.
Clinical Professor of Psychiatry
George Washington University
2021 K Street N.W., Suite 206
Washington, DC 20006

Harry Wexler, Ph.D.
Executive Director
The Psychology Centers
380 Glenneyre Street, Suite D
Laguna Beach, CA 92651

Appendix C

CHAPTER TEN: SECRETS OF PERPETUAL VIRILITY

SHOPPING FOR A DOCTOR/
MALE HEALTH CLINIC

The following are useful questions for a man to ask when auditioning
a sexual therapy clinic or clinician:

- Do you treat the whole man? What different types of specialists are involved? Is there a urologist? A psychologist? A primary care physician? Any patient educators?
- What percentage of your male patients receive hormone therapy? (If it's as high as 20–30 percent, this doctor is throwing hormones around willy-nilly.)
- What kind of reference material or literature do you suggest?
- How many men do you diagnose with high cholesterol or diabetes as a major factor in their sexual functioning problems? (If they say "We don't check for that," then they're not looking at all the issues.)
- Do you have a questionnaire I can fill out at home? (Saves some embarrassment.)

RESOURCES: PHYSICIANS AND THERAPISTS
FOR SEXUAL HEALTH ISSUES

Below are some physicians and therapists with notable expertise
in men's sexual health issues:

Sandra A. Davis, L.S.W., Ph.D.,
Psychotherapist
Shadyside Psychotherapy Associates
4716 Ellsworth Avenue
Pittsburgh, PA 15213

J. Francois Eid, M.D., Urologist
Director of Sexual Function Center,
New York Hospital–Cornell
Medical Center
428 E. 72nd Street, Suite 400
New York, NY 10021

Kenneth Goldberg, M.D., Urologist
Director, Male Health Institute
(outside Dallas)
Baylor Medical Center at Irving
Coppell, TX 75019

Tom Lue, M.D., Urologist
Professor of Urology at University
of California, San Francisco
(Private practice)
2300 Sutter Street, Suite 205
San Francisco, CA 94115

Myron Murdoch, M.D., Urologist
Director of the nonprofit Impotence
World Association Institute of
America
(Private practice)
7500 Hanover Parkway, No. 206
Greenbelt, MD 20070

Norman Orentreich, M.D., FACP,
Dermatologist, Cosmetic Surgeon
Orentreich Medical Group, LLP
909 Fifth Avenue
New York, NY 10021

Dean Ornish, M.D., Internist
President and Director, Preventive
Medicine Research Institute
(Private practice)
900 Bridgeway, Suite 1
Sausalito, CA 94965

Michael A. Perelman, Ph.D.,
Psychologist
Clinical Assistant Professor of
Psychiatry
New York Hospital–Cornell
Medical Center
133 E. 35th Street
New York, NY 10016

Robert Perotti, M.S.W., L.C.S.W.,
Psychotherapist
2530 Crawford Avenue, Suite 304
Evanston, IL 60201

Jon M. Reckler, M.D., Urological
Surgeon
New York Hospital–Cornell
Medical Center
(Private practice)
New York Urological Associates,
P.C.
880 Fifth Avenue
New York, NY 10021

Domeena Renshaw, M.D.,
Psychiatrist
Director, Loyola Sex Therapy Clinic
2160 S. First Avenue
Maywood, IL 60153

Richard F. Spark, M.D.,
Endocrinologist
Associate Clinical Professor, Harvard
Medical School
25 Boylston Street, Suite LO8
Chestnut Hill, MA 02167

Bernie Zilbergeld, Ph.D.,
Psychologist
(Private practice)
1901 Leimert Boulevard
Oakland, CA 94602

Impotence World Association
Institute of America
10400 Little Patuxent Parkway, Suite
485
Columbia, MD 21044-3502
(800) 669-1603
(This national nonprofit health
association provides referrals to
physicians.)

Appendix D

CHAPTER ELEVEN: PASSAGE TO THE AGE OF INTEGRITY

PRERETIREMENT COUPLES EXERCISES

Here is a useful exercise for you and your partner to do separately, then compare notes on, maybe on a car trip:

Ask yourselves three questions:

1. What do you believe are your partner's retirement dreams?
2. What do you believe is the biggest adjustment your partner will have to make to retirement—or to *your* retirement?
3. In what ways can you imagine your intimacy with your partner improving once you retire?

Jot down your thoughts, but don't think too hard about it. Just list whatever comes up. You should not take more than fifteen minutes.

When you have finished your list, go back and number your most important needs from I to 5.

Compare lists with your partner when you have quiet time together. This will give you a platform from which to negotiate and compromise and build bridges to construct a new future together.

Appendix E

CHAPTER TWELVE: PROGRESS VERSUS DESPAIR

WARNING SIGNS OF DEPRESSION

Mood: Have you had two weeks or more when nearly every day you felt down and couldn't snap out of it? An "empty" feeling? Ongoing anxiety? Loss of interest in usually pleasurable activities, including sex? Feeling you have nothing to look forward to?

Thinking: Two weeks or more when you have had difficulty concentrating, remembering, or making decisions?

Appetite: Has there been a period of two weeks or longer when you lost your appetite?

Have there been at least two weeks when your eating increased so much that you gained as much as two pounds a week for several weeks, or ten pounds altogether?

Sleep habits: Have you had two weeks or more when nearly every night you had trouble falling asleep or staying asleep, or woke up very early?

Have you had two weeks or longer when nearly every day you slept too much?

Bibliography

Books

Allen, Tim. *I'm Not Really Here.* New York: Warner Books, 1997.

Anderson, Terry. *Den of Lions: Memoirs of Seven Years.* New York: Del Rey, 1994.

Anderson, Walter. *The Confidence Course: Seven Steps to Self-Fulfillment.* New York: Harper-Collins, 1997.

Arterburn, Stephen. *Winning at Work Without Losing at Love.* Nashville, Tenn.: Thomas Nelson Publishers, 1995.

Bancroft, John, M.D. *Researching Sexual Behavior: Methodological Issues,* The Kinsey Institute Series, vol. 5. Bloomington: Indiana University Press, 1997.

Barnett, Rosalind, Lois Biener, and Grace K. Baruch, eds. *Gender and Stress.* New York: The Free Press, 1987.

Benson, Herbert, M.D. (with Marg Stark). *Timeless Healing: The Power and Biology of Belief.* New York: Fireside (Simon & Schuster), 1997.

Buford, Bob. *Halftime: Changing Your Game Plan from Success to Significance.* Grand Rapids, Mich.: Zondervan Publishing House (HarperCollins), 1994.

Burton Nelson, Mariah. *The Stronger Women Get, the More Men Love Football: Sexism and the American Culture of Sports.* New York: Avon Books, 1994.

Carnoy, Martin, and David Carnoy. *Fathers of a Certain Age: The Joys and Problems of Middle-Aged Fatherhood.* Winchester, Mass.: Faber & Faber, 1995.

Carruthers, Malcolm, M.D. *Male Menopause: Restoring Vitality and Virility.* New York: HarperCollins, 1996.

Chamberlain, Wilt. *Who's Running the Asylum?: Inside the Insane World of Sports Today.* San Diego: Pro Perkins Publishers, 1997.

Diamond, Marion, M.D., and Janet Hopson. *Magic Trees of the Mind.* New York: Dutton, 1998.

Gilmore, David. *Manhood in the Making: Cultural Concepts of Masculinity.* New Haven, Conn.: Yale University Press, 1990.

Goldberg, Kenneth, M.D. *How Men Can Live As Long As Women.* New York: Summit, 1994.

Goldman, Robert, M.D., and Robert Klatz, M.D. *Stopping the Clock: Dramatic Breakthroughs in Anti-Aging and Age Reversal Techniques.* New York: Bantam Books, 1997.

Gottman, John, Ph.D. (with Nan Silver). *Why Marriages Succeed or Fail.* New York: Simon & Schuster, 1994.

Gray, John. *Men Are from Mars, Women Are from Venus: A Practical Guide for Improving Communication and Getting What You Want in Your Relationships.* New York: HarperCollins, 1992.

Harvey, Steven, ed. *In a Dark Wood: Personal Essays by Men on Middle Age.* Athens: University of Georgia Press, 1996.

Hochschild, Arlie Russell. *The Time Bind: When Work Becomes Home and Home Becomes Work.* New York: Henry Holt & Co., 1997.

Hollis, James. *The Middle Passage: From Misery to Meaning in Midlife.* Sunlakes, Ariz.: Inner City Books, 1993.

Hughes, Robert. *American Visions: The Epic History of Art in America.* New York: Alfred A. Knopf, 1997.

Karpman, Harold L. *Preventing Silent Heart Disease.* New York: Crown Publishers, 1989.

Kennedy, Eugene (with Sara C. Charles). *Authority: The Most Misunderstood Idea in America.* New York: The Free Press, 1997.

Kimmel, Michael. *Manhood in America.* New York: The Free Press, 1996.

Latham, Aaron. *The Ballad of Gussie and Clyde: A True Story of True Love.* New York: Villard Books, 1997.

Levant, Ronald F. *Masculinity Reconstructed: Changing the Rules of Manhood—At Work, in Relationships, and in Family Life.* New York: Plume, 1996.

Levant, Ronald F., and William S. Pollack, eds. *A New Psychology of Men.* New York: Basic Books (HarperCollins), 1995.

Levine, Michael. *Lessons at the Halfway Point: Wisdom for Midlife.* Berkeley, Calif.: Celestial Arts, 1995.

Levinson, Daniel (with Charlotte N. Darrow, Edward B. Klein, Maria H. Levinson, and Braxton McKee). *Seasons of a Man's Life.* New York: Ballantine Books, 1978.

Magnusson, David, ed. *The Lifespan Development of Individuals: Behavioral, Neurobiological, and Psychosocial Perspectives.* New York: Cambridge University Press, 1996.

Mailer, Norman. *The Fight.* Boston: Little, Brown & Co., 1975.

McGrath, Ellen, Ph.D. *When Feeling Bad Is Good.* New York: Bantam Books, 1994.

McMurtry, Larry. *Lonesome Dove.* New York: Pocket Books, 1991.

Moyers, Bill. *Healing and the Mind.* New York: Doubleday, 1993.

Ornish, Dean, M.D. *Dr. Dean Ornish's Program for Reversing Heart Disease.* New York: Random House, 1990.

Peck, M. Scott. *The Road Less Traveled: A New Psychology of Love, Traditional Values and Spiritual Growth.* New York: Touchstone (Simon & Schuster), 1988.

Plimpton, George. *Shadow Box.* New York: Simon & Schuster, 1989.

Real, Terrence. *I Don't Want to Talk About It: Overcoming the Secret Legacy of Male Depression.* New York: Scribner, 1997.

Renshaw, Domeena, M.D. (with Pam Brick). *Seven Weeks to Better Sex.* New York: American Medical Association/Random House, 1995.

Rosenfeld, Isadore, M.D. *Dr. Rosenfeld's Guide to Alternative Medicine.* New York: Random House, 1996.

Ross, John Munder. *The Male Paradox.* New York: Simon & Schuster, 1992.

Ryff, Carol D., and Marsha Mailick Seltzer, eds. *The Parental Experience in Midlife.* Chicago: University of Chicago Press, 1996.

Sheehy, Gail. *New Passages: Mapping Your Life Across Time.* New York: Random House, 1995.

Simon, Harvey B. *Conquering Heart Disease: New Ways to Live Well Without Drugs or Surgery.* Boston: Little, Brown & Co., 1994.

Spark, Richard, M.D. *Male Sexual Health: A Couple's Guide.* New York: Consumer Reports Books, 1991.

Styron, William. *Darkness Visible: A Memoir of Madness.* New York: Random House, 1990.

Vaillant, George E. *The Wisdom of the Ego: Sources of Resilience in Adult Life.* Cambridge, Mass.: Belknap Press, 1995.

Wallerstein, Judith S., et al. *The Good Marriage: How and Why Love Lasts.* New York: Warner Books, 1996.

Waller, Robert James. *The Bridges of Madison County.* New York: Warner Books, 1992.

Weiss, Joseph, M.D. *How Psychotherapy Works: Process and Technique.* New York: Guilford Press, 1993.

Wills, Garry. *John Wayne's America: The Politics of Celebrity.* New York: Simon & Schuster, 1997.

Wolfe, Tom. *The Bonfire of the Vanities.* New York: Bantam Books, 1990.

Zilbergeld, Bernie, Ph.D. *The New Male Sexuality.* New York: Bantam Books, 1992.

Magazine and Journal Articles

Brady, Erik. "MARVelous: Four Super Losses Can't Dull Levy's Zest for Life." *USA Today,* July 31, 1997.

Cowley, Geoffrey. "Are Stogies Safer Than Cigarettes?" *Newsweek,* July 21, 1997.

Elias, Marilyn. "Mood a Stroke Factor: Depression May Be Prelude." *USA Today,* April 16, 1997.

Epstein, Randi Hutter. "Do Men Go Through Menopause?" *Frontiers,* July 1992.

Geist, Bill. "Really Big Trucks." *The New York Times Magazine,* October 23, 1994.

Goldberg, Kenneth, M.D. "Impotence Is Often a Sign of Greater Ills." *The Dallas Morning News,* September 7, 1992.

Morris, Michele. "The Trouble with Husbands." *Executive Female,* May/June, 1996.

Kolata, Gina. "Chance of a Heart Attack Increases for Those Who Suffer Depression." *The New York Times,* December 17, 1997.

Latham, Aaron. "Fathering the Nest: The New American Manhood," *"M,"* May 1992.

Perelman, Michael, Ph.D. "Masturbation Revisited," *Contemporary Urology,* vol. 6, no. 11, August 1994.

Sheehy, Gail. "Male Menopause: The Unspeakable Passage," *Vanity Fair,* April 1993.

————. "Men and Women in Middle Life," *Family Circle.* November 1993. (*Family Circle* randomly distributed 2,000 of my life history surveys to members of a reader's panel that was weighted to approximate a representative national sample. Of the 1,024 who responded, 630 were women, 394 were men.)

Simons, Anna. "In War, Let Men Be Men," *The New York Times* (Op-Ed), April 23, 1997.

Thomas, Morgan B. "What Does a Sixty-Year-Old Man See When He Looks in the Mirror?" *Esquire,* May 1987.

Weiss, Joseph, M.D. "Fighting Back to Get Ahead." *San Diego Union-Tribune,* March 4, 1996.

Academic Papers

Alvarez-Buylla; Kirn; Nottebohm. "Birth of Projection Neurons in Adult Avian Brain May Be Related to Perceptual or Motor Learning." *Science,* vol. 249, September 21, 1990.

Baltes; Staudiner. "The Search for a Psychology of Wisdom." *Current Directions in Psychological Science,* vol. 2, 1993.

Blair; Kampert; Kohl; Barlow; Macero; Paffenbarger; Gibbons (of the Cooper Institute for Aerobics Research). "Influences of Cardiorespiratory Fitness and Other Precursors on Cardiovascular Disease and All-Cause Mortality in Men and Women." *Journal of the American Medical Association,* vol. 205, 1996.

Feldman; Goldstein; Hatzichristou; Krane; McKinlay. "Impotence and Its Medical and Psychological Correlates: Results of the Massachusetts Male Aging Study." *The Journal of Urology,* vol. 151, no. 1, January 1994.

Hazzard, William R., M.D. "Biological Basis of the Sex Differential in Longevity." *The Journal of the American Geriatric Society,* vol. 34, no. 6, June 1986.

Lachman, Marjorie, et al. "Rethinking the Gender Identity Crossover Hypothesis: A Test of a New Model." *Sex Roles,* vol. 32, nos. 3/4, 1995.

Lue, Tom, M.D. (with S. Aboseif et al.). "Quantification of Prostaglandin EI Receptors in Cavernous Tissue of Men, Monkeys and Dogs." *Urology International,* vol. 50, no. 3, 1993.

Marks, Nadine F. "Midlife Marital Status Differences in Social Support Relationships with Adult Children and Psychological Well-Being." *Journal of Family Issues,* vol. 16, 1995.

MIDMAC—MacArthur Foundation Research Network on Successful Midlife Development. Chairman, Gilbert Brim. This is a network of distinguished researchers from many disciplines funded by the John D. and Catherine T. MacArthur Foundation to identify the main biomedical, social, and psychological factors that contribute to good health, personal well-being, and social responsibility during midlife. A list of MIDMAC publications is available on the Internet at *http://midmac.med.harvard.edu.*

Morales, Alvaro, M.D., et al. "A Therapeutic Taxonomy of Treatments for Erectile Dysfunction: An Evolutionary Imperative." *The International Journal of Impotence Resources,* vol. 9, no. 3, September 1993.

Orentreich, Norman, M.D. (with J. R. Matias et al.). "The Effect of Testosterone, Cyproterone Acetate, and Minoxidil on Hair Loss in the Androchronogenic Alopecia Mouse." *Clinical Dermatology,* vol. 6, no. 4, October 1988.

Ryff, Carol D. "Psychological Well-Being in Adult Life." *Current Directions in Psychological Science,* vol. 4, no. 4, August 1995.

Williams, Paul. "Evidence for the Incompatibility of Age-Neutral Overweight and Age-Neutral Physical Activity Standards from Runners." *American Journal of Clinical Nutrition,* May 1997.

University of California at San Francisco study by Maradee Davis and John Neuhasu et al. "Living Arrangements and Survival Among Middle-Aged and Older Adults in the NHANES I Epidemiological Follow-up Study." *American Journal of Public Health,* vol. 82, no. 3, March 1992.

Unpublished Works

American Association of Retired Persons survey

American Management Association surveys

American Psychological Association task force findings

International Gallup poll of adults in 22 nations

Loyola University Sexual Dysfunction Clinic study of married men seeking treatment for impotence.

Sheehy's Life History Survey of 110 Professional Men. Conducted nationwide in 1993 by Questionnaire for Men in Second Adulthood. The men ranged in age from 40 to 65; average age 52. Most (87%) were married; two thirds had some graduate training or graduate degrees; the majority earned more than $50,000 a year.

University of California, Los Angeles, 1995 study of men with abnormally low testosterone

U.S. Census Bureau

Index

A

A Better Chance, 143
addictive behavior, 33, 42, 54
adolescence:
  integrity and, 218
  middlescence and, 97
  prolonged, 10, 18, 32–36, 41–44
adulthood:
  new map of, 17–24
  postponement of, 10, 12, 32–36,
    41–44
  pulling up roots in, 41
  responsibilities in, 32–36, 58–60,
    71–72, 104
African-Americans, salaries of, 156
age and sexual function, 187
Age of Integrity, 23, 215–26, 267
Age of Mastery, 12, 155, 156, 161–62
aggression:
  men and, 98, 99, 162
  self-esteem and, 52, 97
  testosterone and, 200–201

aging:
  brain in, 252
  denial and, 236–39
  disability and, 244–45
  exercise and, 247
  expectations and, 12, 146
  grandchildren and, 123
  impotence and, 184, 186, 187,
    196
  and life expectancy, 10–11,
    245–47, 248–50, 253
  and loss of power, 11–12, 137–39
  lusty winter and, 255–58
  personal control and, 140
  physical changes in, 187
  positive approach to, 196
  rates of, 21, 221, 245
  resilience and, 223, 244
  signs of, 123, 218
  stress of, 195–96
  and survival, 244
alcoholism, 126

alcohol use:
    depression and, 230, 232–33
    impotence and, 183, 195
    as retaliation, 158
Alexander the Great, 56
Allen, Gracie, 243
Allen, Tim, 28
alpha males, 180
alprostadil, 204
Alvarez-Buylla, Arturo, 252
Anderson, Terry, 31–32, 190, 191
Anderson, Walter, 167–69
Angell, Roger, 70
anger:
    impotence and, 195–96, 208
    unresolved, 155, 208
apomorphine, 198
Archer, John, 200
Aristotle, 56
atherosclerosis, 246–47
athletic prowess:
    circulatory system and, 32
    decline in, 31
    Marathon Man phase, 32
authenticity, 218
authenticity crisis, 64
autonomic nervous system, 87

                        B

baby-boom generation:
    aging of, 221
    expectations of, 12
    Me Generation of, 12, 46, 58–60
    middle age rejected by, 12, 27
    prolonged adolescence of, 18
    Vietnam Generation of, 12
balance, yearning for, 218
Bald-Headed Men of America, 31
balding, 29–31, 97
Ballad of Gussie and Clyde, The (Latham),
    256–58
Baltes, Paul B., 140
Bancroft, John, 201
Barbach, Lonnie, 178–79

Barbie Doll fantasy, 179
Bellow, Saul, 249
Benson, Herbert, 84, 196
Bergman, Steven, 147–48
Berman, Len, 189, 191
Biondi, Frank, 80
Blair, Cherie Booth, 18–19
Blair, Tony, 12, 18–19
Bollinger, Lee C., 119–20
Bradley, Bill, 119
brain:
    chemistry of, 234–35
    physical structure of, 161–62
    plasticity of, 252
    regeneration of, 251–53
Braveheart, 65
Bridges of Madison County, The (Waller), 50
Brokaw, Tom, 96
Bronfman, Edgar, Jr., 116
Brook, Peter, 118
Brooks, Gerald, 219–20
brothers, chosen, 76
Brown, Ray, 100–101, 102, 107–8,
    148–49
Bruno, Peter, 179
Buchanan, Pat, 70–71
Buford, Bob, 76
Buhler, Charlotte, 22
Burns, George, 243
Bush, Barbara, 226
Bush, George, 225

                        C

cancer, 145, 203
Capps, John T., III, 31
career coaches, 131–32, 138, 141,
    261–62
careers:
    blind pursuit of, 5, 11, 29, 34, 46,
        142
    competition in, 182
    contraction of, 150, 221
    dropping out of, 105, 150
    of dual-career couples, 182

job market and, 161, 222
postcareer, 222–24
putting in perspective, 62
retirement from, *see* retirement
subjective factors in, 142
traumatic experiences in, 111
of women, 19, 52, 149, 150, 158–59
work addiction and, 40, 41
see also corporate world
Carrey, Jim, 72
Caverject, 204
centenarians, resilience and self-reliance
of, 244
Chamberlain, Wilt, 179
change:
break down and, 22
cultural, 6, 10, 17, 50–51, 52, 71, 76
fear of, 21–22, 50
growth and, 5, 28, 134
honor and, 65
life review and, 84, 104
in lifestyle, 198, 203, 205, 238–39,
247
as loss vs. opportunity, 5
in men vs. women, 5, 21, 51
need for, 50, 84
as occurring through life, 134–35
permission to, 132, 142, 144
preemptive, 133, 144
pursuit of one's passion in, 144–45
resistance to, 7–8, 99, 130–31, 209,
232
stress of, 195–96
as window of opportunity, 5,
133–35, 160
Chapin, Harry, 38
children, 36
connectedness and, 166
deaths of, 123, 171
departure of, 20, 35, 155, 163–64
divorce and, 165, 166
energy needed for, 182
fatherless, 19, 166
gifts to, 251

letting go of, 167–69
relationships with, 166, 168
witnessing the birth of, 59
cholesterol, 194
chosen brothers, 76
Churchill, Winston, 23
Cigar Aficionado, 54
cigar smoking, 53–55
Clinton, Bill, 12, 18–19, 31, 34–35,
96, 163
Clinton, Chelsea, 35, 163
Clinton, Hillary Rodham, 18–19, 163
closeness, *see* intimacy
coalescence, integrity and, 218
cocaine, impotence and, 195
cock walk, 204–5
Coleman, Paul, 252
Coles, Robert, 249
communication:
depression and, 128
intimacy and, 34, 159, 211
in male bonding, 74, 76, 81,
170–72, 180
with mothers, 189
with physician, 190–91, 198
with spouse, 7, 34, 86, 90–91
competition, 57
in careers, 182
with father, 43
with friends, 169
money as goal of, 123
round of eight in, 111, 120
testosterone and, 101, 200
with women for careers, 6, 110–11
connectedness, sense of, 147–49
with children, 166
through crisis, 153
connectivity, network of, 139–41
control:
of emotions, 126–27, 147–48
fear of losing, 30, 187, 208–9, 238
longevity and, 248–49
loss of, 40, 41–44, 141
power and, 97

control *(cont'd)*:
  self-awareness and, 217
  separation and, 147
  system of selves for, 140
coolness, defined, 86
corporate world:
  careers in, *see* careers
  contract workers and, 122
  downsizing in, 47, 49, 81–82,
    110–11, 121–22, 124–27,
    128–31, 133–34, 141–43, 187,
    222, 259–61
  dropping out of, 105, 150, 157
  fastest-growing fields in, 52
  father figures in, 6, 141
  global marketplace in, 52
  heart attacks and, 81–83
  job market in, 161, 222
  leadership qualities in, 148
  mentors in, 147
  networks in, 148
  reentering, 150
  reorganizations in, 79–81
  retirement from, *see* retirement
  waistband status in, 30
Couenhoven, Paul, 71
couples therapy, 160
cowboys, as macho men, 69
Cox, Winston, 78–82
creativity, development of, 98, 132–33,
  147
crisis therapy, 141
cultural change, 6, 10, 17, 50–51, 52,
  71, 76

                              D

daimon, 254
Darkness Visible (Styron), 229–30
Davis, Sandra A., 207
death:
  of business partner, 60–61
  close brush with, 106–7
  fear of, 21
  of friends, 20
  of grandchild, 123
  incomplete mourning for, 230
  of life partner, 255
  mortality and, 48, 78–81, 123
  premature, 246–47
  risk of, 21
  of son, 171
  of uncle, 62
  see also losses
de Gaulle, Charles, 23
depression, 227–40
  antidepressants for, 234–35
  cancer and, 145
  communication and, 128
  exercise and, 247
  heart disease and, 83, 145, 235–36
  immune system and, 145
  impotence and, 183, 195–96
  incomplete mourning and, 230
  "Is that all there is?" and, 190
  multiple causes for, 235
  new age group for, 126
  prevention of, 233–36, 255
  and rebirth, 132
  as recurrent illness, 234
  reverting to immaturity in,
    232–33
  self-destructive behavior in,
    125–27, 230, 232–33
  social isolation and, 126, 127
  of Styron, 229–30
  suicidal, 227–28, 230–33
  warning signs of, 268
DHEA (Dehydroepiandrosterone),
  187, 202
diabetes, impotence and, 195
Diamond, Marion, 162, 252
diet, impotence and, 194
Diller, Barry, 112–16, 117
Diogenes, 251
disease, *see* illness
divorce:
  fatherless children of, 166
  fathers' rights in, 59

independence in, 89–90
joint legal custody in, 165
learning from, 103
Mr. Mom and, 164–66
of working women, 159
dominance:
    "alpha male," 180
    relinquishing of, 140, 196
    self-esteem and, 52, 56–57
    in social hierarchy, 99
    testosterone and, 187
Dominant Male Model (DOM), 72
Drucker, Peter, 120
drugs:
    depression and, 230, 233
    impotence and, 195, 208
Dutiful Sex, 182

E

Eastwood, Clint, 50, 70
Edex, 204
Edwards, Jim, 27
Eid, J. Francois, 185, 203–4
eight-hundred-pound gorilla, 14–16,
    206
Eisner, Michael, 72
Ellsworth, Earl, 171, 172
emotions:
    connecting with, 148–49
    "cool" vs., 86
    expression of, 34, 86, 126, 147
    groundedness and, 165, 166
    immune system and, 145
    impotence and, 195–96, 208
    masking of, 7–8, 16, 126–27,
        147–48
    sports and, 67
    stonewalling of, 85–88
    unresolved, 155, 208
employer, as corporate father, 6, 141
empty-nest syndrome, 155, 163–64,
    172
End of Manhood, The (Stoltenberg), 50
entrepreneurship, 122

erectile dysfunction (ED), see impo-
    tence
erection, as reflex event, 206–7
Erikson, Erik, 22, 34, 147, 218
Everson, Susan, 235–36
evolution, aggression in, 52
exercise, 239, 247, 248
exit events, 20, 99, 131, 144, 254
    see also losses
expressiveness, development of,
    132–33, 147

F

fantasy vs. reality, 28, 179
Farrakhan, Louis, 73
fathers:
    being defined as, 18
    births of children witnessed by, 59
    catch-up, 164
    children without, 19, 166
    competition with, 43
    corporations as, 6, 141
    empty-nest syndrome of, 163–64
    loss of, 35, 37–40, 106, 147, 168
    as Mr. Mom, 18–19, 36, 59,
        71–72, 164–66
    nurturant, 71–72
    paternal sense of, 168
    power struggles of sons and, 36–37
    reconnecting with, 104–6
    reluctant, 58–60
    as role models, 36, 42, 55–56, 57,
        88, 163, 189–90, 219
    roles of, 167–69
    sacrifices of, 72
    sexual vitality of, 189–90
    Silent Generation, 38
    single, 164–66
    take-out, 165
    World War II, 38
father's rights movement, 59
Fearless Fifties, see fifties
feelings, see emotions
Felker, Clay, xi–xiii, 119

Fenwick, Henry, 223
fertility, male menopause and, 185
Fiedler, Arthur, 248
fifties, 22–23, 93–173
  Age of Mastery in, 12, 155, 156,
    161–62
  beyond power in, 108–12, 118–20,
    137–39
  brain-sex changes in, 161–62
  coach in, 151–55, 172–73
  comeback in, 127–28
  connecting in, 139–41, 147–49
  destructive defenses in, 125–27
  downsizing and, 128–31
  empty-nest syndrome in, 163–64
  father hunger in, 166
  father role in, 167–69
  finding your passion in, 144–45
  former pro football star in, 102
  Gender Crossover in, 103, 149–51,
    154, 158–59, 160–63, 173, 208
  in graduate school, 103
  impotence in, 185, 186, 188–89
  influence in, 116, 118–20
  journalist in, 103–6
  letting go of son in, 167–69
  life expectancy and, 10–11, 247
  love and war in, 146–73
  mature masculinity in, 100–102,
    108, 119
  mellowing out in, 162–63, 190
  men friends in, 169–72
  in the military, 136–37
  money realities in, 135–36
  Mr. Mom in, 164–66
  premature retirement in, 102
  professor in, 106–8
  Prospero's passage in, 116–18
  Protean Man in, 98–100, 140
  rebirth in, 131–33
  redirecting your life in, 121–45
  regeneration in, 22–23, 116–18
  safety net wife and, 157–59, 160–61
  Samson complex in, 97–100
  search for self in, 112–16
  sex withheld in, 155–56, 172–73
  spiritual dimension in, 133,
    141–43, 160
  Surfing Sex in, 183–84
  team building in, 127, 139–41
  time warp in, 96
  tolerance in, 102
  window of opportunity in, 133–35,
    160
fight or flight response, 87, 90, 235
financial resources:
  assessment of, 135–36
  income, 18, 52–53, 156, 158
  midlife realities of, 135–36
  in retirement, 222
  safety net wife and, 157–59,
    160–61
Finch, Caleb, 253
First Adulthood:
  challenge and risk in, 32
  end of, 99
  false self in, 34, 113
  onset of, 10
First Wives Club, The (film), 89
Fisher, Mike, 102
flexibility, 140, 224
flexible network society, 76
flooding, with stress chemicals, 87, 90,
  91, 235
Florio, Steve, 108–11
Flourishing Forties, see forties
Foreman, George, 67–68
forties, 22, 25–91
  Age of Mastery in, 12, 156
  angst of idealist in, 47–48
  authenticity crisis in, 64
  cigar smoking in, 53–55
  current manhood models in, 69–77
  decline in athletic prowess in, 31
  defining manliness in, 55–58
  false self confronted in, 52–53
  father-son power struggle in, 36–37
  freedom in, 32–36

hard time for men in, 50–51
heart attacks in, 81–85
honor among men in, 64–66, 71
impotence in, 183, 186
"Is that all there is?," 28, 190
loss of father in, 37–40
manhood on trial in, 45–77
manly sports in, 66–68
Marathon Man phase of, 32
Master's Tournament Sex in, 183
middle age in, 10
midlife delinquent in, 41–44
money as goal in, 123, 134
mortality in, 29, 63–64, 78–81
prolonged adolescence and, 27–44
Protean Man in, 140
reluctant father in, 58–60
sole breadwinner in, 47
spirituality in, 62–63, 72–76
stonewalling in, 85–88
traumatic career experiences in, 111
vanity crisis in, 29–32
"When you comin' home, son?,"
    37–38
wives' development and, 88–91
Yuppie catch-up in, 46, 58–60
Foster, Vince, 230–31
Franklin, Benjamin, 23
freedom zone, 34
Freud, Sigmund, 54
friends:
    competition with, 169
    deaths of, 20
    male, 43, 169–72
    need for, 143
    with one's children, 168

G

Gates, Bill, 72, 120
Geist, Bill, 17
Gender Crossover, 103, 149–51, 154,
    158–59, 160–63, 173, 208
generativity, 147
Gibson, Mel, 70

Gilmore, David, 55–57, 98
Gingrich, Newt, 70–71
Glaser, Milton, 5, 21
Glenn, John, 243
Goldberg, Kenneth, 192, 198, 204
Goldman, Robert, 190–91
Goldstein, Irwin, 192
Gordon, Albert H., 249
Gore, Al, 31
Gottman, John, 87–88
Graf, Peter, 140
Graham, Bob, 142–43, 169, 187
grandchildren, 123, 124
Green Berets, 180
"a guy thing," 3–16
    achievement as goal, 8
    aggression, 52
    blind pursuit of careers, 5, 11, 29,
        34, 46, 142
    changed playing field, 6, 17
    decline in athletic prowess, 31
    doing one's duty, 16
    doubled life expectancy, 8–10
    eight-hundred-pound gorilla, 14–16
    fear of impotence, 12
    fear of loss of power, 11–12
    "Gut it through," 20
    hiding one's feelings, 7–8, 16
    lack of communication, 7
    linear reasoning, 8
    male menopause, see male
        menopause
    need to know and fear of knowing,
        13–14
    postponement of responsibilities,
        10, 12, 32–36, 41, 71–72
    raising one's guard, 21
    refusal to change, 7–8
    self-image, 13–14
    waiting it out, 16

H

Halftime (Buford), 76
Hazzard, William, 246–47

health, *see* illness
Heaney, Seamus, 107
heart disease, 81–85, 145, 194,
    235–38, 244, 246–47
Hillman, James, 254
Holland, Bo, 103, 107
Holt, Robin, 121, 133
homosexuality, as sin, 75
honor among men, 64–66, 71
hope, search process of, 145
hormones:
    DHEA, 187, 202
    longevity and, 246
    sexual function and, 187, 190,
        199–200, 208
    see also testosterone
hostility, and impotence, 196, 208
Hughes, Robert, 229–30
hypertension, and impotence, 183

I

idealists, 47–48, 62
I Don't Want to Talk About It (Real), 231
illness:
    impotence and, 183, 185, 193,
        194–96
    "killer cells" and, 145
    loss and, 20
    prevention of, 198, 203, 205,
        238–39, 247
    risk factors in, 84, 194–96
    stress and, 83, 145, 151–55
    as wife's nightmare, 20–22
    see also specific diseases
immaturity:
    prolonged adolescence and, 10, 18,
        32–36, 41–44
    reverting to, 232–33
immortality, children as guarantors of,
    36
immune system, stresses to, 84, 145
impotence:
    affairs and, 209–10
    aging and, 184, 186, 187, 196

alcohol use and, 183, 195
anger and, 195–96, 208
anxiety and, 210
baldness and, 30
couples work on, 205–9
drug use and, 195, 208
as eight-hundred-pound gorilla,
    14–16, 206
erectile dysfunction as, 185, 186,
    188–89, 201
expectations and, 178–81, 187, 206
habit of, 192
hostility and, 196, 208
hydraulics and, 192
hypertension and, 183
illness and, 183, 185, 193, 194–96
industry built around, 193–94,
    196–98
male menopause and, 14, 15–16,
    178–81, 185–89
medical help for, 190–91
obesity and, 173
onset of, 12
physical causes of, 187–88, 196, 203
sexual ignorance and, 181
smoking and, 183, 193, 194
stress and, 182, 187–88, 195–96
testosterone and, 201
treatments for, 202–5, 210–11
"Use it or lose it" and, 199
widower's, 199
independence:
    of debt-free life, 135
    divorce and, 89–90
    resilience and, 244
    vs. responsibility, 32–36, 41–44,
        71–72
    of women, 89–90, 157
influence, power and, 23, 116,
    118–20, 216
Influential Sixties, *see* sixties
initiation rituals, 89
injections, for impotence, 203–4
Integrity, Age of, 23, 215–26, 267

Internet, 76
intimacy:
    basic need for, 52, 147
    expression of, 34, 86, 159, 211
    withdrawal of, 206
irrelevance, fear of, 23, 218
isolation:
    fear of, 61
    individuation and, 147
    self-imposed, 20
    social, 126, 127, 165
    stonewalling and, 85–88
"Is that all there is?," 28, 190

J

Jacobs, John, 102, 135
Jagger, Mick, 219
job market, 161, 222
jobs, see careers; corporate world
Johnson, Philip, 249
Jung, Carl, 22

K

Kaplan, Helen Singer, 203
Karpman, Harold L., 83
Kemeny, Margaret, 145
Kimmel, Michael, 56
Kline, Kevin, 72
Koten, John, 129
Kramer vs. Kramer (film), 71

L

Lachman, Margie, 162
Lafavore, Michael, 189, 191
Lalli, Frank, 225
Lanin, Lester, 248–49
Latham, Aaron, 256, 257
leadership, networks of, 148
Lee, Peggy, 28
Leno, Jay, 245
letting go, 28, 238
    of "big-shot" ego, 218
    of growing son, 167–69
    of the past, 105

Levant, Ronald F., 57, 158
Levinson, Daniel, 22
libido, see sexual drive
life:
    compartmentalization of, 143
    integrity vs. despair in, 218
    making a difference in, 221
    as process, 209
    redirection of, 121–45
    resilience for, 217, 239–40
    review of, 84, 104
    simplification of, 163
    twilight of, 254–55
    unauthenticity in, 219
life expectancy, 8–11, 215
    activities and, 22–24, 248–50
    goals of, 253
    marriage and, 255
    of men and women, 245–47
    retirement and, 223
lifestyle:
    illness and, 198, 203, 205, 238–39,
        247
    middle-class, 18, 61
Lofton, R. J., 98
longevity, see life expectancy
losses:
    of children, 20, 35, 147, 155,
        163–64, 171
    of control, 40, 41–44, 141
    of dreams, 127
    as exit events, 20, 99, 131, 144, 254
    of fathers, 35, 37–40, 106, 147,
        168
    of idealized self, 127
    illness and, 20
    of job, 47, 49, 81–82, 110–11,
        121–22, 124–27, 128–31,
        133–34, 141–43, 187, 259–61
    as little deaths, 102; see also death
    of mothers, 172, 230, 231
    of power, 11–12, 125–27, 137–39
    of relationships, 147
    spiritual hunger and, 253

losses *(cont'd)*:
    of status, 20, 136
    stress of, 20, 83, 145
love, in twilight of life, 254–58
Lovett, Joe, 95–96
Lue, Tom, 186, 195, 197, 198, 202,
    204

M

McCartney, Bill, 73, 74–75
McCartney, Paul, 219
McGrath, Ellen, 235
McKinlay, John, 187
magic bullets, 196–98, 207
Maguire, Jerry, 72
Mailer, Norman, 50–51, 55, 66, 68,
    249
Mainehardt, David, 65
male menopause, 175–211
    couples work on, 205–9
    DHEA and, 187, 202
    as eight-hundred-pound gorilla,
        14–16, 206
    expectations and, 178–81, 206
    fear of, 8, 13–14, 23
    impotence and, *see* impotence
    intelligent behavior about, 189–91
    magic bullets in, 196–98, 207
    as MANopause, 185–89, 194
    medicalization of, 194–96, 206
    as mindbody syndrome, 4, 23, 192
    mind over manliness in, 191–92
    perpetual virility and, 193–211
    reduced sexual activity in, 15–16,
        198–200
    sexual life cycle and, 177–78
    testimonial woman and, 209–10
    testosterone and, 200–202
    treatment for, 202–5, 210–11
    as unmentionable passage, 14,
        185–89
Male Paradox, The (Munder Ross), 57
Malone, John, 72

Mamet, David, 64, 66
Man for All Seasons, A, 65
Manhood in America (Kimmel), 56
manliness, 45–77
    addictive behavior and, 33
    as "Big Impossible," 58
    changing attitudes about, 50–51
    cults and codes of, 51
    cultural definition of, 57–58
    current models of, 69–77
    defining and proving, 20, 55–58,
        97–100, 107, 125
    expectations of, 179–81, 206
    "killer" state of, 57
    mature, 100–102, 108, 119
    mind over, 191–92
    of New Father, 59
    new ideals of, 77
    nurturing and, 98
    selfless generosity in, 98, 119
    smoking cigars and, 53–55
    sports and, 66–68
    traditional model of, 58, 77
    wuss state vs., 57
    and youth, 97
MANopause, 185–89, 194
Manuck, Stephen B., 86
Marathon Man phase, 32
marker events, unpredictable, 3–4
Markovitz, Gary, 11
Marlboro Man, 69, 193
marriage, *see* relationships, male-female
Marron, Donald, 111
Marx, Groucho, 193
masculinity, *see* manliness
Masculinity Reconstructed (Levant), 158
massage, 185
Master's Tournament Sex, 183
Mastery, Age of, 12, 155, 156,
    161–62
masturbation, 199
Matisse, Henri, 250
Matsumoto, Mel, 219

maturity, physical vs. emotional, 10
May, Lee, 101, 102, 103–6, 144, 160
May, Lyn, 105, 160
Mead, Margaret, xiv, 149–50
meaning, search for, 34
meditation, 43, 84, 254
Me Generation, 12
    focus on careers by, 46
    as playing catch-up, 46, 58–60
mellowing out, 162–63, 190
Meltz, David, 100, 101–2, 106–8, 144
men:
    aggressiveness of, 98, 99, 162
    bonding of, 74, 76, 81, 170–72,
        180
    as breadwinners, 45, 47, 151,
        157–58
    changes in society for, 50–51, 52
    college enrollments of, 52
    emotions hidden by, 7–8, 16,
        126–27, 147–48
    forces of femininity and violence
        within, 168
    friendships between, 43, 169–72
    heroes of, 56
    honor among, 64–66, 71
    incomes of, 18, 52–53, 156, 158
    insecurity of, 56
    as made not born, 55, 56–58, 168
    male identity of, 146–47
    neediness of, 159
    nurturing by, 71–72, 98, 119, 147
    other men's opinions of, 66
    "real," 51, 55, 119
    role expectations of, 57
    role reversal in, see Gender Crossover
    rules lacking for, 57
    separation anxiety of, 159
    sexual life cycle of, 181–85
    stonewalling by, 85–88
    in work force, 150
    see also fathers; "a guy thing";
        manliness

Men's Health, 29–30, 189
men's magazines, 51
Messenger of God (MOG), 72–76
metabolism, slowdown of, 186
Michelangelo, 250
Michener, James, 249
middle age, 10
    boomers' rejection of, 12, 27
    stereotypes of, 97
middlescence, 97, 218
midlife:
    activities after, 22–24
    benefits of, 60
    major task in, 41
    male menopause in, see male
        menopause
    as "male middle-life slowdown,"
        186
    money realities of, 135–36
    as opportunity for growth, 34, 160
    "pacesetters" in, 148n
    personality changes in, 34
    potency crisis in, 178
    transformative women and, 43–44
    transition into, 36, 49
    women in, 7, 21, 89, 149–50, 155
midlife crisis, as turning point, 34
MIDMAC (MacArthur Foundation
        Research Network on Successful
        Midlife Development), 140–41,
        162
military:
    downsizing in, 136–37
    ideals in, 63
    women in, 18, 69–70
Million Man March, 73
mind, power of, 12, 192
MOG (Messenger of God), 72–76
Molt, Edward, 122
Monet, Claude, 250
money:
    debt and, 135
    as goal, 123, 134

Moonstruck (film), 21
Moore, Demi, 54
More, Sir Thomas, 65
Moriarty, Erin, 15
Morning Flag-flying Test, 199
mortality:
    Aha! moment of, 78–81
    dealing with, 110
    jolt of, 29, 48, 60–64, 78–81, 123
    see also death
mothers:
    communication with, 189
    continuity of experience in, 21
    empty-nest syndrome of, 163–64
    loss of, 172, 230, 231
    single, 19, 166
Motherwell, Robert, 229
mourning, incomplete, 230
Moynihan, Daniel Patrick, 19
Mr. Mom, 18–19, 36, 164–66
    as New Father, 59
    Sensitive New Age Guy as, 71–72
Muhammad Ali, 67–68
Munder Ross, John, 51, 56, 57, 159,
    168
Murdoch, Rupert, 72, 112–13, 117
Murdock, Myron, 188
MUSE (Medicated Urethral System
    for Erection), 204

N

Nelson, Mariah Burton, 67
Nelson-Palmer, Col. Mike, 136, 137
nervous system, 87, 162–63
networking, 127, 132, 139–41, 143,
    147–49
Neugarten, Bernice, 22
Newhouse, S. I., Jr., 109
New Male Sexuality, The (Zilbergeld),
    155
New Passages (Sheehy), 13, 99, 148,
    159
New Psychology of Men, A (Pollack and
    Levant), 57

nurturing:
    by men, 71–72, 98, 119, 147
    by women, 98
Nyberg, Leroy, Jr., 186

O

O'Connell, Bill, 64–65
O'Dell, Joe, 122–28, 227
Ornish, Dean, 82, 194, 195, 198

P

"pacesetters," 148*n*
Paige, Satchel, 45
parenthood; *see* fathers; mothers
Partner and Leader (PAL), 76
passages:
    to Age of Integrity, 215–26, 267
    to Age of Mastery, 12
    to First Adulthood, 10
    from First to Second Adulthood,
        12, 28, 34
    middle, 140
    midlife crisis vs., 34
    of Prospero, 116–18
    Second Adulthood, 10–11,
        95–120, 259–62
    six A.M., 189
    transitional periods as, 8, 36
    uncertainty in, 41, 49
    unmentionable, 14, 185–89
Passages (Sheehy), 4, 63, 89
patriarchy:
    dominance and submission in,
        56–57
    outdated concept of, 6, 36, 50
    regeneration of, 73–76
Paxil, 235
Peck, M. Scott, 134–35
penis, 206–7
    muscle of, 201–2
    steely, 204
    stimulation of, 199, 208–9
    see also impotence
Perelman, Michael, 180–81

Perotti, Robert, 208–9
Perrine, Steve, 29–30
personality, changes in, 34
Phillips, Ed, 164
physical attributes:
    balding, 29–31, 97
    careers and, 30
    male grooming industry and, 29–30
    moral superiority and, 17
    self-confidence and, 49
physical condition, and impotence,
    187–88
physicians, 265–66
    communication with, 190–91, 198
    depression and, 234
    mindbody connection and, 192
Picasso, Pablo, 23, 250
Plimpton, George, 66–67, 68
Pollack, William, 57
postpatriarchal man, 18–19
    fatherhood of, 19
    in Fearless Fifties, 22–23
    in Flourishing Forties, 22, 60
    as Protean Man, 98–100
potency, see impotence; manliness; sex-
    ual drive
power:
    of "big shots," 137–39
    control and, 97
    defined, 108
    as extension of self-knowledge,
        117–18
    greater than oneself, 120
    influence and, 23, 116, 118–20, 216
    loss of, 11–12, 125–27, 137–39
    moving beyond, 108–12, 116
    separation and, 147
    of sons vs. fathers, 36–37
    transformation of, 12
    transitory nature of, 119
    of young men, 97
prescription drugs, 195, 235
primitive peoples, 89
Promise Keepers, 73–76

Propecia, 30
Prospero's passage, 116–18
Protean Man, 98–100, 140, 216–17,
    218
Prozac, 208, 235
PSA (prostate-specific androgen)
    blood test, 203
Psychobiology of Aggression, The (Archer),
    200
psychological causes of impotence,
    182, 187–88, 195–96
psychotherapy, as initiation ritual, 89
Puder-York, Marilyn, 160–61
puer aeternus, 35

R

Racing Car Sex, 181–82
Ramey, Estelle, 87, 253
RAMM (Resurgent Angry Macho
    Man), 69–71
Real, Terrence, 231
rebirth, 131–33
Redstone, Sumner, 72, 80
reflexology, 185
regeneration, 22–23, 116–18, 251–53
relationships, male-female:
    breakup of, 147
    communication in, 7, 34, 86, 90–91
    couples therapy for, 160, 263
    double desire disorder and, 181
    of dual-career couples, 182
    empty nest and, 155, 163–64, 172
    Gender Crossover and, 103,
        149–51, 154, 158–59, 160–63,
        173, 208
    impotence and, 205–9
    intimacy in, 159, 211
    life expectancy and, 255
    out of sync in, 149–51
    as partnerships, 18–19, 107–8,
        132, 142, 147, 158–59
    power struggles in, 156, 208, 210
    preretirement couples exercises, 267
    renegotiation of, 155

relationships, male-female *(cont'd)*:
  in retirement years, 224–26
  in the twilight of life, 254–58
  withholding sex in, 155–56, 172–73
relaxation response, 84, 196, 254
religion, study classes, 76
Renshaw, Domeena, 178, 181, 199,
    206–7
resilience:
  defined, 217
  discovery of, 12, 140–41
  independence and, 244
  for life events, 217, 239–40
  in retirement, 223
  sources of, 217
responsibility:
  of fatherhood, 58–60, 72
  feeling stuck with, 104
  of grandparents, 124
  postponement of, 10, 12, 32–36, 41
  vs. independence, 32–36, 41–44,
    71–72
Resurgent Angry Macho Man
    (RAMM), 69–71
retirement, 23
  couples exercise before, 267
  early, 220, 222–23, 225, 250
  fantasies about, 224–26
  fathers as role models for, 219
  flexibility in, 224
  forced, 169, 240
  internal mission for, 223
  as living death, 109–11
  new careers in, 222–24
  premature, 102
  redirection vs., 220–21
  resilience and, 223
  self-funding of, 122
  uprooting in, 225
Richards, Keith, 219
risks:
  of change, 21
  as opportunities, 112, 190
role reversal, *see* Gender Crossover

Rose, Charlie, 146, 229
Rosenfeld, Isadore, 83–84
Russert, Tim, 75

S

sacrifices:
  of fatherhood, 72
  of "guy things," 166
  of starting over, 139
  of women's careers, 60
  for your dream, 135
safety net wives, 157–59, 160–61
Samson complex, 97–100
Scheibel, Arnold, 251–52
Schuller, Robert, 170
search process, hope alive in, 145
Second Adulthood, 259–62
  Age of Integrity in, 23, 215–26, 267
  connecting with one's father in,
    104–6
  defining moments of, 95–96, 110,
    113
  exit events in, 99
  Fearless Fifties, *see* fifties
  female menopause in, 99
  flexibility in, 140
  Flourishing Forties, *see* forties
  Influential Sixties, *see* sixties
  longevity and, 245–47
  physical changes in, 183
  power defined in, 23, 118–20
  Protean Man in, 98–100, 140
  pursuing your passion in, 144–45
  reinventing yourself in, 22, 99
  rules lacking for, 57
  search for meaning in, 34
  social entrepreneurs in, 120
  stages of, 22–24
  use of term, 10–11
  wisdom in, 120
  wives and, 173
self:
  authentic, 34, 64, 114
  expectations of, 140

false, 34, 52–53, 64, 82–83, 113, 114
  idealized, 127
  individuation of, 147
  redefinition of, 116, 139
self-assessment, 134
self-confidence:
  image and, 49
  mature masculinity and, 108
  testosterone and, 200
self-destructiveness, 34, 125–27, 158, 232–33
self-esteem, 52, 56–57, 97, 140
self-image, challenge to, 13–14
self-knowledge, power as extension of, 117–18
self-realization, 113–15
Sensitive New Age Guy (SNAG), 71–72
separation anxiety, 159
servant-leaders, 76
seventies:
  longevity in, 247
  lusty winter of, 255–58
  rediscovery of love in, 255
  return to college in, 250–51
  Snuggling Sex in, 184–85
sex:
  and age, 187
  as mechanistic problem, 194
  for procreation, 182
  as regimen, 182
  withholding of, 155–56, 172–73
Sex Hormone Binding Globulin (SHBG), 183
sex therapy, 206, 210–11
Sexual Diamond, 161–62
sexual drive:
  double desire disorder and, 181
  erectile dysfunction and, 185, 198–200, 203
  expectations and, 23, 178–81, 206
  foreplay and, 184, 207
  health and, 193, 194–96

  obesity and, 173
  of one's father, 189–90
  slackening of, 12, 15, 21, 49, 177–78, 189, 206, 208
  see also impotence
sexual dysfunction, see impotence
sexual life cycle, 181–85
  Dutiful Sex, 182
  male menopause and, 177–78
  Master's Tournament Sex, 183
  Racing Car Sex, 181–82
  Snuggling Sex, 184–85
  Surfing Sex, 183–84
sexual prowess, see virility
Shakespeare, William, 72, 116–18
Shanken, Marvin, 54
Shaughnessy, Rick, 37–38
SHBG (Sex Hormone Binding Globulin), 183
Sherwin, Barbara, 208
Sienkiewicz, Mark, 74
Silent Generation fathers, 38
Simon, Harvey B., 83
Simons, Anna, 180
six A.M. passage, 189
sixties, 213–40
  Age of Integrity in, 23, 215–26, 267
  authenticity in, 218
  backing up in, 231–33
  balance in, 218
  coalescence in, 218
  denial in, 236–39
  depression in, 227–31, 232–36
  impotence in, 184, 186, 187
  irrelevance feared in, 23, 218
  postcareer careers in, 222–24
  progress vs. despair in, 227–40, 268
  Protean Man in, 218
  recognition in, 120
  resilience in, 217, 239–40
  retirement in, 23, 219–21, 224–26
  spiritual hunger in, 253–54
  Surfing Sex in, 183–84
  well-being in, 216–19

Smith, Rick, 46, 58–60
Smith, Walt, 172
smoking:
    cigars, 53–55
    impotence and, 183, 193, 194
SNAG (Sensitive New Age Guy),
    71–72
Snuggling Sex, 184–85
social entrepreneurs, 120
social isolation, 126, 127, 165
Soder, Dee, 141–42
Solti, Sir George, 248
Sorel, Eliot, 14
Soros, George, 120
South, Terry, 28–29, 65–66
Spark, Richard, 187
spirituality:
    fifties and, 133, 141–43, 160
    forties and, 62–63, 72–76
    inner resources of, 231
    sixties and, 253–54
sports, manly, 66–68
Stevenson, Chuck, 14
stoicism, 20, 57
Stokowski, Leopold, 248
Stoltenberg, John, 50
Strand, Mark, 175, 254
stress:
    depression and, 231
    events of, 83
    fight or flight response to, 87, 90,
        235
    flooding and, 87, 90, 91, 235
    illness and, 83, 145, 151–55
    impotence and, 182, 187–88,
        195–96
    of loss, 20, 83, 145
    mellowing out and, 162–63
    mental reaction to, 83
    physical reaction to, 86–88, 145
    psychological, 182
    unawareness of, 20
Stricker, David, 171
Styron, William, 229–30

substance abuse:
    depression and, 125–27, 230,
        232–33
    immaturity and, 42
    loss of control and, 40, 41–44
    as manly, 33
suicidal depression, 227–28, 230–33
superachievers, 231–33
suppositories (MUSE), 204–5
Surfing Sex, 183–84
Surrey, Janet, 147

                            T

take-out fathering, 165
Talese, Gay, 50
Tarloff, Erik, 28
teachable moment, 119
team building, 127, 132, 139–41,
    143, 147–49
Tempest, The (Shakespeare), 72, 116–18
Tennyson, Alfred, Lord, 213, 220
testicles, size of, 201
testimonial woman, 209–10
testosterone:
    aggression and, 200–201
    cancer and, 203
    competition and, 101, 200
    dominance and, 187
    drop in levels of, 173, 183, 187,
        196
    longevity and, 246
    measurement of, 173, 186,
        199–201
    "normal" levels of, 189, 201
    replacement of, 201, 203, 208
    sexual activity and, 199
    sexual function and, 187, 196,
        200–202, 208
    surges of, 87
    technical menopause and, 15
therapeutic touch, 185
Third Age, 251
thirties:
    deadline decade of, 63

Dutiful Sex in, 182
focus on careers in, 46
living at home in, 41–44
testosterone in, 101
traumatic career experiences in, 111
Thurber, James, 66
Thurmond, Strom, 249
Tiefer, Lenore, 206
"Time Flies Test," 145
Toscanini, Arturo, 248
transformative women, 43–44
transitions, *see* passages
treatments, 202–5
    injections, 203–4
    resistance to, 211
    suppositories (MUSE), 204–5
    testosterone, 201, 203, 208
    therapy, 210–11
    vacuum pumps, 205
trophy wives, 138–39
Trump, Donald, 72
Turner, Ted, 120
twenties:
    Racing Car Sex in, 181–82
    time spent on sex in, 183

U

"Ulysses" (Tennyson), 213, 220
Updike, John, 217
"Use it or lose it," 199

V

vacuum pumps, 205
Vaillant, George E., 217
vanity crisis, 29–32
Vasile, Andrew, 171–72
Vasomax, 197–98
Viagra, 197
Vietnam Generation, 12
virility, 193–211, 247
    DHEA and, 202
    loss of, 13, 185
    magic bullets for, 196–98, 207
    male menopause and, 185–89

perpetual, 6, 23, 193–94, 264
proving, 96–100
relationship with wife and, 205–9
testosterone and, 200–202
treatments for, 202–5
see also manliness
von Furstenberg, Diane, 115

W

Wallace, Irving, 168
Wallace, William, 65
Waller, Robert James, 50
Wallerstein, Judith, 159
Washington, George, 23
Wayne, John, 70–71, 136–37
Weinstock, Anne, 138–39
Wexler, Harry, 42, 234–35
Wills, Garry, 70–71
window of opportunity, 133–35
wisdom:
    and experience, 120
    unconventional, 243–58
wives:
    communication with, 7, 34, 86,
        90–91
    dependency on, 130, 131, 142,
        157–59, 208, 238
    depression and, 236, 255
    development schedules of, 88–91
    and Gender Crossover, 103,
        149–51, 154, 158–59, 160–63,
        173, 208
    intimacy and, 86, 206
    nightmares of, 20–22
    partnerships with, 107–8, 132, 142,
        158–59
    postmenopausal, 150, 207–8
    safety net, 157–59, 160–61
    sexual needs of, 207
    of superachievers, 231–33
    trophy, 138–39
    virility and, 205–9
    working, 18, 102, 149, 156, 158–59
    see also women

Wolfe, Tom, 72
women:
    in Age of Mastery, 156, 161–62
    arousal of, 182
    "ballsy," 180
    career sacrifices by, 60
    careers of, 19, 52, 149, 150,
        158–59
    change as a given for, 21
    college enrollments of, 52
    competition with, 6, 110–11
    as counselors, 138
    divorces initiated by, 89
    emotions aired by, 126
    estrogen and, 208
    friendships of, 21, 169
    honor and, 65
    incomes of, 18, 52–53, 156, 158
    independence of, 89–90, 157
    at menarche, 56
    menopause as marker for, 57, 99,
        155, 164
    in midlife, 7, 21, 89, 149–50, 155
    in the military, 18, 69–70
    mothers' communication with, 189
    as nurturers, 98
    positive changes for, 5, 51
    postmenopausal zest of, 150
    as returning students, 250–51
    role reversal in, see Gender Crossover
    as single by choice, 159
    as single mothers, 19, 166
    stereotypes defied by, 58
    subservience of, 50, 56–57, 73
    testimonial, 209–10
    transformative, 43–44

    youthful beauty of, 31
    see also mothers; wives
women's magazines, 51
women's movement, 6, 18
work:
    contract, 122
    as defining identity, 221
    "dinosaurs" at, 110
    job market for, 161, 222
    manliness defined by, 125
    passion of, 106
    resigning from, 105
    stimulation of, 225, 249
    see also careers; corporate world
World War II fathers, 38
World Wide Web, 76
wunderkinder, 231–33

X

X chromosome, 246

Y

Y chromosome, 245
Yen, Samuel, 202
youth:
    independence and, 32–36
    manliness and, 97
    perpetual, 6, 23–24, 241–58
Yuppies (Me Generation), 12, 46,
    58–60

Z

Zen Buddhism, 63
Zilbergeld, Bernie, 155
Zoloft, 235

About the Type

This book was set in Centaur, a typeface designed by the American typographer Bruce Rogers in 1929. Centaur was a typeface that Rogers adapted from the fifteenth-century type of Nicolas Jenson and modified in 1948 for a cutting by the Monotype Corporation.

About the Author

GAIL SHEEHY, the author of twelve books, is best known for her landmark works *Passages* and *New Passages,* as well as the book that broke the silence about menopause, *The Silent Passage.*

Ms. Sheehy is also a political journalist and contributing editor to *Vanity Fair.* The mother of two daughters, she divides her time between New York City and Berkeley, California, where she lives with her husband, editor and university lecturer Clay Felker.

The New Map

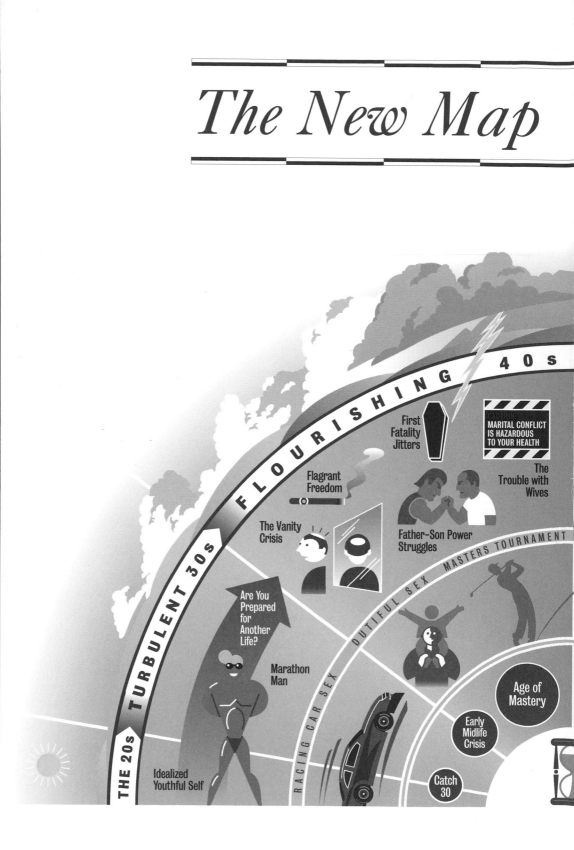

FLOURISHING   40s

First
Fatality
Jitters

CAUTION
MARITAL CONFLICT
IS HAZARDOUS
TO YOUR HEALTH

The
Trouble with
Wives

Flagrant
Freedom

The Vanity
Crisis

Father-Son Power
Struggles

DUTIFUL SEX   MASTERS TOURNAMENT

TURBULENT 30s

Are You
Prepared
for
Another
Life?

Marathon
Man

RACING CAR SEX

Age of
Mastery

Early
Midlife
Crisis

THE 20s

Idealized
Youthful Self

Catch
30